'14   £2-95

Modern Fishing Classics
General Editor: Antony Atha

AT THE TAIL OF THE WEIR

AT THE TAIL OF
THE WEIR

BY

PATRICK R. CHALMERS

ANDRE DEUTSCH

First published 1932

Reprinted 1984 by André Deutsch Limited
105 Great Russell Street London WC1

ISBN 0 233 97690 6

Printed in Great Britain by
Ebenezer Baylis & Son Limited
The Trinity Press, Worcester, and London

TO

M. I. BUCHANAN

IN MEMORY OF THE MANY LYRICS AND THE MANY
BOTTLES ENJOYED WITH HIM DURING
FORTY YEARS' FRIENDSHIP

FOREWORD

Patrick Chalmers is one of the best-loved sporting writers of the early part of the 20th century. He was born in 1872 at Brechin in Angus, where he was brought up and learnt at an early age to fish and shoot. After school at Rugby he came to London to work in a merchant bank, and when he retired in 1922 he lived for the rest of his life at Goring-on-Thames in the house he had bought on his marriage in 1917. He died in 1942.

At the Tail of the Weir is his tribute to the Thames and its fish. It is a lovely book, typical of Chalmers, who had an enormous knowledge of nature, ornithology and all field sports, which he wore lightly and dispensed with such a sure touch. I think of him as a fisherman first and foremost. He was a keen shot, as his verse bears witness; he was an immensely knowledgeable stalker. But I think he was primarily a fisherman. And, I think, he would rather, given the choice, have finished on the Thames with his Hardy spinning rod, or his 'lesser' spinning rod, or his trout 'live and bait' rod, or his fly rod 'for chubbing, a pukka four-piece, eight-foot fly rod', or perhaps, best of all, his 'commonplace rod', than on the Spey or the Dee with some more important-sounding piece of equipment in his hands. I think that it would have been more in keeping with his temperament, closer to Old Isaak. I suspect that secretly he looked on salmon fishing and the like as modern sport with less of a history and technique.

Often with Chalmers you do not realise that you are being instructed. You are beguiled by the effortless beauty of the prose. Here he is on the subject of catching barbel: 'So, quietly, drop the bare triangle into that straggle of bright silk-weed. And quietly lift it out again. You see that the hook has baited itself? The little green streamer that now hangs so drippingly upon it is lure enough. So float it quietly down upon the current and the first eleven-pounder that it meets with will, I hope, gently inhale it.' It all sounds so easy that the veriest tyro could do it in his sleep. But it isn't.

What else do we learn? We learn some of the history of the Thames. We learn of its fish; the pike, 'the tyrant of the river', bream, tench, chub, roach and perch; we learn of the romantic eel; we learn how all these fish should be caught; and above all we learn of The Thames Trout—the only trout which should be spelt with capital letters and is found, so we read, in the weir pools. We also learn of the birds, the flowers of the Thames and—surprisingly enough—how to cook the fish.

The Thames and its fish have changed in the 50 years since *The Tail of the Weir* was published in 1932. In the past 20 years 104 species of fish have been identified in its water, far more than Chalmers wrote about. As I write, I look at a picture of Mr Russell Doig, who has achieved fame on the 23rd August, 1983 as the first man to catch a salmon on the Thames by rod and line since 1833. Chalmers had strong views on salmon in the Thames and Mr Doig has not followed his advice, which was to put the salmon in the pot and tell no one. It will be interesting to see whether his predictions, which you can find on page 226, will be borne out. Somehow I doubt it, but I do know that Chalmers would have applauded the immense work of conservation and against the pollution of his beloved Thames of which Mr Doig's salmon is only the outward and visible sign.

Antony Atha

CONTENTS

PAGE

INTRODUCTION

I. LONDON'S RIVER - - - - - - I

II. THE THAMES WE FISH IN - - - - 20

III. A THAMES ANGLER'S OUTFIT - - - 39

IV. THE PIKE - - - - - - - 58

V. AND STILL THE PIKE - - - - - 74

VI. THE BARBEL - - - - - - - 87

VII. THE THAMES TROUT - - - - - 106

VIII. THE BREAM - - - - - - - 131

IX. THE TENCH - - - - - - - 143

X. THE CHUB - - - - - - - 155

XI. THE ROACH - - - - - - - 170

XII. THE EEL - - - - - - - 184

XIII. THE PERCH - - - - - - - 197

XIV. THE CARP AND SOME OF HIS SMALL RELATIONS 209

XV. AN EXERCISE IN THE OBSOLETE: A WEIR
ALSO A WERE-WOLF - - - - 223

XVI. THE FLOWERS OF THAMES - - - - 239

XVII. THE BIRDS OF THAMES - - - - 248

XVIII. A KETTLE OF THAMES FISH - - - - 264

INTRODUCTION

With a ripple of leaves and a tinkle of streams
The full world rolls in a rhythm of praise,
And the winds are one with the clouds and beams—
Midsummer days ! Midsummer days !
A soul from the honeysuckle strays
And the nightingale as from prophet heights
Sings to the Earth of her million Mays—
Midsummer nights ! O midsummer nights !

W. E. HENLEY.

OOKS are like people and no man introduces another man to a friend unless the introducer first knows the introduced. In the same way you cannot introduce a book to a public unless you yourself know the book as a preliminary. And you cannot know a book until that book is written and read. Therefore before you introduce a book you must read it, and before you can read it you (or preferably someone else) must write it.

And so all men who write introductions to their own books leave the writing of these ' allow me's ' until their books are written. Which is the only possible way.

When I sat down to write about an angler's Thames I thought my task was going to be an easy one. I had practically virgin water to work on. For during the hundreds of years that men have fished in the river there has been only one small book produced on Thames angling, one small, old book—Mr. Engle-field's most lovable *The Delightful Life of Pleasure on the Thames and An Angler's perfect Sport*, which is a long title for a little volume.

There have, here and there, been allusions to Thames trout fishing, notably by Mr. Francis in the Badminton Library, and again by Mr. Sheringham who frankly admitted that he had not the patience for it. Indeed in his *Fishermen's Tables* he is impatient of Thames as a fishing river. Here, for instance, is his ' carp table ' :

> ' one day = eighteen hours (summer time)
> eighteen hours = one potato
> ten years = one carp '

and here's his ' Thames Trout Table ' :

> ' Fifty bleak = one season.'

Just that and nothing more.

And so I thought that I, since I had Father Thames practically to myself, was going to have a facile time with him. But I soon found how wrong I was.

To begin with, what is a fishing book *for* ? Well, its uses are two. It may teach, or aim to teach, how fish may be caught and where. Or it may be a sort of Song of Solomon in praise of the angle and one's own prowess therein—*My Fish and how I have Caught Them* is a usual title for the latter type of book. And of these two kinds the last is the better fun to write and, infinitely, the better fun to read. For of the catching of fish there is no new thing to be said. *The Badminton Library*, *The Lonsdale Library*, Mr. Sheringham's *Elements of Angling* furnish all that any fisherman needs to ask.

Many wise men write fishing books and many wise men read them. But there is, and I regret it, among the *cognoscenti*, a leaning towards making of a pastime a science of the schools. With deference I say to my masters, ' simplify, simplify.'

For fish do not alter. They do not as a race learn by adversity, nor do they become educated of fishermen by the years. Naturally the older fishes in much fished waters become gut shy and more careful than they were at the beginning of the season, but they do not transmit their experience to their spawn and a feeding fish can usually be caught by anybody who will take a little trouble to do so and to keep, at the same time, out of sight. And he can be caught in exactly the same methods as employed by Walton our founder and enjoyed by Cotton his friend and ours. There is nothing new in the angle. The pursuit of fishing has been made, perhaps, by lighter rods and finer tackle an even more delectable pursuit than it used to be. Yet of that I am not quite sure. *We* with our featherweight ideas would no doubt grumble if we must go to Tweedside with the ponderous eighteen-footers that served Harry Otter and our own fathers. But did these latter enjoy themselves less than we of to-day do? And do we catch more fish than they did for all our finnicky new fashions and finesse ? No, in both cases.

And why would it be otherwise ? Our fathers fished the same waters as we do. Thames does not alter nor Tweed. And it is the same fool salmon who passes under Berwick Bridge as passed under it a hundred years ago. And it is the same roach at Remenham who remains to be gulled by the same gentle that did business with him when Farmer George reigned at Windsor.

And so I discovered that, after all, there was nothing usefully new for me to say about catching Thames fish. And very sorry I was. But it is a bad thing to put your hand to a plough, or to a pen, and then say that, furrow or foolscap, you find the task too hard for you. And therefore I got remembering what men of old have said to me of roach and dace, of chub and barbel. And, like Mr. Stevenson's 'gangrel Scot', I have added to the honest whisky of others

> 'A hash o' leemon peel,
> And ice an' siccan stuff,'

just to eke myself out with. And thus I have made a book, a 'sort of a book,' about Father Thames and found great fun and comfort in the making.

I say 'about Father Thames,' for now that I read over what I have written I am not sure, though fish and fishing predominate, that this is a fishing book within the popular meaning. It is however the book of a Thames fisherman about a river to whom he owes a content that he has never found elsewhere.

And when I come to think of it I doubt if any one man could write the perfect book of Thames angling. Thames is England and Thames would require a committee of his sons, and hers, dead and living, to do him justice. And his fishing book should be a book for his fishermen rather than a treatise on how to catch his fish.

In fact the book that I have in mind would have no fishing within it. It would be a book of the poetry of green places and old elms and Elizabethan manors.

It would have the *clonk clonk* of down sheepbells to hear and the songs of the larks at Moulsford. It would have the drip and the dip of the paddles of mills which have turned, slowly splashing, since the days of Doomsday Book. It would have the songs of the broken water under the weir's sill and the voices of rooks high up in a spangled December twilight. Age would be in it and Youth and the pretty girl with the rose in her bonnet from *Twickenham Ferry*. No one man could write it and no one man would want to. But all men, for it would be a little book, would carry it in their pockets when they went riverwards with a rod.

And, within the book, a singer would sing, ' Sweet Themmes! runne softly till I end my song,' and softly may he run, say I, until the songs of all men are ended.

P. R. C.

Goring-on-Thames,
    May 1932.

AT THE TAIL OF THE WEIR

I. LONDON'S RIVER

And still when mob or monarch lays
Too rude a hand on English ways,
The whisper wakes, the shudder plays
Across the reeds at Runnymede,
And Thames, that knows the moods of kings,
And crowds and priests and suchlike things,
Rolls deep and dreadful as he brings
Their warning down from Runnymede !

RUDYARD KIPLING.

WERE the average man or woman to name the most famous river in the world it would I think be the Thames that he or she would mention.

Thames and Tiber have the distinction of the masculine—Father Thames and Father Tiber—all other streams, from Mother Ganges downwards to the wee-est West Coast water, are feminine if not in grammatical law at least by the loving custom of anglers, and other waterside fellows.

Tiber, however, owes his name and fame to Roma Dea whom Romulus built upon his banks. Also to Lord Macaulay and Horatius, who both did much to make a man of him. Without these three Tiber would be a tiresome old school-book river, historical perhaps but muddy always.

Old Father Thames, on the other hand, has made great the London that he adorns and because of him Oxford remains for ever the world's centre of youth, learning and athletics. He is the river of a sea-borne commerce compared with which those of Carthage and Tyre might, in their days, have come home in an Usk coracle. He is the river of Politics, at Runnymede, at Westminster ; England was and is and shall be made. He is the river of Pastime and the Father of the Eight Blue Blades that, dipping and swinging together, have sent their rhythm round the world. And upon his lowlands at Windsor was the power of the Corsican broken. Or so said His Grace of Wellington who had, you will admit, a better right than most men to express an opinion.

Thames also is the benevolent doyen of the punt for two. He presides over summer evenings, swifts, cockchafers, the sun that dipped an hour ago behind Streatley Hill, and Damon and Phyllis who drift down to Whitchurch in the cushioned canoe.

And if, some day, our old gentleman becomes the Old Gentleman indeed and, in a terrible Bank holiday hour, arises and overwhelms the Gods of Tin, whose temple is the gramophone box and who, braying to Heaven's rafter, destroy his Arcadies, why, the sooner the better, say I, or the art of Compliment and that of the Conversation of Lovers will be lost.

Thames too is the river of fishermen. Buy any comic paper and read it in the train to Tilehurst ; walk abroad and through the T.C.C. gate and on to the towing-path and you will require no word of mine

to assure you of the angling aspects of the Father of
Streams who is entirely the River of the People.

The Thames and the Tiber, so unlike to look at,
have another possession of common fame. They have
each the fame, in song and in story, of a Bridge. For
what bridges are so nursery-quotable as London
Bridge and the bridge of the Dauntless Three ?

The Thames is the Artery of England ; he flows
through the very green heart of her from where he
rises, among the wild roses at Ashton Keys, until he
lifts the keels of her great liners and goes seaward at
Gravesend. The length of him from where he rises,
a little clearness of sherry-brown water, darting minnows and brook-cresses, to his deeply rolling and
stately finish is 209 miles. He has made history and
he continues to make it. He is locked now and har-
nessed and restrained, he may be mistaken, sometimes, for the family butler of Lord Desborough. He
is not so really but remains the river that the Romans
knew, the river that the saints and the pilgrims
forded below Goring, the river of whom his Conservancy are the servants and he the lord.

Until he goes to Oxford the Thames, like any other
stripling, is but a boy, rather a studious boy, mild
and gravely merry among the roses and rectories of
Buscot and Bampton. But after Oxford he is grown
up and come to his strength. His bridges grow with
him, they become great in span and wear townships
at either end of them—Crowmarsh Gifford, to wit,
and Wallingford ; Goring and Streatley, Pangbourne
and Whitchurch, Caversham and Reading and so
downstream, away to Battersea and Clapham, to
Westminster and Lambeth.

And of the rivers which are the tributary rivers of Thames? There is the Colne above Oxford, the Windrush, the Evenlode, the Cherwell. And nothing more of much importance, except the pretty little and well-stocked Pang, until he reaches Reading where another vassal attends him, the lovely Kennet famous for mighty barbel in the mill-tails and for the big trout who may, when the mayfly is up, be taken on sea-trout gut and a big, dry Green Drake.

At Shiplake the Thames meets two more of his dependants, the Loddon and St. Patrick's Stream. Below Sunbury he is joined, from opposite directions, by a second Colne upon the left and by Wey upon the right. And, at Hampton Court, by the Mole. And, Mole accepted and absorbed, some fifty miles further on Thames goes to sea, receiving in the tideway the homage of Brent and Wandle, Ravensbourne and Lea, Darent, Inglebourne and Medway.

I wonder what else need be said of the river in which I hope that we shall catch a fish or so presently? It *is* necessary to know a little of the river one is going to fish in, is it not? But perhaps it is *not*, for I admit that no one will catch another roach for being able to say that the river in which he fishes rises 700 feet above the sea level and that from the ridiculously jumpable he attains to sublimity at the Nore and a width of five and a half miles.

Or would such a knowledge of the schools as is the knowledge that our river owes his name to the portmanteauing, in ages forgotten, of Thame and Isis help you to one more barbel out of him that you would otherwise have failed of?

Or did I tell you, presuming you did not know it,

that it was Julius Caesar who first addressed Father
Thames respectfully, and as one Dignitary to another,
as Tamesis, would that wisdom help you, next May,
to achieve the big trout that lives just below Marsh ?
The trout that took the place of the eleven-pounder
that—perhaps I'd better tell about that fish before
I go any further. But, or ever I do so, I would say of
Thames another thing, that he is Father of all the
Fishing Stories that are not told in a brogue, Scots or
Irish. It was just below Wallingford Bridge, for
instance, that the Bloody Limit story started. And
every funny fishing, or boating picture, drawn by
Mr. John Leech, with the exception of those of Mr.
Briggs and his salmon, are Thames pictures.

I wonder who possesses the originals of the Leech
angling sketches ? The Fly-fishers' Club *ought* to but
I do not think that they do. Of them all I'd prefer
the ' Delicious Repose ' picture, I think. You remember it—the roach anglers in the parlour of the
anchored punt, the swifts, the summer day, the five-
gallon jar of beer, and the top-hatted Destruction,
blindly about to batter their ancient peace, amid-
ships and unawares ?

And I must have another John Leech to go along
with my ' Delicious Repose.' In procession they pass
before me ; ' Setting trimmers for jack ? Oh yes,
great fun, but why does not Charlie pull up the anchor ? ' ; Mr. Briggs, his little boy Walter, and the
pike that flies at him and ' barks like a dog ' ; Mr.
Briggs punting Mrs. Briggs and about to fall out of
the punt ; a charming gudgeon-fishing party, ' fairy
Mary, me and the man,' says the refrain of the verses
that it illustrates ; they pass, reluctantly. And

I am left, and I think rightly, with the picture of the two pretty girls in the mushroom hats who sit, I know the very river garden that they sit in, who sit to sketch the beauties of the summer Thames.

These two rosebuds supply the answer to the caption, ' Who is this ? This is Mr. John Chub pulling with those long, steady strokes,' etc., which appears under the picture of a fat gentleman stroking a double sculler and catching, at the same time, a most almighty crab. There is never a fishing rod in the picture so I cannot claim my second choice as an angling example. But it is Thames and the very essence of high Victorian summer, the reeds up, green and rankly bending in the current, blue dragon-flies, and the upper blue swept of swifts.

I wonder if the summers of the sixties were more golden than those of to-day ? I fancy that the August river was then a more peaceful place than the gramophones and the motors have made of it for us. But when a man looks back most everything is golden—Youth for instance and the Girl in the Boater Hat who met you at Waterloo (by the book-stall) when Weybridge was out of Town and the river at Shepperton as rural as at Rushey.

In one of Mr. Gilfrid Hartley's books he refers to the music in the names of the Highland Deer Forests —Auchnashellach, Gildermorie, Rhidorroch, Fan-nich, Inverlael. In those names are all the musics of the brae—the roaring of the great harts in the sunny September corries, the voices of a hundred running waters, the wild challenge of a grouse cock on a boulder—all, all. Even the tinkle of the six shillings

change out of the two ten-pound notes, that your
return railway ticket to Inverness will cost you, is
within them.

But, if you'll take your Thames weir ticket, the
10s. pass that franks you, for the fishing season, upon
the Conservancy's bridges, works and precincts
generally, you'll find a string of river pearls that
give you the poetry of green places, the heart of
England, indolent, unbridled June, mays and wild
roses and the slow, cool eternities of dripping, dipping
mill wheels. Hambledon, go the names, Mapledurham, Hurley, Abingdon, Boveney, oh, ' almost singing themselves they go.'

And the other Thames names—are not they England too, are they not kingcups, rooks in April
elms, the white owl sweeping and a nightingale in
the dark ? Listen to them, Bablock Hythe, Bray,
Long Wittenham, Bisham, Hedsor, Iffley, Medmenham—I could fill a page with such music and, reading,
you would remember, in the sound of it, the big
trout below Marsh that I wanted to tell you of. I
tell the tale as it was told to me, I do not vouch for
the truth of it, I only say that you will learn, when
you fish for a much fished for Thames Trout, that he
is an exceptional fellow and, like Habakkuk, *capable*,
almost, *de tout*.

The eleven-pounder lived, when first I heard of
him, *above* Marsh Lock. He was a glorious fish,
short, thick and deep, as I know because once in May
he followed my spinning-bait almost into the bank.
He meant business ; like a bullet he came, full speed
and wide open. But he came too late. Perforce
the bank stopped my minnow's flight. The trout,

undeceived, turned aside from the sham with a flounce and a wallop, that, literally, splashed me with Thames water, and was gone.   Later in the summer it was told to me that a young Scotchman, going from Shiplake to Henley, approached the lock in a rowing boat.   As he came, he, resting upon his oars, sought in his flannel trousers for the three coppers which his lock ticket must, presently, cost him.   He found but two pennies and so he must break into a sixpenny bit.   In his hand he held the little coin when, to avoid the wash of the steam-launch *Wargrave*, he picked up his oars all of a sudden.   The sixpence fell into the water.   The young man, like the Scot in the comic papers, looked outboard as his sixpenny piece spun, silverly dropping in the slow current, down into green deeps.   He saw a great fish shoot across the path of his little silver coin and absorb it as though it were a silver dace that wobbled so seductively.   That was all.

Next June the Best Thames Angler Ever anchored his fishing punt on the bright shallows below the Lock.   The bright shallows where the spawned barbel, rolling like cats roll sidealong in the sun, clean themselves and preen themselves at the tail of the weir.   Then, standing up, the angler tossed a spinning-bait hither and yon.   Presently, as the blue phantom sped among the piles of the footbridge, a yard-long shadow dashed aslant at it.   The little rod bent into a kicking arc, the reel shrieked, and forty yards away—but you've read this sort of thing before, I think ?

To make a long tale short then, an hour or so later when the Trout was opened in the kitchen, within him was found, and sent upstairs to his captor upon a salver, three coppers and a lock ticket.

As I said, I do not vouch for the exactness of the story, but it is one upon which Father Thames prides himself, and if it isn't true it at least ought to be.

When I began to tell this tale of a trout we had been thinking of the tributary rivers of the Thames, had we not ? What about the hill ranges that feed him with these rivers ? Well, Father Thames takes his toll from the Cotswold waters, and the waters of the Chilterns, from the cress beds of the Cumnors, from the trout streams and the springs and the fountains and also from the little waters of the waterless downs, especially from the little Upland Eve of the Legend. Especially from the brook who was once the little girl whom the blue butterflies loved, a myth of Hellas gone straying to Berkshire and to be found in the shadow of Old White Horse of Uffington.

These hills send down to Thames a largesse of shells. Some day I am going to make a collection of the Thames shells. At present I have little knowledge of them and it is as dangerous to play with a little knowledge of river shells as it would be to make a fireside toy of a ' dud ' howitzer shell. However, I do know that though the Thames has mussels, the mussels, unlike the mussels of Tay, Spey and South Esk, are without pearls. I cannot say why this is. The Thames mussels seem of a finer leaven than the Scotch. They are smaller, they are thinner of shell and the shell itself is a smooth pheasant-egg sort of brown to see and to handle. Whereas the Scotch shell is a black and a rugged jewel-case and as stern and wild, in comparison with the Thames variety, as is Caledonia herself when compared with the Vale of Windsor.

But the Thames has many shells besides that of the mussel. There are probably half a dozen to a dozen varieties of shells. And I know the English names of none of them. Possibly they have no English names, only Latin ones. Of which I know but one, which is *neretina* and which may not be Latin after all. So I will call them all, with the exception of the mussel, the shells of water snails. But they are of various sizes, some as small as number four shot, some as large as walnuts. Some are shaped like the cockles that the ghost of Molly Malone still sells in Dublin's fair city. Some are pointed like distaffs. Some look like periwinkles for tea. Some are tight curled like the flatly-worn horns of Silvani and Satyrs and Pan people. And the colours of them are delicate and lovely—rose, purple, green, black-and-white, olive— some day I am going, with their assistance, to make a photograph frame, like the frames we used to buy at Torquay in 1888, and in it I shall put the picture of my best beloved.

For I should like to find a pretty use for these jewel things of the Thames Valley. At present, so far as I know, the only one usable is the mussel who walks on one foot. He only has one and you can see his foot's marks in the river mud any time you like to walk along the towing-path. When he walks he looks very like a unit of the oysters that Mr. Tenniel drew for Alice in 1856, supposing it to have unfortunately lost one of its legs. The mussels then are useful to the otter, who loves them like the Walrus loved the oysters. As you walk you may see where

the otter has dined.   He has had a four-pound chub,
you can weigh the fish by its own scales which are
littered upon the grass.   Among them are the
crunched and ejected shells of perhaps a dozen
mussels which the otter has enjoyed, succulent,
yellow and delicious, along with his fish.   I wonder
if the otter collects the mussels first, lays them on
his landing place and then goes chubbing ?   Or if he
first catches his chub ?   We'll think about the otter
presently, but while we are under Thames water with
the shells let us think about the insects of Thames,
the beetles and larvæ that live upon his bounty.

You will find them mostly in the backwaters and
quiet weedy places of mud.   Places where the shod
punt-pole, down driven, frees pockets of a gas that
will ignite if a lighted match is applied to it ;   which
is as easy a way of setting the Thames a-fire as
there is.

Anybody who has read *The Water Babies* knows
how a dragon-fly hatches and that he goes first as a
devouring crocodile in the deep and then like an
eagle in the air.   And that he is the foundation of all
the Fairy Prince transformation stories in the world.
On the Thames it is never summer until the swifts
come and the green and blue dragons begin to haunt
the bulrushes, one the male fly the other the female
and which is which any book on insect life in pond
and stream will tell you.   These two slim-bodied little
creatures are the two Thames dragons that are com-
monest of all.   And they mean midsummer and are
never far from their parent the river.   Their big
brothers come later and are to be seen in woods and
forests quite as often as upon the banks of the river.

To me these great jewelled wonders, so dashing and fierce and harmless, except to mosquitoes and gnats, mean September and the heats of September, the end of the trout fishing and the renewed frequency of the gun.

Dragon-flies all are like sundials : they only count the sunny hours, and because this is so I love them.

The biggest beetle but one in the Thames is the Brown Water-Beetle, a fine and ferocious creature of an inch and a half. He is heavily armoured. He eats everything carnivorous that he can kill, tadpoles, newts, snails and little fish such as minnows and small ' bait.' He can walk and climb and, of course, swim. He can fly too, and when he is tired of Cleeve mill-tail he climbs up a bulrush stem, lifts into the dark blue summer dusk and alights, for all I know, at Mapledurham. And if you are fond of watching people fight, and I admit the fascination of the scrap voluntary and of obligation, I commend to you a meeting between two male Brown Water-Beetles.

He is a murderous brute, both in the grub or larval form and as the perfect insect, but he is of character. He is long-lived, for a beetle, and his allotted span is three years. Next time you go to Mapledurham lie upon your face and be looking at him in the clear brown water of the mill-tail, after the miller goes home and the leat ceases to run, and I think that you will find him not the least interesting exhibit in Father Thames's aquarium.

The biggest beetle of all that may be found, from Lechlade to Chertsey, is the Great Water-Beetle. He is dark green and about two and a half inches long. He is a vegetarian and as peaceful as he is great. He goes in constant fear of the Brown Water-Beetle and well he may, for he has no means of defence and the Terror from Cleeve kills him on sight and then eats him.

He makes a pleasant pet, so I am told. At least a well-known journalist of my acquaintance risked his own life for that of his dear *Dytiscus* in the Dublin Rebellion of 1916. He walked slowly through a storm of bullets carrying from his burning home the glass aquarium which held his Great Water-Beetle, and all was well. But personally I have never found the Great Water-Beetle so interesting as the Brown Killer.

There are other insects and water peoples of all sorts in Thames, but the dragons and the two big beetles are, unless to the microscopic mind, the most entertaining. And no one would take a microscope with him when he went to angle. And in this chapter I am trying to introduce the river and its interests to the angler, the tyro of Thames, who will presently be thinking of putting his rod together and walking down to the landing stage.

What then have I left out in these brevities ? The birds and the flowers ? Why then I mean to make a whole chapter upon these a little later on. The amphibians ? Well, the summer Thames is full of tadpoles—see them under the boards at the ferry landing stage, the brown water is living with the waggle of the gollywog atoms, with the embryo frog, with the toad to be.

And in a week or so the summer grasses will be alive with tiny frogs, the prettiest, daintiest little creatures that come up from the water. Not even excepting the mayfly of which the Thames is prolific. The mayfly which, except in the very highest reaches of the river, the trout never seem to take. The coarse fish, the smaller among them, roach, dace and small chub, gorge themselves on the drake. But the big chub, the five, six or seven pounders, do not seem to have the mayfly habit. And once only have I seen a big trout feeding on mayfly.

It was above Whitchurch weir, under the trees on the Berkshire bank. The trout lay on the top of the water, he was probably twelve pounds in weight, he was certainly as long as an umbrella. The fly came down in hosts and he sipped and sucked and sipped again, his olive neb just stirring the calm surface, his great square tail occasionally awash. You could have counted his spots, he was very, very big. And he would have been a gift for a fly angler. But who would take fly to the river before the chub was in season ? Not I, anyhow. So I pulled a spinning-bait across his nose and put the judicious epicure down at once.

I never saw him again, but I think he was the same trout who that season lived, and fed, off the landing stage at The Swan. This fish would in the early summer mornings chase the ' baits ' among the fleet of anchored boats off the hotel landing stage. And, colliding with skiff, sculler and luxury punt, would set the whole argosy rocking at their rope ends. But I could never catch him—not I. It was difficult to keep a bait spinning among all the shipping, and the trout usually fed most actively on the mornings that I was not there to offer him a second helping.

But the frogs now—the baby frogs in the June grasses ? I have little to say of them except be as careful not to tread on them as you would be if they were young pheasants and not young frogs. And never use them as bait for a chub on the 15th of June or on any other day. A chub will take a fly just as readily as a frog, and a frog is no lure for a man who was once a child to use. And if you ask me why this is so I will refer you to '*Heigh Ho, says Rowley,*' as illustrated by Mr. Caldecott, and leave it at that and to your own conscience.

Are leeches amphibian? And if so are they of Thames? I think they are of the river though I have rarely seen them. Those I have seen were amphibian. They were attached to the person of a bather who had, in the glorious summer of 1911 when the lasher at Shiplake was shrunken to a splashing spoonful, bathed in the weir pool (against all T.C.C. laws and the might of its lock keepers) and been injudicious enough to sit down upon the sill while what was left of the lasher played upon his brown shoulders. He sat among leeches who attached themselves to him as and where was convenient.

The Thames, however, has other dangers for bathers to brave than the occasional leech. He is a river of octopus weeds. He is a river of treacherous bottoms. His weirs are full of kelpies. Some people call these kelpies cross-currents and under-tows, but they are kelpies all the time. So a boy or a girl who goes bathing, or boating or angling, in or upon the lilied river should not only be able to swim well enough to win Humane Society medals but also be the keeper of his or her head in all emergencies.

And the latter may be various. A young lady who is a friend of mine took a notion to sleep in her punt. She moored it in shallow water alongside a daisied meadow. A nightingale sang her to sleep. When she woke she lay in a foot of mud and a cart horse was in the punt. But camping out for the sake of camping out is a poor game anyhow. And the mention of bathing takes me back to the otter.

The Thames is full of otters who enjoy, and rightly, the protection of the Conservancy. Otters only annoy me when a hunting otter shoots up among the white waters of a weir when I am fishing. Then every trout, at once, will go off his feed. But I do not think the otters kill many trout. I have rarely seen the remains of a trout, otter-destroyed ; chub seem the usual diet of Thames otters, chub, pike and moorhens. Frogs too ; last summer I met in the dusk a big dog otter frogging up the ditch that runs down to the river near Hardwick. He was as surprised to see me as I was to see him. He loped across the grass like a great cat and went, unsplashing, into the river as smoothly as oil.

But though otters are plentiful they are not often seen. Occasionally perhaps when you, upon a summer evening, have anchored the punt below the weir and wait there for some big trout or other to show, you will see an otter. The last one I saw so was at Temple weir, below Cleeve. The river was low ; only in the ' lion's mouth ' was the water pouring through the boards. Without stirring a ripple an otter landed, ran up the steps, like, said my companion, a brown spaniel dog, and slid noiselessly into the calm river beyond the pool. I saw the wave of his passage for a moment, then the water deepened and I saw no more.

The closest sight of a wild otter that ever I had was at Hambledon. I was fishing ; a friend with me went for a swim. He was a young Irishman and I

presently heard him whoop. Stark naked he came
bounding triumphant down the towpath holding up
for my inspection an otter cub, about as large as a
half-grown kitten. As he came, pinkly dripping, the
brave old mother otter dashed out of the reeds where,
exploring, he had found her cub. She pursued chat-
tering with rage. Whether she would have attacked
or no I cannot say, for the kidnapper dropped his
prize and ran the faster. The mother snatched her
treasure by the scruff of its neck and went overside
with it before you could say *lutra*.

An otter cub, a bitch cub for preference, will make
a charming pet to the man who will take trouble.
But I implore those who cannot make sacrifices of
rest and time not to attempt it. A loose-box is required, a paddock, a pond, and pounds and pounds of
food per diem. Fish, rabbit and milk, a pet otter
will eat. And it requires to eat twice its own weight
daily. Of all the fish, eel is the most preferred by
the otter. And a good choice too.

Of the other fur-coat fays of Thames is the vole,
the common brown vole, for I have never seen the
black vole hereabouts. Also there is that little black
velvet wonder, the water shrew-mouse. He is more
often seen in the tributaries than in the main river.
But I have spent half an hour in watching a water
shrew-mouse in one of the shallow streams that at
Hambledon splash down among the green eyots from
the weir to the river again. I will not tell you what
it did—the Messrs. John Sobieski and Charles Edward
Stuart shall tell you that :

' A shrew-mouse came out from its little door and
dropping into the stream, darted up the current to

the throat of the pool, where it fished with great vigilance and velocity, then, suddenly rising to the surface, like a little black cork, ran along the water like a spider-gnat, climbed the margin of the gravel, and sitting on its hind legs, ate what it had caught, wiped its face with much assiduity and again plunged, and repeated its fishing. When it had exhausted the best of one part it descended to another, generally rising on the surface and running down with the current, tumbling through the little rapids and rolling over the stones like a tiny black ball. Having entered the new basin, it ran down to about the middle, and, turning sharply, dived against the stream and shot up the water, fishing it with great activity, to the entrance of the throat. We watched it for more than half an hour, at only a few paces, sometimes only a few feet, distant, till the light beginning to fail, it disappeared up the stream.'

And as for the vole—the harmless, delightful, brown velvety vole, the little eater of salads whom the ignorant call water-rat, what of her ? I will tell you :

> There was once a well-connected
>   Little Naiad, but a prude
> Was she too, for she objected
>   To what artists call ' the nude ' ;
> She would turn a trifle redder
>   Than the wild-rose by the road,
> When a sister took a header
>   Garbed in that old fearless mode.
>
> When her sportive mates and splashful
>   Took the clear Cephissian tide,
> She would potter, being bashful,
>   In the reedy river-side,

For it seemed to her audacious
  Bare as little frogs to be ;
'*What if Pan*—? ' she thought. ' Oh, gracious !
  Oh, my gracious, goodness me ! '

One fine morn, when skies shone bluely,
  Came a piping, sweet and clear ;
'Twas a blackbird, really, truly,
  But she said, ' That's *Him*, oh dear !
Piping on the oat, his plaything.'
  Swift, to Dian's Virtuousness,
Prayed she, ' Since I be a-bathing,
  Mayn't I have a bathing-dress ? '

Hear the Chastity's replying :—
  ' You shall have a magic gown,
Velvet that shall ne'er need drying,
  Of an unobtrusive brown ;
Modesty's own self they'll rank you
  When you swim.' Then, bless my soul,
Ere the child could murmur ' Thank you,'
  There she was—a water-vole !

And to-day, in cool recesses
  In between the lily stems,
You may see her nibbling cresses
  In the care of Father Thames ;
Swimming shyly and discreetly,
  Timid as when Time began,
And, although she's clothed completely,
  Diving when she sees a man.

And now that I have a little introduced you to
Father Thames and to some of his folk, shall we think
about catching a fish in him since that, after all, was
what we came out to do ?

II. THE THAMES WE FISH IN

Then since we're of the Faithful, vowed to follow
Old Thames's placid flow,
We'll breathe of his leviathans that wallow,
In bated tones and low.

P. R. C.

THE Thames is, as an angling water, a much neglected river. You do not think so when you see the rows of bank anglers that sit in each other's pockets, upon his bank. Each of these sportsmen has two rods out, one with a legering tackle baited with lobworm and probably festooned with weed ; the other, a roach pole, baited with crust or gentle or elderberry. They catch, as a **rule**, little. Indeed it seems that they are out for the ' delicious repose ' of the angle and not for the sport thereof. They come early, they stay late. They smoke, they make tea, they gossip. Here and there among them is a sweet-hearting couple, here and there a family party, baby, dog and all. It is a day out of doors, it is a picnic, a holiday. It is beneficent but it is not the angle. The fish they hope to catch are, upon the leger, and in order of precedence, an eel, a barbel, a possible but improbable trout. It is hoped for the roach pole, that it may achieve roaches. And the fish, if any, that are caught are thrown on to the bank to die by degrees. No angler is, I am sure, a cruel man on purpose. But many Thames anglers of the bank ignorantly suppose that a fish tastes better if it is left to die at its leisure and they act in accordance with this epicurean belief. But, for the most part, if they depended for their supper upon their baskets they would be very hungry before the morrow's breakfast time.

Sometimes a bank angler puts out a live-bait in hopes of a jack and sometimes a jack justifies his hopes. Indeed one of the best pike I ever saw out of the Thames I saw taken thus by a bank angler above Shiplake Hole. I never heard the weight but I judged it to be not far off a score of pounds.

And sometimes the ' banker ' with the live-bait does better still. A most reliable professional fisher-man tells me that on the last day of the trout-fishing season of 1909 he saw a bank angler playing a big fish below Whitchurch Bridge. He went to his assistance and the amateur claimed to have hooked a big pike. Said the professional, ' Never saw I a pike play thus.' And as he spoke the ' pike,' rolling, showed a rood of spotted flank. The trout weighed eleven pounds and some ounces.

Now what follows is, I firmly believe, no lie but a true thing. Upon the last day of the trout-fishing season of 1910, the same bank angler, fishing in front of the reed-bed below the bridge at Whitchurch, hooked a big fish upon a live-bait intended for a pike. The same professional saw his fortunate plight and once more came to his assistance. This time the trout weighed nine pounds. Here is coincidence indeed !

Is there any magic in it ? Do similar conditions influence a repetition, or a continuation, of similar things ?

On the Christmas Eve of 1872 an absent-minded professor of philosophy drove from the railway station to the house of a Christmas host. His host's coachman drove him in a dog-cart behind a chestnut mare with a white foreleg. The frost froze, the moon shone and, as the mare went raking down Roseacre Hill just before you get to the lodge gates, the guest said to the coachman, an old friend, ' John, do you like eggs ? ' ' Yes, Sir,' replied John.

The conversation languished ; whatever train of thought had inspired the philosopher's enquiry was followed, if at all, by that learned man in complete silence.

On the Christmas Eve of 1873, the same savant, off the same train, was driven to the same hospitable house by the same coachman in the same dog-cart and behind the same old mare with the white off fore. The frost froze and the moon shone. And as the mare came raking down Roseacre Hill the professor, who had been silent for a mile and more, turned to the coachman and said, ' How ? ' ' Poached, Sir,' unhesitatingly replied John.

You can't account for it, can you ?

Before I, for the nonce, leave the bank anglers, I want to remember a bank angling scene that once amused me. It was on the reach below Wargrave. An angling competition was toward. Twenty anglers, at intervals of five yards, sat in a row upon the tow-path side. Behind them, in the meadow, the Conservancy's men had for some good purpose been removing turves which they had piled up (fragrant of green earth and the loam, and roly-poly as Swiss rolls) into little stacks of neatness.

There is, or was, a sailing club at Wargrave and one of the boats was out. The two young men who manned her were evidently not anglers. I have no personal skill in sailing boats and little knowledge of the tongues and technicalities of Poseidon. But this is what I think happened.

The crew tacked and went about, the boom swung over and, with her lee scuppers shipping it green, the boat came tearing past the competitors within a yard or so of the bank. The anglers, accustomed to such incidents and regarding them as a part of the fun, raised their rods and poles as one man. Presently the boat did it again, without attracting criticism. But when for a third time in fifteen minutes she sailed, galloping, among the quill floats, the landlubbers murmured. And on the boat's fourth coming there was a pithy exchange of compliments.

Now there stood behind the line a benevolent spectator, a professional fisherman of the neighbourhood. He had the round, pale eye of a jackdaw or a practical joker. The boat gone by, this one whispered to the anglers who, acting on advice, each provided himself with one of the turves I have told of. For a fifth time the boat went about, the boom swung over and, lee scuppers as before, she tore past the competitors within a yard or so of the bank.

' And forthwith, thick as hailstones, came whistling through the air '—but I expect you can imagine what occurred. But you cannot imagine how like that pretty ship looked to all muck heaps, as likewise did her two pretty men.

And what happened when she came by again ? She did not come by again.

I said just now that Father Thames was neglected of anglers and to prove my words I have spoken of anglers, anglers in bulk, ever since. What I really meant to say was that the Thames does not seem to attract the same class of fisherman as he did in our fathers' day. He is a great river and a beautiful. He has in his pools and shallows and shadowy caves every fresh-water fish in the kingdom, with the exception of the char and the rudd. The grayling ? I have myself caught a grayling or so in the river, at Whitchurch, and I've no doubt but that the pretty creatures, for a grayling is a handsome dame in spite of what Mr. Caine has cruelly said of her, came to me from the Pang (where grayling do abound) for my catching in Thames proper and in support of my claim that she is a Thames fish.

Thames, then, has his fish of all sorts, in almost unbelievable profusion. He has to each species specimens of unusual size. There is no river in the kingdom that can beat the Thames for the multitude and the magnitude of its fishes. I make a mental reservation, however, in slight disparagement of the average size of Thames pike, to whom I hope to refer later.

And the char that Thames lacks, this char, this lovely rainbow thing, is a lake fish and not a river one at all.

And as for the rudd—well, if you are particularly keen on catching a rudd in the Thames all you need do is to say that your next roach *is* a rudd. No one will bother to contradict you, least of all myself. The rudd is anyhow a contemptible little fish with a maximum growth of two and a half improbable pounds and a back fin about an eighth of an inch closer to his tail than is the dorsal of a roach. And now you know as much about the rudd as I do.

We will return therefore to our fathers' day, or if you are, as I hope that you may be, much younger than I am, to our grandfathers' day. To about 1865 anyhow.

Those were the palmy days of Thames angling. Every riparian village had its professional fisherman. Railways had made the middle Thames accessible. Men came to Thames in the London train full of cash and credulity. Important fishing centres, Maidenhead, say, or Henley, had probably four or five professionals. And each professional had a lucrative clientèle, a waiting list perhaps, of what Mr. James Englefield has called ' fortunate aspirants for trouting and other Thames honours.'

I do not know why all this has altered. Men in those days came to fish in the Thames as contentedly as Harry Otter went once to Melrose. And they considered a big barbel, or a big trout, as good as, or even better than, ' the never ending monster of a salmon ' that, as it came from Sandy's coarse linen bag on Tweedside, was torch to Mr. Scrope's tinder. And well they might, for this inspiring monster was but twelve pounds. And twelve pounds is a quite possible poundage for either a Thames barbel or a Thames trout.

Perhaps it is that easier travel and more delicate tackle have altered matters ? To-day, like Ariel, we may fly from Thames to Tweed and from Tweed to Tay and from hence to ' a' the various river Dees,' to any whither, in fact, that our angling fancy leans to.

But more probable is it that the Thames has lost his wonted popularity because of the light fly-rod. In the days when the engines employed for the catching of trout and salmon upon the fly were the ponderous beams that contented our ancestors the thrill of the fly was lost in the wood. And so you might as well fish with bait and be catching something bigger than brown trout.

The Thames is not a fly river in the general sense of the word, and with the coming of the light rod the method of the fly came to its easy own in its own places. Fly fishing is of course a prettier sport than bait fishing, but it is at the same time a less artistic one. I hold that the truly expert bait fisherman is a finer artist than the first-class fly fisher. Though I will admit that the dry-fly magician, the man who can, with seven ounces of split-cane, send a ' Tup's Indispensable ' at the end of four yards of 4x gut anywhere, to do, in all conditions, any jiggery-pokery round-the-corner job required of it, is the best man of all, though not by much.

I will say too that it is the light rod that has put trout fishings and salmon fishings to prohibitive rents. And I will return contentedly to the Thames as I know him to-day.

I have said that in him we may catch most everything except the char and, of course, the salmon and the sea-trout. And we may perennially fish in him ; with the exception of the fortnight that lies between the 15th of March and the 1st of April. His seasons are, for trout, from the 1st of April to the 11th of September. And I should be glad to see the Conservancy alter these dates. I think that the trout season might well be from cowslipped middle April to the 30th of September and the fall of the leaf. The river is usually too heavy for successful trouting before mid-April, before the sweet of the year. And the trout do not spawn till November-December. Indeed the Thames trout, who seem to go a little out of condition in July and August, have a second blooming in September and you will spot a big fish moving and feeding, after the 11th of the month, that you have seen no fin of since the first week in June. A sight for Tantalus.

For the coarse fish the season is similar for all. You may catch an inch of minnow to an ell of barbel from the 15th of June to the 15th of March.

And here again to criticize, if I were the T.C.C.'s angling expert I would make the season, for all but the chavender or chub, open on the first of July and close on the 28th of February. The chub I would allow to be catchable as at present for the joy and freshness of midsummer mornings. And for the joy of the fly-rod, for the joy of the walk to the river at

4 a.m.   The stillness, the greenness ; how green they
are then, how very very still !   And the punt that
presently we step into, how it drips with the dew, how
its wet boards have the vague, unforgettable river
smell that I must always associate with the Thames,
with the dawn of another midsummer day, and with
chub.

But I would have the chub's close season begin on
the 1st of March like that of his river mates and yeoman companions.

The motor, like love, makes most things bearable.
You may live in London and yet, thanks to Mr.
Morris or Mr. Rolls, get in a half-holiday afternoon
with the angle rod on any weir of the lower or middle
Thames of which ' kubber ' may have come to you
per first post and upon a post-card.

' Dear Sir,' the post-card will say, ' I saw a big
trout feeding in the middle run at tea-time yesterday.
He is ten pounds.   Emmie says she saw him Sunday
too.   I'll have some bait if you let me know.   Yours
respectfully,   W. FLOATCAP, Lock keeper.'

That'll fetch you, I think ?   But though the car
will do wonders, the jolliest life for the Thames
angler is to live on the river.   Or if this may not be,
to have a week-end cottage to keep his rods in and
to come to when the week's work is done.

London is full of anglers, full of anglers who, like
yourself, think that they cannot afford to fish except
for a brief three weeks in the year.   Therefore you
rent a salmon river or a beat on a salmon river, or a
rod upon a beat of a salmon river.   And to the
Whaupie you will go full of optimism and golden
imaginings.   And for the first fortnight the weather

will be just right for cricket or lawn tennis and claret
cup. Blue sky there will be and a slight blue haze
where the stack of Lochnagar is dim and blue and
far away. The Whaupie ? Well, just look at her—
an emetic to see—a huddle of boulders something like
St James's Street when it is up. Oh yes, the children
can wade about in Hell's Hole or Meg's My Lady and
find pearls if they want to. Yourself can answer
letters about your overdraft or take the car into
Edzell and play a round of golf and lose half-a-crown.
For the last week you can put on your oilies and be
taking a walk. There is of course a certain wild
grandeur about a Highland river in spate and, if you
are lucky, you may find a drowned sheep—braxy it is
called.

And so home to Scarsdale Villas, Kensington, and
to the office on Monday morning. The friends in
Throgmorton Street to whom you hinted, last
month, that—well, they are a disbelieving lot and
why, if they wanted a salmon as much as all that,
could they not buy one at Messrs. Sweeting's or somewhere else where salmon are ?

Thames, unless in terrific flood, will not thus dis-
appoint in sport, or in that appearance which is hopeful of sport.

But where shall our cottage be to be most central,
to be within a walk of weir pools and barbel swims ?
For the man who may not walk to the river loses
something of the finer bouquet of fishing. I can
never be quite sure whether it is better to walk to
the river after breakfast, the whole day before you,
the incense of a cigar to mingle with the freshness of
the lilac and the sweetness of mays and the chestnut

time, or to walk thither in the dawning, a shadow yourself in the harmonies of grey and green ? I have asked myself these questions every June since the perfect summer of 1911 which caught me and made me a Thames angler.

However, I think that if I had to choose a week-end cottage on the Thames, with Thames angling in my mind, I would choose Shiplake. Shiplake is not the beauty spot that many Thames villages are, but that is, maybe, because Shiplake is no longer a village. But seventy pounds per annum ought there to get you the cottage that I mean you to have.

You will probably come to Shiplake by car ; if you do not the railway service is excellent. Once there the weirs at your walking disposal are, Shiplake, Marsh, Sonning and Hambledon, and the last named is the second loveliest weir on the Thames. Eight or ten miles off is Marlow, a glorious horseshoe of winking water, a quarter of a mile of tumbling trout stream in the middle of a pretty town. Above Marlow are Temple and Hurley weirs, but the former is what a Scotch ghillie would call ' gey foul ' with snags, piles and boulders and it is difficult to fish.

The Shiplake-Henley district is good trout water both in the weirs and the open river. Shiplake Hole for instance is for ever haunted by one or two really big trout, is excellent pike water, and moreover holds a few carp. But it is a difficult place to fish. And there are, in the neighbourhood of Shiplake, many famous barbel swims. Also, between Shiplake and Henley are one or two good bream pitches. The bream is a patchy sort of fish and seems to confine himself to certain localities, and the reach that I have named is one of his stamping grounds.

At Henley, close to Shiplake, there still remain one or two professional fishermen. It is well for a beginner to employ a professional ; from him he will learn, if not much about angling, at least where to angle and where not to. The charge for such a Mentor is 10s. a day. If you have a good day make it 15s. And, if he nets a real big trout for you, make his fee a sovereign. In the fee you pay him is included the bait he provides and uses while out with you. If you want any for your private use, when out without him, pay him half-a-crown a dozen for live-bait, and what you will for worms, paste, etc. The beer consumed at lunch and other times is your charge. Usually Mentor's pocket lunch is his own affair but it is well to ask first.

But tea, if he has tea, you must pay for. All lock keepers sell teas and mineral waters, and tea is a jolly meal taken in the flower garden of the lock, a tame jackdaw to be impudent for cake crumbs and the thunder of the water reaching you softened and grogged by the apple blossoms between you and the white plunge and green turmoil of the fall. If you have been standing above a weir pool for two or three hours the rest and the laying down of the rod for half an hour will be pleasant things.

Upon some people a too prolonged gazing into the peacock tails and the spouting green water just under their boots has a Folkestone to Boulogne effect. Let you therefore, if you introduce a new friend to the river, have a bottle of aspirins in your tackle box lest the tyro succumb to a grandeur too great for him.

And, prentice hand or practised, don't be wanting a pair of smoked-glass spectacles to wear against the May sunshine and the might thereof tossed back from the broken fountains of the pool.

If you fish, say, Marlow or Hambledon weirs you will be the better of waders or high boots. At Marlow indeed these are indispensable, as the weir cannot be fished at all except by wading.

Let us suppose, however, that you prefer to catch fish to more lovely surroundings even than those I have been describing to you. I would, in this case, recommend to you Goring, or the neighbourhood of Goring.

But you will not catch quite so many fish. You will not have the same freedom of access to good water. Whitchurch weir and Mapledurham weir are both private fisheries, the only two on the Thames, I think. Goring weir itself is small and one requires waders in order to fish it properly. And it is a Hardy's heaven, a tackle-maker's paradise of a place to lose Blue Phantoms in at a dollar a time.

Cleeve, just above Goring, is smaller still. Both these weirs, however, are the abodes of big barbel and chub of a magnificence. Above Cleeve, and within reasonable distance of Goring, is Benson weir, a mightiness of water that fishes best in the late summer. It is apt to be heavy early in the trout season and, of late years, it has become infernally popular. It requires no waders and there were five anglers busy on it last time I went there. I made the blasphemous sixth.

I do not care what the copy-books say. Personally I hate, instinctively, the stranger that I find fishing

the bit of public water I had meant to fish myself.
The stranger, of course, hates me just as much as I
hate him. But we soon make friends over a joint
loathing for the third fellow who happens along and
puts a rod up.

It was at Benson that I lately played the angler in
the Bloody Limit story. I had had the weir to myself
from 9.30 a.m. till afternoon. I had gone empty and
unrewarded. At 2.45 an old gentleman (the Boy with
the Bent Pin) arrived. He carried a jam-pot—
Apricot Jam said the label upon it—and therein was
water and two discouraged-looking minnows. He
prepared his tackle and, attaching a minnow to the
trace, he cast it into the pool, and then, laying his
rod down, he lit a pipe and sat in the shade to read
the newspaper. My boatman said, ' The old party
has hooked a fish, Sir, a chub, I think.' He called
the owner's attention to the rod. The old gentleman
had no net so I sent my own with compliments and
in due course the chub was out and (for it was the
close season for chub) in again, although the angler
seemed not a little loath to see it depart. My boatman was, however, a river keeper and a disciplinarian.

The angler mounted his remaining minnow,
dropped it into the river, and returned to the leading
article. In a moment or two he had hooked another
fish, and, once more, I sent salaams and the landing-
net. A curve in the weir pool hid the proceedings
from me, but presently my boatman came back. He
looked a little shaken, a little hysterical. ' It's a six-
pound trout, Sir,' he told me ; and he added, as
though it was something original that he said, something new, ' I call it, Sir, (he said) the *limit*.'

So I think that I have shown that when Whaupie has ' never a fish intill her ' that Father Thames, whether you go to him from Town, from Maidenhead, from Henley, from Reading, has plenty of fish and plenty of free water. So why not be up and fishing him ?

And while you are putting a rod up I will tell you a story which has little to do with fishing but of which the mention of Reading, the mention of Goring-on-Thames, has reminded me :

Clive Winser-Brown was the name on his gun case. I know nothing else about him except that he was talkative, and that he travelled with me in the train from Reading to Goring-on-Thames, that short journey. We spoke of cheap shooting. He told me that sometimes he took one of the mysterious rough shoots that are advertised so often to let by the day.

' Does that include a dog, and so on ? ' I asked.

' A dog ? ' he said. ' Oh yes, occasionally they provide a dog.' He shuddered slightly.

' Would you like the window shut ? ' I asked him.

' It wasn't *that*,' he said, ' it was —— ' he paused.

' Yes ? ' said I, interrogatively.

' You mentioned a dog,' said he. He went on quickly. ' Last Christmas week,' he said, ' I took, with accommodation, two days' rough shooting in Essex. Sarah, here, went with me.' Mr Winser-Brown indicated the small Cocker bitch couchant at his boots.

' The accommodation was a house big enough for ten, but I was the only guest. An old house, a tumble-down old house of the grange type, it was. A tumble-down, rather daft-looking, old couple caretook it.

It had belonged (so said the chauffeur who brought me from Braintree—I always talk to chauffeurs) to an eccentric old gentleman who had lived there alone. He had fallen, so said the chauffeur, oh, yes, *fallen* down his own front door steps and broken his neck. His name was Massingbert, and the chauffeur said that he was a scholar and that he liked his glass. I always talk to chauffeurs.

'It was a wet and windy evening. The rickety gate of the short avenue was shut. Upon it was a chipped blue-and-white enamel plate that said, "Beware of the Dog." I read it by the headlights as my driver swung the gate open.

'The house was surrounded by elms that roared and swished. There was a balustered flight of twelve, steep, stone steps from the gravel approach up to the hall door. At the top of these steps, one on each side, were two stone pedestals. The one on the right was moss-grown and void. Upon the left pedestal sat, *not* lay, a very large stone dog. Lichens and moss had made that stone dog look leprous and patchy. Its ears were flat-shaped and rather rounded ; its stone eyes were as big and as expressionless as saucers.

'The driver rang the bell. Sarah, tuck-tailed, refused to get out of the car. I lifted her out, but she jumped back again. I noticed a lettered stone above the lintel : *Cave Canem*. Massingbert was a scholar, you remember. The old couple both came to the door and took my traps in. I paid the chauffeur and lugged Sarah out of the cab and up the steps.

'There was a good fire in the sitting-room, but the house felt damp. I asked the old woman who brought me dinner—oh, quite a decent dinner—if she and her husband kept a dog. She said that they did not. She said, whatever made me ask that? I mentioned the avenue gate and the inscribed keystone. " Poor Mr. Massingbert's fun, Sir," said she, " bless you, there's no dog here o' ours. '

' (What station's this? Pangbourne? Thanks.) Now, I noticed nothing funny until I took Sarah out at ten o'clock. She seemed frightened to go down the steps. " Silly little fool," said I, and packed her under my arm. Half-way down I couldn't help but look back—don't know why. I told you about the stone dog? Blessed if I didn't imagine that the image was cocking its ears and lifting up one of its front paws. But I saw that I was mistaken at once. Some effect of the moonlight, I thought. For the moon was up and galloping in a sky of clouds. It was when I was on the bottom step but one that I heard a bit of mortar, or something of the kind, fall behind me. Again I had, sort of *had*—if you understand, to look round.

' You've seen a big dog get off a sofa who'd no business to be on it? Sort of slinky and slyly? That's how I imagined, just for one moment, that the stone dog was getting down off its pedestal. But I saw at once that I was mistaken—what with the moonlight and all. It was obvious, however, that Sarah didn't want to go out ; so why should she ? said I. I started to go back up the steps. When I was half-way up I thought that I'd go down again and get in at the kitchen door rather than—mind you I don't deny that I was perhaps shaken a bit by what I thought I'd seen.

' This time I walked down the steps without inter-ruption and on to the wet gravel. When I'd gone twenty yards I looked round, same as before, sort of. The top of the steps was white, brilliant white, with the moon. The left pedestal, where the stone dog had sat, was as empty as the other one. The steps were in deep shadow. In that shadow *there slunk a deeper shadow*——'

' This is Goring,' said I ; ' I get out here. What was the shooting like ? '

' To tell you the truth,' said Mr Winser-Brown, ' I didn't wait to see ! '

But before you begin to fish in the Thames I will say that you will be wise to make yourself a proficient, even a skilled boatman, punt pole, paddle and sculls. A swimmer of course you are, and by being boat perfect you will obtain that independence which puts the final polish on Thames fishing. When you can manage a heavy fishing punt in a heavy weir pool with the delicacy of touch with which a great horse-man will coax a terrified eighteen-month-old filly running for the first time, will handle some sulky six-year-old rogue till he is handier than a Park hack, you may call yourself a freeman of the angle and of the Thames.

The late Walter Coster of Marlow, best of Thames professionals, was the most consummate artist in a fishing boat that ever I saw. He could take his punt anywhere and make it do anything. The most timid, and a weir pool can, in certain conditions, look alarm-ing enough, was care free when Walter was Palinurus. Aim then to be as good as he was and you shall catch the fish that I shall fail of.

The best sort of boat to possess is a punt which is also fitted with oars. She must be broad of beam and the possessor of a ' well ' for bait or for such fish as you wish to keep alive with a view to their restoration later on to the river. She must have an anchor, or suitable weight, and twenty yards of rope to come and go on.

The ideal fishing boat would be, I have always thought, a motor launch fitted accordingly. Therein the angler might go from reach to reach without delay and, if he towed a dinghy behind him and felt like getting into it and dropping quietly round the shallows below the weir the while he cast a Coachman to the fat, grey chubs under the willow bushes, why, there would be nothing to prevent his doing so.

A weir itself is usually best fished off the footbridge or by wading upon it.

Thames fishing requires four rods at least. You will want—but I will tell you about that in the next chapter. And as to the sizes of the fish that we are going to catch with our rods, the legal sizes, the limits, are they not clearly set forth upon the notice boards of every weir on Thames ? To these boards then I straitly commend you.

III. A THAMES ANGLER'S OUTFIT

It is there that we are going
With our rods and reels and traces.

RUDYARD KIPLING.

 THAMES angler will, without undue
ostentation, require more rods than will
his brother who fishes in fashionable
streams, by fashionable methods, for
fashionable fishes.

I will not include in a Thames angler's outfit a
roach pole. There are more ways of catching roach
than the bank fisherman's way, and the pole, though
ornamental, is only useful for bank fishing. Its use
upon the bank is undoubted when its occasion occurs.
Which it does when the angler upon the towing-path
finds it necessary to reach out over a reed-bed or to
make himself ' fine and far off.'

A roach pole is 18 ft to 20 ft in length. It is a
piece rod in four or more pieces, two of them hollow
and pack-upable, and it is often of exquisite, silk-
bound workmanship. It is a Londoner's rod almost
entirely and I do not think that it has any general
use in rivers other than London's own. A roach pole,

in a fishing family, is frequently an heirloom. And I have no doubt that such a rod is an expensive one to buy and I am pretty sure that you could not buy one in Pall Mall.

This however need not matter since you will probably decide to leave poles to the expert. My chief objection to the pole fashion is that you have no reel. The line, a few feet of fine silk, is attached to a ring at the end of the pole's top joint, which is usually made of cane and whalebone. This line is fastened to an equal length of fine gut. It will thus be seen that the angler has small chance, wanting a reel, of landing any fish, larger than a roach, which he may hook. Smashed he is, almost inevitably. I say ' almost ' for I believe that occasionally the big chub, bream or barbel who takes the gentle, or whatever lure the angler may incline to, is duly landed. How such a triumph can be accomplished I cannot tell, but fishing miracles, as all fishermen know, did not cease with the Miraculous Draught. The absence of the reel has given to this pole method of roaching the cheerful title ' tight line ' fishing.

The roach pole is the symbol of the London bank angler. And the bank angler is himself the symbol of all Thames angling. And Thames angling is ? The crisp lisp of water in the reed-beds, the cuckoo with her tune changing, the haunting, hunting scream of the swifts, the croak of a water-hen in the frost, the rooks that caw together and go home at the same time as you do of a frosty winter evening—these are Thames angling, and for the sake of it and the sake of these things which are its own, I will say, as well as I can who have small knowledge of the pole, how to fish for roach by means of one. But not yet, for the roach shall find room later on.

The man who goes to fish in the Thames then, the man who is not a ' banker ' and does not intend to specialize in roach, will require, without undue extravagance, five rods. These shall be a spinning-rod of the greater method and another of the lesser. Also a rod to ' live-bait ' for trout with and a fly-rod, such as he would take to any trout stream. And a commonplace rod whose uses I shall touch upon presently. The angler will require reels to suit and of these too I shall talk anon.

Yet it is impossible for me to be dogmatic and say you *must* have this or you *must* have the other. I daresay it does not matter a bit what you have or do not have in the way of rods and reels. But I will tell you what I have and you can please yourself as to whether you follow my fashion or your own.

My bigger spinning-rod is a two-piece Hardy rod which stands twice as tall as I do when I put it together. It is a cork-handled split-cane of the most princely. I use it for Scotch salmon and for Hampshire pike as well as for Thames trout. I bought it, paying the best part of a tenner, in June 1911 and in a moment of youthful enthusiasm, and it will last me till I go to the Styx and it to my godson.

This is how my large spinning-rod occurred. I had newly come to the Thames, knowing nothing of the Father of Streams as a river to fish in, but only as a romantic old gentleman who loved to encourage ' punts and pink parasols, gold water dreams '—not, thanks be, that I needed encouragement along those lines. I was leaning upon the footbridge below Marsh, and thinking what a likely-looking ' lie ' for a salmon was the jade-and-white water beneath me just before it swished under the boards to spread far and wide over the shining gravels below the bridge.

At this moment a young gentleman rode up on a bicycle. He had a fishing rod. He was the first Thames angler that I had ever seen, for it was June, as I have said, early June, and between seasons for the ' coarse ' fisher.

I watched, in all curiosity, the newcomer as he put up a small, stiffish rod. This done he impaled a dead bleak upon a flight of hooks, impaled it without the removal of a single bright scale. He gave, I noticed, to its green-and-silver tail a coquettish little bend. He attached it to his casting line and drew it through the current, where, lo ! by some magic it revolved with the flashing speed of clockwork.

There then followed such a display of angling dexterity as I had never before seen. The fisherman swung his rod, ever so little it seemed, and the bleak flew hither and thither in flights of fifty yards, sixty yards, seventy yards. Enchanted, I must needs up and ask a question, and my delighted interest not displeasing the angler, I was invited to witness more marvels.

For the young man was able to use his rod with the accuracy of a rifle, that is he was able to put his bait, within a radius of some seventy yards, exactly where he wanted to put it ; and he did so, for my pleasure, times and again. Falling to an inch, he caused it to flicker, like a silver flame, in and out of a forty-yard-off fastness of black piles and broken water. He cast from the Nottingham reel, he cast from the coil, he cast from the hand.   He cast ambidexterously.   He cast to the exact here, to the precise there, and to the strait and narrow and absolutely impossible everywhere.   Then, as a grand finale, he dropped the bleak, *plunk*, into a borrowed washing basket at sixty paces and four times out of six.

He told me that this accuracy which was his, and which he said, untruthfully, might be acquired by practice, is what makes a master and catches the fish which we others do *not* catch.   And he proved his words by inviting me to see a room full of stuffed Thames trout, fishes that gave to wonder why we Londoners go so far and pay so much to catch salmon when such a freedom as this is at our very doors.

Next day I bought my spinning-rod and, from Chertsey to Lechlade, I have followed Father Thames with it, season by season, since.   But *still* I cannot mount a dead bleak upon a Thames flight so that it will spin and not wobble, nor can I drop the same into baskets at sixty yards.   Nevertheless, I have had fun with my purchase and, by assiduity, a few great trout.

My lesser spinning-rod is, like the greater, two-piece also.   She is greenheart and, standing as high as my shoulder, she may weigh 4¾ oz.   But I have never weighed her, of course ;   who weighs their rods or their lady loves ?   Not I, anyhow.

But this rod cost me about a guinea, and if I tread on her and she break, which the gods forbid, I shall be able, perhaps, to replace her with her twin sister and, like the lover in the lyric, ' forget my Clementine.'   She wears rings of porcelain and is sneered at by the Hardy dame, whose rings are of agate.

Now the reason for two spinning-rods upon the Thames is in this wise. The Thames is a big river and it is necessary to make, sometimes, as long a cast as your powers permit. The 'sometimes' happens when, of a sudden, you see a feeding fish fifty yards away and it becomes a question of cover him now or, probably, never. A two-handed rod will throw a bait further than her single-handed sister can throw one.

And on the Thames, the objection of the indolent angler to the heavier rod does not arise. The angler who fishes a salmon river, when she is in spinning ply, must continue to cast, to chuck and chance, all day or until he's into a fish. A heavy rod, he will say, gars his back ache. And so he will go up to the hut and get a cup of tea and tell the pretty lady with the teapot about the fifty-pound salmon he lost in September 1899.

On Thames's green side a man uses his spinning-rods by fits only and starts. Sometimes he will spin a weir pool over, sometimes he will search the hundred yards or so of main river wherein a heavy trout has lately been seen to stampede the splashing bleak shoals. But in either case the spinning-rod will be laid down in twenty minutes' time.

Of course when spinning for pike upon a winter's day is the angler's object, the big rod must be in more continuous use. But even now it will only be employed to drop a spoon, or a sprat, into likely-looking eddies and backwaters and not for the wholesale, whole day, broadcast of the same that the search of the salmon demands.

As a rule the Thames angler treats his spinning-rod

as his emergency need. It leans, ready for action, against the railings of the footbridge above the pool, it lies, equally ready, upon the sun-blistered thwarts of the punt. A spinning-rod is, in spite of the fact that it is for occasions only, almost as essential a thing to the angler as is a rifle to the deer stalker. Yet not quite for it is not unsportsmanly to kill pike or trout in the Thames with a live-bait, which is the only alternative method to spinning. But it would be highly unsportsmanly to shoot a stag, or a roebuck, with a shot-gun.

The little spinning-rod enjoys her vogue in the cramped seclusion of mill-cuttings, under the timber of weir-bridges and where the angler must walk along ledges beneath the masonry of T.C.C. works. Also is she in evidence when he must cast from close at hand among the bubble-shoots of mill-tails, among the worn, moss-grown piles.

In fact her occasions are where exactness and accuracy are most essential and in every crabbed and confined fastness where a big trout lurks nose to river, where a great pike, the cruellest, most hypocritical of fishes to see, has his lair, and where the striped shoals of the perch follow the tiny silver spoon with the triangle to it.

The reels that I use on both these rods of mine are the wooden Nottingham reels that are ' braked ' by thumb. They cost about thirty shillings each. But there are many excellent and almost fool-proof reels, such as the Silex, which many men prefer to spin with at three times the price. Possibly I too should prefer a Silex if I was in a far country and one reel had to last me long and be in continuous use. On the

Thames I have shown that a spinning-reel is never in long continued action and that it does not go *too* often to the well.

I use, upon both reels, an undressed silk spinning-line. I have forgotten what the makers, Messrs. Allcock, say of its *size*, but it is about twice as thick as sewing thread and as strong as a Clydesdale. I have a hundred and fifty yards of it on one reel and a hundred upon the other. I use no ' backing,' and I am careful to test the last three yards of the reel line before I use it again and, if these offend me, I cut them off.

And I am always careful when the day's done to pull these, and all other fishing lines, off the reels to dry either on a ' winder ' or laid upon a bed or beds. For half an hour will serve to dry the wettest line, and the bed will not be wanted till supper's done.

I always take a spare reel to the river with me. And of the baits and traces and weights that catch me my trout and my pike I will tell when we begin to fish in earnest ; it is of rods and reels and lines that I am thinking at the moment.

Next to the spinning-rods comes my trout live-baiting rod. Perhaps it is extravagant of me to have a special rod for this ploy when my commonplace rod would do as well. But I do, in fact, use a four-piece fly-rod of 10 ft or so, cork handle and split-cane and perfect in all ways except that one of its stoppers has been lost and another, of amateur make, substituted therefor. I use a Nottingham reel and a hundred and fifty yards of the spinning-line that I described just now. And when live-baiting I test the ultimate and penultimate portions of my line as before, and anoint

(with vaseline) the last thirty yards that, resisting
water-log, they may the better float. To trace and
tackle I will return when we, presently, walk out on
to the footbridge with the sun on our backs and a
swift swooping about us.

My live-bait rod, a Hardy, has for the last thirty-
five years been in all sorts of use. It has been, and it
is, a ' lucky ' rod and long may it flourish. Well,
that's three of the five wands.

The next is a fly-rod, for chubbing, and of course
when I come to think of it the live-bait rod would
serve equally well. But I have a pukka, four-piece,
eight-foot fly-rod, just the same as yours, and an
aluminium reel that carries thirty-five yards of
tapered and waterproof trouting line and makes, unlike the free-running Nottingham, a merry music
when I hook my chub. To whom, too, I will refer
later.

I am left now with my commonplace rod. This rod
is a twelve-foot four-piece greenheart and I bought it,
cork handle and all, for thirty shillings in 1911. I
can throw a reasonably good spinning-line with it. It
does to live-bait for trout with at a pinch. But I find
it a little heavy. It's real uses are twofold. It does
well, propped upon the stern of the punt, to live-bait
with for pike on a mild January morning, the river
clearing after flood and, in the shelter of the mill-tail,
the air as balmy as May—almost. And, see, how
orange and blue is the kingfisher who sat on the stone-
work and, now, flits to the main river, a streak of
sapphire, a spark of blue !

And the commonplace rod is just the one to lend
to beginners, not so heavy as to be wearisome, not so

fairy light as to dissatisfy a lad with the 'cast' parental rod he has at home. He can live-bait with it for pike or for trout, I will tell him how in good time. He can spin with it like a Dervish. He can even, on a summer day, catch chub upon my commonplace rod and a Coachman fly. And I have never lent this rod of mine, and its Nottingham reel, without it having both inspired the lendee with a becoming gratitude and been his medium of a not unbecoming sport, sport, on at least one occasion, even extending to the extent of a 'beginner's luck' fish.

These will be the limit of the rods you'll be wanting, and a margin too you'll say. Take care of them tenderly ; after use dry them meticulously and never put them into anything but a dry cover. And do not, when you have so put them to bed, leave them, higgledy-piggledy, to lean heaped in a corner of the hall. All well regulated rod covers have a loop to the ends of them. And why ? Because a rod keeps her figure and youthful symmetry best when (despite the example of poor *Thrawn Janet*) she hangs up by this convenient loop. Therefore keep your rods hanging when you are not using them, which will not, I hope, be often ; for, as I have shown, you may fish in Father Thames for something or another during fifty weeks of the year.

Tackle to employ is best treated of at the river side as I have already hinted. But the Thames angler will land few fish without a landing-net. The Thames, you see, has few facilities for beaching even a half-pound roach. And the net is really a very important item of Thames outfit, more important indeed is it upon the River than on any river that I have fished

in. A gaff on the Thames offends my eye and those
of the gods. Some Thames anglers carry a gaff. But
who would gaff a trout ? And you will not catch a
Thames pike worthy of the steel as long as the gods
see you carrying the ' cleek ' thus cock-surely. So the
net it must be. And make no mistake, do you hook
a fish of *any* sort you will want a net. If you fish
from the bank, the banks of Thames are, remember,
high banks and you cannot lift your fish, weigh it but
a poor half-pound, on to the grass without extreme
danger of breaking the light tackle upon which you
have hooked it. Do you fish from a boat the same
danger is equally obvious. And on a weir the landing
of any fish other than a gudgeon would be, without
a net, the sheerest impossibility.

And, you ask, what sort of a net do I recommend—
what sort of a net do I, myself, use ? Indeed I keep
three landing-nets and I maintain that three are
necessities. When I walk down the towpath with a
spinning-rod, and without a lady of my house to
ghillie me, I carry a net slung inconveniently upon
me. It is a net that folds on a knuckle and you are
supposed to straighten it out with a jerk when you
want it. When I have successfully done so the handle
of the net is four-foot long, which is not usually
enough to be useful.

So the lone hand netting of a Thames fish, when
the fisherman is on the towpath, is difficult. My
advice is to play the captive until he has scarce a
kick left, lay the rod upon the bank with the reel-
handle uppermost, just in case, take the line in the
left hand and the net in the right and, yourself lying
down, net your fish out as cannily as maybe. If he

is a truly big fish I fear you will have a lot of trouble unless you can attract the attention of another angler. It is as well, if you have time and opportunity, to drop a stone into the bag of the net ; this will give it due depth in the water and make it an easier matter to tumble your fish into it. It is as well that this should be done his head first.

But be careful always, when netting a fish for a friend, never to lift the net until the fish is over it. Let me illustrate, since one picture is worth a page of precept.

An excellent judge of Thames trout and the weight of them, and incidentally an artist at achieving their capture, tells me how one June evening he hooked in a weir pool a trout that took him nearly twenty minutes to bring within reach of the net. Yet at length the great fish lay beaten, eighteen (the angler estimates), eighteen glorious pounds of him. The lock keeper took the long-handled net and lay down upon the coping. The angler said, ' Lay the net in the water, I will bring the trout to it and do not you lift until I tell you.' What follows would be best forgotten—' if forgetting can be willed.' Nevertheless to point my moral I will say that no sooner was the great, olive-green neb above the net's rim than the *retiarius*, overcome by the sight of such a potential trophy as was here, made a lifting scoop at it as though he would catch a butterfly. And he fouled, with the meshes, the Thames flight on which the trout had been hooked. The fish floundered heavily, it pulled the hold out and the current bore it outwards into the deep. The watchers saw it right itself slowly on to an even keel ; its great fins stirred, and the chance of a fisherman's lifetime, which had been the angler's, was now gone.

The man with the roach pole who takes up his stance in the morning and stays there till it is time to catch the 7.25 has no bother with his net. It has a long handle, six foot, I daresay, and upon the grass it lies beside him till he wants it. He has only to carry it from and to the station, he has only to make a long arm with it from where he sits, upon the Sunday paper, and he lifts out his roach. Roach anglers seem to expect nothing better than roach. Their nets have the circumference of soup plates, so when they *do* get anything bigger than two pounds there is as much trouble over packing it into their receptacle as there would be in getting a pint of stout into a sherry glass.

When you fish from a boat let your landing-net be long-handled, six foot at least, and of the salmon capacity. But let its meshes be small so as it may accommodate whatever may come to it. It is maddening to see an eel wriggle through a mesh, or a half-pound dace drop through the same.

The fashion in boat-fisher's nets seems, for all my good advice, to be for short handles. Upon the folly of this I will, once more, give the example which is better than counsel. I will quote this time from Mr. Barrington's delightful *Seventy Years' Fishing*, which is not, unfortunately, a lifetime spent on Thames.

' Though frequently on the Thames for many years I never saw a trout killed. Once, however, whilst sculling a little above Walton Bridge, I watched, for twenty minutes or so, a most interesting struggle between an unusually large one and a punt angler. The angler, who was after roach and dace, had hooked a small fish when, as it was being drawn in, it was seized by a trout, which was allowed to gorge it; then the excitement began. Either the bait was too far down to be ejected, or the roach hook had got hold. The trout ran all over the river, where it pleased, followed by the puntsman, who had cast loose from the ryepecks, to which he had fastened up, and wonderfully well he managed his punt.

' The angler seemed to have but little line on the reel, his tackle being only intended to deal with roach and small fish: nothing but the skill displayed by his attendant could have saved him from disaster, long before the end of the fight. At length the trout came to the surface, all but beaten, and was gently conducted towards the well of the punt, over which the professional was leaning with a landing-net such as is commonly used on the Thames, *i.e.* having no length of staff, but a mere handle of about two feet. The fish, catching sight of the enemy, made a final effort; the angler had shortened his line and in so doing brought the gut through the top ring; something stuck for a moment, a break naturally ensued, and the trout was gone. The angler flung down the rod in despair, whilst the puntsman cried out to me, " He wound hisself up too tight, and that fish weighed 11 lbs. I have known him all the season." '

But the real difficulty is the netting of a fish off a weir. The angler who fishes much for trout is the angler who is here most concerned. He should have a net with a great capacity, of course. And it should have a handle of twelve feet. I recommend him to have such a handle built for him in two pieces that, fitted together at the river, make transport as easy as may be. Once upon the weir the net, for all its size, is no great trouble so long as you do not forget to take it with you when you move from the ' lion's mouth ' to the ' tumbling bay.' Let the bag of the net be deep and ample. Do not forget the stone that gives weight to the proceedings. Or ever you begin to fish study your immediate surroundings and make up your mind where you will most easily net the ten-pounder that you will before long hook. Place the net where you can lay your hand on it when the moment comes. And the moment must *not* come until the trout is well and truly beaten. When it *is* beaten, hurry slowly ; for who knows what may happen on a short line and who can speak with certainty of a hold before the fish is out of the river ?

But now that you have the big trout in the quieter water between the two runs, now that he ' lies floating many a rood,' get on with it calmly but quickly. You are possibly separated from your fish by six feet of sheer and solid masonry. Kneel upon the brink and take your rod in your left hand. Take heed to keep the gut trace clear of the wall and of the probable concrete ledge below the wall. Take the net in your right hand and lay it in the river as horizontally as is possible. Now move right hand and left hand towards each other, and may the gods be with you. As soon as the fish is netted lay your rod on the coping and with both hands lift the net and its burden up and out. Carry it a yard or so from the edge. Remember that the coping slopes and that a fish can roll and that a six-foot drop back into the river will break any trace. Therefore, while the fish is still in the net, let him be visited by the priest, ay, or ever you remove the hook from his mouth.

And now, with knees and hands which shake a bit, I expect, and a face, could you see it, of the colour of butter (well, a big trout always serves *me* like that), you may sit down and smoke a cigarette and admire yourself and your trophy.

As a matter of fact I possibly have been theorizing for the last few hundred words. In general practice the angler who hooks a trout off a weir blows the whistle which he carries, and the lock keeper, or the lock keeper's lad, runs hot-foot to his assistance. So do not forget the whistle as part of your Thames outfit. Silver shrill, its panic note will carry above the plunge and thunder of great waters, whereunto never voice can reach.

I fancy that I have now touched upon all the main essentials of Thames angling. I spoke of waders ? So I did. You will never require these unless you fly-fish for dace in tidal water or unless you fish a weir, and not always then. Stocking waders will serve you well. The water you wade in may be swift but it will never be deep. You will be walking as a rule on a made pavement and therefore there will be no grit or gravel to get into your brogues and wear your waders out before their time. So you may, if you will, dispense with the socks that you would wear over your trouser waders did you go to the bonny banks of Whaupie.

Whole-piece waders, by which I mean waders on to which the brogues are built, will do on the Thames, but I prefer the ' stocking ' sort. Because if the whole-piece wader springs a leak then the brogue is put out of action too, and that's a double catastrophe where one would have served. Moreover, you cannot turn whole-piece waders about when you want to dry them. And a man should cherish his waders and dry them inside out and outside in, always, after a wearing. But you will only wade in Thames water in the summer time, for in winter the weirs and their wadeable places will be too heavy for either safety or sport. Still, waders must surely be a part of the Thames angler's kit.

And what else will he be wanting ? He will want a tackle box. I set beside me on weirs or carry in my boat a small leather despatch box made originally for the baser uses of books and correspondence. There is room within it for three reels, a box of artificial minnows and the usual offices—traces, floats, spoons, weights, flights according to fancy, snaps, hooks and a reel of cotton. You'll soon know all that's required of your box. And a disgorger is required. Never go to the river without one. It saves the life of many an unsizeable fish. If, however, it has been forgotten, your knife (which you will carry in your pocket) will cut you an eight inches of willow twig with a tiny fork, like that of a fairy catapult, at its ultimate extremity. This fork, passed into the jaws of the fish and pressed gently upon the bend of the hook, will soon jolly the hold out. Whereupon the little fish must be held under water, head to the current, until he gives a wriggle, slips through your fingers and is gone. Never *throw* a fish back to the river. Lovingly handle it, in the nursemaid manner that I have prescribed, until its strength is renewed to it by the water. To be thrown back will possibly cause it, it being weak and tired, to drown and thus will a potential trophy untimely die and you, a slayer of infants, be ' a fool unto thyself.'

What else is wanted ? Well, in summer, if it is a summer like that of 1931, you will want a light ' oily ' coat and a pair of ' leg overalls.' These, rolling up small, will, when not in commission, easily go into your waterproof bag. In winter you will want all the clothes and sweaters you can put on and a hurricane smock over all. The leg ' overalls ' too, as once in May.

I mentioned a waterproof bag. This is wanted not to carry fish in but for luncheon (if you eat it), 'oilies,' and (if you are walking the bank with a spinning-rod where a tackle box would be a burden to you) for an extra trace and a change of baits. You can always put your fish therein too. But if you are being lucky you will find it too small. Almost invariably, however, you will find that your Thames fishing is done from a boat or from a weir. In a boat you will put your fish into the ' well,' to be enlarged, for the most part, later. On the weir, lay your big trout down in the lock-keeper's shed upon plucked grass or, preferably, on nettles, and hap (as they say in Angus) the whole in two sheets of newspaper. He, or they, will do nicely so, till it is time to go home.

If you put, all alive-o, a big trout, pike, chub or barbel into the punt's well, be careful how you open the same. I have seen a tragedy. A beginner caught a beginner's luck pike. I do not know how big it was for it was never weighed. It was put into the well. The captor was warned that it was unwise to remove the cover of the well and gloat. He did so neverthe-

less once, and twice. When, like the young man in
the auction rooms of Madrid, he for a third time
' lifted the lid,' the pike had recovered its spirits and
strength. Seeing light in its darkness it leapt with a
wallop that landed it on the side of the boat, off
which it fell, with another wallop, into the water.

Really I think that I have now named all your re-
quirements except the actual fish. Patience of course
you will require, and perseverance. Also a high heart
and a pretty content in all the petty miseries of
angling. Which are far worse to bear than the
grievous misfortunes of the game. And one thing
more. You will probably lose less tackle in the deep,
main Thames than in any other river that you could
name. Yet a weir pool eats wagtails and spinners, a
weir pool is the grave of the white-metal spoon. You
will want *all* your patience and one or two little
chaplets of willow. In fact when you get hung up, do
not, cursing like a cockatoo, tug at your tackle. Be
gentle with it to the point of *laisser faire* and anon the
current shall set you free. If it does not, slip one of
the little wreaths I have named over the butt of the
rod and let it run down the line on to the trace,
where, in some mysterious way, it and the river working in unison will, seven times out of ten, save the
situation and your half-crown phantom. Make two
of these wreaths before you begin to fish and it is
possible, quite possible, that you will require neither.
To make them, cut a yard of willow twig, bend the
points together and lash them tight with the untrust-
worthy link or two that you have just cut off the end
of your spinning line. So shall nothing be wasted
and you may, at long last, begin to try for a fish.

IV. THE PIKE
(*ESOX LUCIUS*)

Hist! there's a pike, see, nose against the river,
Gaunt as a wolf, the grim, old privateer?

AUSTIN DOBSON.

Y gardener, who is an angler too, tells me that he has read in a printed book that the pike has seven hundred and three teeth in his ugly head. I presume that the writer of the book has counted them to see. I have not but I should, at a guess, have estimated for about seven thousand, had you asked for my opinion while the removal of a spoon-bait from among them was in process.

I was once badly bitten by a pike. In a salmon river of Angus that I used to fish long ago there was, no doubt there is still, a long, deep pool above a salmon dyke. This pool always had a pike or two in it though I never saw a man jack of them in any other part of the river. Sometimes, for want of a better employ, I would fish for these pike, spinning with a silver spoon. On the occasion of my accident, for the poor fish did not bite me on purpose, I had caught a pike of 10 lb. I was spinning from a coble employed on the pool as a ferry boat. This little ship was kept padlocked to a post but it had a long chain and you could stand in the stern of it and cover every likely corner of the pool by throwing a length of line. When I caught the pike I killed him and laid him on the seat of the boat and went to take the hooks out of his mouth. But I had not killed him dead enough—a pike has more vitality, I think, than any fish other than eel—and as I fumbled among his molars, canines and incisors with a canny finger or two, he gave a flounder and fell off the seat and almost took the top of my right thumb along with him. I spouted blood till I nearly had the boat swamped, and if you do not believe me I have the mark to show you in proof that my words are true.

But they have taken me a far cry from the green Berkshire banks off which I must be fishing this morning. I implied just now that the pike was an ugly fellow. Before I go further I wish to eat my words. A pike in autumn and winter is an extremely handsome fish in the rather rococo style. His lines are those of a racing car, he is deep in his jade-brown flank, he is thick in his back of olive-green. His belly is as palely golden as the best butter. He has the *driving* appearance of a torpedo. Indeed his caudal, dorsal and anal fins, great fins all, contagious and of a similar and balanced appearance, remind one a little of the screw propeller of a torpedo. He is built, in fact, for pace, power and a flying start as you would

expect him to be, he who must exist by murder and
piracy. His flat skull and jaw, Dr Turrell has said,
accentuate his speediness.

He has the appearance of a courageous Uriah Heap.
The adjective is my own, the simile that of Mr Sheringham. He is the tyrant of the watery plain. I
have forgotten whose copyright that is, but it is not
mine.

Esox then is, on the whole, a rather fine-looking
fish and a yeoman fighter.

> Not a Galahad, mayhap,
>   Gently born, would I acclaim him,
> But a very decent chap
>   And a stubborn, I would name him ;
> And I fancy (mind the pile ;
>   There he shows—one sullen flounder)
> You will say it's been worth while,
>   Ere we net that thick ten-pounder.

But the first step to netting your pike is to hook
him, as Mrs. Beeton might have said. And the first
step to hooking him, say I, is to begin to fish for him.

And since it is a Thames pike that we want it is to
Thames that we must go. And, for some reason
which I am at a loss to conjecture, the Thames, a
great river with abundant food, spawning facility,
and an enormous stock of pike, lacks in really big
fish. I have never personally killed a Thames pike
of over ten pounds. A friend of mine who must have
landed, in his fishing life, at least a thousand Thames
pike has had but two of this vast number that pulled
down the scale below the twenty-pound notch. I
know of a pike of twenty-nine pounds taken at Goring
some twenty years ago and that is the largest Thames

pike that I have knowledge of. I have, as I have said, never killed a Thames pike of over ten pounds. That, maybe, is because I rarely use live-bait for jack and I think that the very big fish take a spinning-bait less often than a live dace. But even so the live-bait does not accomplish much bigger things than the dead or artificial lures. But I have caught a Dead Sea Apple fish that probably weighed twenty pounds.

You ask me of Dead Sea Apples ? Listen and you shall hear :

In green and white the deep water plunges under the footbridge and spreads into streams of weir pool, and an angler on the bridge contemplates a cheerful red float that, forty yards away, nid-nods on edges of duller emerald and pearl.

Of a sudden this float swims from its stance, and when it has proceeded ten yards the angler strikes. Look, he has certainly hooked a large fish, for his rod bends and his reel most rapidly revolves ; while the fish, boring prodigiously into the current, goes downstream as though the devil had kicked him. Fifteen minutes later, with sullen flounder and exhibitions of a thick olive-green back, a twenty-pound pike comes stubbornly to the capacious net, without which no provident Thames angler goes.

Now it is no mean accomplishment to have achieved so goodly a pike on such fine tackle and in such heavy water. And yet the angler and his attendant lack in animation, and the interested lock-keeper is surely being sympathetic. For it is lilac time and pike are sacrosanct, and only a spotted trout may to-day be lawfully ours. And this large pike has taken our trout bait, and now that the hook has been removed, with all gentleness, from his jaw, he who would have made the fortunes of a February day must go free. Nevertheless, please to slide him into his Thames *above* the lasher and not *below* it, lest he there live to be the bane of trout and to increase our estimate of his present bulk upon the pink fleshes of *fario*.

*　　　*　　　*　　　*　　　*

On this mild and springlike morning our punt is moored in the main river. The rod we use to-day is a stiffer rod, a sturdier rod and a heavier by far than that we were handling just now. And yet it is bucking in our grasp as though its weight were but five ounces, while fifty yards from the point of it a huge trout leaps and leaps again. Nevertheless, presently the net is under him and he is our own. There are experts in the punt who estimate his nobility at eleven silver pounds. Surely, then, our reputations are made ? Well, so they might have been in the May month, but to-day, mild and springlike though it be, is but a February day.

And so our trout is a Dead Sea Apple after all, a Dead Sea Apple that has fallen to a pike-spoon. And now that he has been nursed awhile, nose to current, he too must go free and unfished for until the cuckoo calls.

*　　　*　　　*　　　*　　　*

This honest angler thinks that he has hooked a specimen trout, which will look well in a glass case with, maybe, a mayfly in its mouth. And who will blame the fancy, since April is up and blossoming, and the beautiful pool in which he is fishing (with a live bleak) is famous for the size and quantity of the trout he so desires. And has not the fish he is playing (helped a little by the stream perhaps) just taken forty yards off his reel in the most spritely fashion ? Yet why, after so gallant an effort, does so gamecock a fighter cease to fight and come heavily to hand, rolling in weary bronze and much pallor of belly ?

The reason is, alas, obvious, for it is a loggerhead chevin of the off-season who has taken the lure, and no trout at all. And yet the fellow is not without a certain dignity as he lies goggling upon the coping, while those present, condoling with his captor, agree in voting to his misfortune a magnitude of eight pounds, and in naming it, with many an ' if only,' a record chub even for Father Thames.

Perhaps, since there presently paddles away a shadowy shape among the schools of fry below the steps, perhaps, next July, as in summer indolence a portly Presence lies sunning upon the ' apron,' perhaps it may be that a Coachman dropped in front of a pompous nose—Well, we shall see.

* * * * *

Dead Sea Apple fish, then, are the big fish taken out of due season. Noble fish which must be put back into the river along with the repute that might, a month earlier, a month later, have been, because of them, the angler's.

Two other big Thames pike I have heard of. These are a male and a female fish each weighing a little over forty pounds, spawners which, many years ago, were sinfully caught by hand in a flooded ditch near Wallingford. If the weights are right, or approximately so, these are, by ten pounds, the heaviest pike that Father Thames has ever told me of.

The methods of pike fishing are two : spinning and live-baiting. We will look at the latter way first since ninety per cent of the pike caught in the Thames are taken upon a living lure. Generally the bait is an eight-inch dace or roach which the angler either catches himself, on crust or gentle, or buys from a professional fisherman.

The usual manner of fishing the live-bait is the float manner. The paternoster is rarely employed. The reason for this is that the paternoster, a swivelled trace with a weight at the end and the single hook, on six inches of gut, attached to the trace a foot or more above the lead in the manner of a ' dropper ' fly on a trout cast, is only superior to the float style of fishing in weir pools and among weed beds. It may be dropped, upon a commonplace rod, cannily among dangerous piles and awkward corners. When it is felt that the lead has touched bottom, raise the point of the rod till you have the line taut. Keep out of sight, if you can, and when you have held your bait in position for a minute or two without result lift it up and drop it between the next pair of piles. If here you get, what the Thames fisherman calls a ' knock,' which means a bite, lower the point of the rod for about ten seconds to give the pike time to turn the bait in his mouth, which he does very quickly (head first), and then strike hard. I use a single bait hook, one of the medium size, and I fasten it below the dorsal fin of the dace. As I have said, the paternoster is not greatly used on the Thames. At the time when most men go pike fishing the weirs are too heavy to show sport and, were they not, a weir ticket is essential, which almost certainly the pike angler, unless he follows in his season the Thames trout also, has not troubled to provide himself with. And the weed beds in winter time, in pike time, are negligible as annoyances. So in practical Thames politics we can rule out the paternoster.

In practising the float method of the live-bait a boat is nearly always to be preferred. There are places where the angler may cast his tackle into deep water and, keeping it close to the bank, may walk with it downstream until something happens. Bank anglers, as we have seen, may throw out a live-bait and hope the best for it, while they themselves continue with the roach pole. But the boat is the common form.

And the live-bait rod is our commonplace rod, though upon the thwarts may lie one or other of our spinning pair. It will be found pleasant to have a chuck or two presently, pleasant to get out of the boat and restore circulation by a brisk walk up the frosty towpath with the spinning-rod to accompany you and search out any likely eddy or golden reed-bed's lee upon the way. And, quite frankly, I hate live-baiting for pike, though illogically, for trout, I freely use the method. I think the difference is that the dace and the roach attached to the heavy pike tackle look so tired and uncomfortable. A bleak or a gudgeon upon light tackle seems by comparison to be almost enjoying the novelty of its experience. And on the first symptoms of boredom on the bait's part I let it go. I never put a bait back into the can but always into the river, where it goes off with a dash.

I cannot believe that the bait suffers pain as we understand pain. I cannot think that it realizes fearfully the purport of its restraint. When, too, a trout takes a live-bait it may well happen that the trout, hooking itself, ejects the bait unharmed. I have seen this occur when the bait has been taken close to me. I have seen bleak and gudgeon swim away in no wise, apparently, worse for the encounter. The pike on the other hand has time to kill or injure the bait he takes before you strike him. All live-bait fishing is cruel, but we can make it less so if we release the bait when it is obviously tiring, and if at the end of the day we turn the little fish that we have over loose in the river again.

Do not keep the residue of your live-bait from day to day unless you have a proper aquarium for them. The best and simplest sort is perhaps the well of a punt that is moored in a sharp stream. The fish will keep there without hardship for two or three days. But look at them daily and any that seem to be dwamly restore to the river at once. I have a bait aquarium made, like a meat safe, of perforated zinc. This, on a tow-rope, in the tail water of a weir or a mill-race, keeps the captives in excellent health. But it is only rarely that I use it for I like to see the bait that are over and above go back to Thames at the end of the day. The bleak dart hither and thither like dogs let out of kennel, the gudgeon make straight for cover, a moss-grown pile, or wall, and into the moss they burrow like so many rabbits. And you, their liberator, feel yourself, do you not, to be another St. Francis ?

But to get on with our fishing. And that expression reminds me that years ago I was fishing for trout with the late Walter Coster. Coster was a man of solemn appearance. He dressed in rusty black and wore a bowler hat always. We were anchored at the entrance to the backwater that runs from the weir alongside the lawns of The Angler Hotel. A party in a smart private launch came upstream, for the hotel, at a rate of knots. Behind Coster's punt was a gravel shallow cocking up goldenly out of the deep, foam-laced current. Coster did not speak, but he motioned with his hand to imply that caution was required, that there were breakers ahead. The young men and maidens on the launch thought that they were being haughtily instructed by a menial. Thought that they were being asked to keep out of an angler's way and water. The launch shot past. ' You have not bought the river,' said the lad who steered her, ' get on with your fishing and be damned to you.' Coster did not look up. Twenty yards away the launch, still at a rate of knots, rammed the gravel and went aground with a grunt. Coster did not turn his head. But I turned mine and saw the launch peck and pant to back off the shoal that she had fouled. She failed to do so, profanely.

' Hi, gov'nor,' said one of the marooned, ' give us a tow off ? '

' I'll get on with my fishing,' was the robust retort.

But after one of the party had gone outboard and up to his middle in the loose, shifting gravel and failed to push *Naiad*, or whatever her name was, off and into her draught, the fishing-punt's anchor was slowly, very slowly, weighed. And still in silence was a salvage effected and the salvagees' offer of a fee waved aside. It was renounced with the same solemn gesture that they had misinterpreted in the first instance. And, then, still in silence, Coster ' got on with his fishing.' And it is perhaps time that we got on with ours.

The commonplace rod, then, as when we tried the paternoster. The Nottingham reel, as before, with its undressed silk line the ultimate ten yards of which you may rub with vaseline. Attach thereto two yards of salmon gut mounted on swivels and weighted according to taste and water to be fished. I find the ' envelope ' leads of Messrs. Hardy the simplest and quickest to put on and take off. They are extremely cheap and may be had in every variety of size. For the colour of my float I prefer red to white. A big red float is, like Pitti Sing, ' a cheering sight to see ' ; something about the height of a hock tumbler I mean but rotund as a claret glass.

This big float may be attended by two or more little floats—about the size of a shilling—which are placed at intervals of a foot or so above their principal. The function of these lesser floats, they are known as pilots, is, I believe, to prevent the bait, when cast out, fouling the line or swimming over it if the latter becomes water-logged. They are useful I think chiefly in lakes ; in rivers the stream keeps, or should keep, the sequence, line, float, trace and bait, in due position. But pilots add to the prettiness and pretensions of pike fishing and are employed, as ornaments, by many Thames anglers of artistic taste.

The hook that I use is a single, strong bait-hook, with a shank of an inch or thereabouts. This is tied on six inches of gimp. A pike, as we have seen, has seven hundred teeth and may, when hooked, bite through salmon gut easily enough. On the other hand he may not ; I have landed dozens of pike on the finest gut, fellows who have taken my trout tackle. But in pike fishing, as in most other things, it is better to be sure than sorry. This single hook I fasten just below the dorsal fin of the bait and I am then ready to begin.

The actual fishing of a live-bait for pike requires little skill. In the Thames it is rarely necessary to cast the bait because the stream will carry it where you will. If to cast is necessary, pull the requisite line off the reel and coil it upon a clear space, say the flat lid of the punt's well. Lift the bait up and swing the point of the rod, gently, underhand, and forward. Weight, bait and float will carry the coiled line in the direction required and you may then sit down and wait events.

The pike never takes a live-bait with the *stramash* of the trout. When you are fishing a weir pool from the footbridge and you hook a pike the common form of it is thus. You will notice that your float is under water. You will think that the under-tow has carried your tackle in among the moss-grown piles that guard the weir's apron and that there it has fouled. You will tighten gently and feel a living, but loglike, re-sistance. You will have hooked a pike, for no other fish that swims the river acts thus sluggardly towards you. Here in the anchored punt the first indication of sport will be a gentle rock-a-bye motion of the big red float, imitated, in pygmean tremblings, by its system of little scarlet pilots.

While you watch these tremors with anticipation I would say that your punt will be anchored twenty or thirty yards from where you expect the pike to be. And a pike of course may be anywhere. But the likeliest lies are in quiet eddies, close swirling under banks and at the ends of reed bed and eyot. Upon a clearing flood the pike come into lock-cuttings, mill-tails, and backwaters of all kinds to be at ease and near the small fishes that come haunting there too. In such places you will sometimes take, in a suitable water and on a suitable day, half-a-dozen fish without moving your stance.

And a suitable day I have most often found to be a mild winter morning, grey and soft. Indeed the best day's pike fishing ever I had was once upon a third of February, Spring already in the air and a bud on the sallow. This was the day on which I caught the Dead Sea Apple trout under the ' Vicarage Bough ' on Henley Regatta course.

Usually I think that pike take more freely in the morning than in the afternoon, and yet last Sunday, March 6th, I saw a catch of eleven pike, largest ten pounds, taken, all of them, to the bite of an acidulous East wind, at the end of Goring mill-tail between 3.30 p.m. and freezing six o'clock. 'The Pike,' as Mr. Punch has told us, per his Mr. Leech, ' is a voracious fish and takes readily in cold weather.' And the angler, in the picture, is breaking the ice with a pick-axe. This is not entirely the spritely invention of a great humorist.

The January day had come in bitterly and the two anglers who had pulled down on the flood from Mouls-ford found that the backwater, above the building yards at South Stoke, was frozen over by a thickness of ice. ' The Pike,' quoted one fisherman to the other, ' is a voracious—— '

No sooner said than the other, Mr. Leech in mind, urged the punt into the ice field while his friend laid about him lustily, if not with a pick-axe, at least with a ryepeck. Gradually an acre of ice was broken. But a welter of broken ice is to the angler little better than frozen over. The anglers slapped their arms till their fingers tingled and they whistled for a wind. And a wind came ruffling the snipe marshes and ' crisping the lazy dyke.' And it blew the ice packs jumbling and jingling out of the backwater and into the river. And, out of the backwater too, eight handsome pike were achieved in an hour. Which proves, if it proves anything, that Mr. Punch, occasionally, jests seriously and to a purpose.

Now while I've been talking the floats have continued to wobble and now the parent float moves away a yard, two, three yards and then under it goes. Not with a quick bob and curtsey, the mode of lesser fishes, but with a stately circumstance. Get a taut line with care therefore and strike hard—strike really hard. And you will have hooked your pike, I fancy.

But keep on striking if you suspect the fish of not being truly hooked. Pike are sometimes prone to hold the bait in their mouths and swim with it a space and let it go. If you have the hook home in him for keeps you will get a sort of figure-of-eight pull.

Be suspicious always of an even strain and hit him once more and mak' siccar.

But had the float moved, instead of downstream or side along, *upstream*, your strike must be administered so that the bait is not pulled away from the pike's hold. A taut line, as before, then, and the point of the rod at as right, or as left, an angle from the pike as possible. And then hit him as usual. If you cannot see the sunken float itself it may be that the pilots will indicate to you in which direction the fish is moving ; if they too are below surface the line is tell-tale enough for any man with eyes.

Once hooked on a bait a pike is usually as good as caught and in the playing of him an ordinary skill suffices. You don't want me to tell you to keep a tight line, to keep the point of the rod up, so I'll only say the sooner the hooked fish is out of the river the less water he'll disturb and the sooner you may try for another. And, once more, let your landing-net be capacious and of a long handle. You will probably kill all the pike you catch that are sizeable fishes, so whack this one on the head with one of the empty bottles or ever you take the hook out of his mouth.

I have said that I use a single hook for this form of angling. Many more anglers than I use the Jardine adjustable snap. It's a jolly name anyhow. I have said that my aim is not to be *too* instructive. So I will not expound upon this tackle further than a brief statement that it consists of two triangles mounted on gimp, the upper of the two ingeniously contrived for adjusting itself, with your assistance, to the size of the bait employed. This top triangle is inserted under the bait's dorsal fin, the lower beneath the corresponding pectoral. And now proceed as before.

Gorge-bait fishing is nowadays rightly considered by the Conservancy to be illegal. I will not dwell upon it here. Its only merit was that the natural bait employed was dead. The pike took it, the float went under. The angler laid the rod down, looked at his watch and whistled the popular tune of the moment—*Tommy make room for your Uncle*. In five minutes' time, *i.e.* after the pike had swallowed, most thoroughly swallowed, the bait, the angler hauled him out. The angler then, or his attendant, performed what deer-stalkers call the gralloch, which alone enabled him (as with a moment's thought you will recognize) to recover his tackle.

Once an elderly angler told a little boy how a pretty lady, standing on the footbridge below Goring lock, had dropped her diamond engagement ring off her lily-white finger and into the river. Next day the angler caught a pike upon the gorge-bait, not then illegal.

' What,' said he to the little boy, ' do you think I found inside the pike ? '

' Guts,' said the little boy promptly.

' Exactly,' said the elderly angler ; ' and so the pretty lady never saw her ring again and had to have a new one or else she couldn't have been engaged any more.'

I think that's all that is essential to the live-bait.

This, perhaps, further, if you are not getting ' knocks ' do not be lazy about lifting anchor and punting up to Winney's Weg and trying a new pitch. And every now and then, and nothing happening, take the trouble to wind in and examine your bait. Possibly you will find a streamer of weed caught up on it. I have never known a fish to take a bait to which a salad has attached itself. It looks too unnatural, I suppose. The pike is a voracious fish but he shuns mayonnaise.

V. AND STILL THE PIKE

Down the wind with rod and traces
To the changeless changing places
With a pocket full of spinners, and a little net and bag ;
Just a whisper on the margent,
' My device is gules and argent,
Yes ! and I will follow softly with the spinner that can wag.'

CHARLES MARSON.

HAVE said that the shortest method with a Thames pike is the way of the live-bait. But occasionally the pike will take anything from a mayfly, or a bunch of gentles, to a cygnet. I have caught a pike on the Thames on a small Alexandra fly ; I have seen one, of 16 lb., caught on a Jock Scott in an Angus salmon river. I believe that the Great Pike of Loch Ken who weighed 72 lb. and whose head—*nine* inches across is that gaunt head—may still be seen at Kenmure Castle, Galloway, was taken by the gamekeeper who caught him upon a large, brown, single-hook fly.

I have seen Thames pike and trout take infant

74

water-hens and infant voles, and not so infant as all that either. I once, at the Forfar end of Rescobie Loch, shot a teal which fell in the water. Or ever the keeper's curly, red dog, cleaving the deep, could reach it an enormous swirl spread and widened and the duck was gone.

But I do not think it follows that because a pike takes a large bait he is himself large. Long ago I watched a fisherman playing a 6 lb. grilse on the Shannon. Suddenly the sparkling liveliness of its play was changed to a dull resistance. In a moment or so this heaviness passed and then the angler literally pulled his fish ashore. It was dead and the imprint of great jaws marred the flawless silver.

' The largest pike in Ireland ! ' cried the angler and would have gone home at once for trolls and pike tackle.

But I had seen the pike take the grilse across its silver self. Far from being a big pike I don't believe it would have made 15 lb. Which is less than nothing for an *Esox* of Erin.

Therefore when you land a pike of 5 lb. and he torn and worried, do not therefore say of his wounds that for certain some leviathan lives hard by. It may be so, but a pike, and indeed all fish, are poor judges of their own cubic capacity. Judge not the size, then, of any fish by evidence other than that of the eye and the fish's actual self. Worst of all is it to say that the pike who has just broken you by sheer physical strength is a very large one. Your friend will spin over the spot and catch the brute forthwith. It will have your phantom in its mouth and it will weigh 3 lb. 5 oz.

For pike will come again and again. I caught the same small, unseasonable fish four times in half an hour as I spun for trout at Mapledurham one April day. I knew it by the works of another; it had a triangular tear below the dorsal that was unmistakable. When I had taken the hooks from it for the fourth time I put the little glutton back to river above the lock, or nor I nor my friend would have had, that morning, peace for our lawful occasions.

An unlawful way to catch Thames pike is by what is called trailing. It is a confusing thing, but this trailing is what on Loch Awe, where ' the ferox rins,' is called *trolling*. Which is what, on Tayside, is only *harling* after all. But trolling, on the Thames, is, speaking pedantically, live-baiting. To trail is, shortly, to throw out a spinning-bait behind the boat and row upstream as fast as you can. I do not know why the Conservancy object to this.

Two young men and a maiden, brothers and sister, went with one spinning-rod and a large blue phantom to Staines. It was on an August day and a pike was the secondary objective. The first was a Sunday on the river in a Canadian canoe with cushions. This, the latter named, the Sunday, was a complete success; the pike they failed in. At four o'clock there was a thunderstorm. The sister lay down in the canoe and the brothers covered her with flannel coats and *The Sunday Times*. Then, shirt-sleeved, they went to it with the paddles like the Canadian Boat Song. The nymph upon the floor held the rod. Illegally she paid off line till she had thirty yards out with the four-inch, weighted, blue phantom to spin at the end. And the thunder rolled and the big rain came splashing down like tepid half-crowns. To dig of paddles the canoe raced for shelter and tea. Suddenly the lady and the reel screamed together like the morning stars. Over the canoe's stern the rod's point, kicking convulsively, was being dragged into the water. Then, fifty yards away, a fish, great and very silver, leaped and leaped again. There was no net, there was nothing but the rain and the thunder and the shouting of the captains and the conflicting advices of the same. But the trout, he had taken good and proper, was landed. And he weighed 6 lb. 4 oz. and tasted far better than salmon.

There is yet another way which Conservators deny and I agree with them. This is trimmer-fishing which is not fishing at all but only rather fun. Take half a dozen flat pieces of cork cut circularly to about twice the size of a soup plate. Paint upper sides white and lower sides red. Put pegs through the centres, and to the *tops* of these fasten a yard or so of line, trace, single hook and live-bait. Launch forth the argosy and watch it as it floats slowly down upon the gentle stream. A pike will presently take hold of one or other of the voyagers. But how will you, in your boat, know that ? Because the trimmer that has been attractive will turn over and run, blushing redly for its sin. And you will now row after it and catch it when you can. I need not say, I hope, that I have never practised this method on the Thames. But it is a fascinating game for little boys on lakes which it is desired to stock with trout when ' those damned pike ' have been taken out from among the lily-beds.

And so, at long last, we come to the only reputable way of catching a pike, we come to spinning and the spinning-rod. Of the spinning-rod we have seen. Of the art of spinning there is little new to be said. You swing the rod gently forward, you carry through (as they say at St Andrews), the line flies out (or else it over-runs) and in the former case you will be spinning well enough to catch salmon, if the Thames had salmon, or to catch almost as many pike as the next man.

If the reel over-runs, and there is no such thing as a quite fool-proof reel, take the trace off the line, take the reel off the rod and as patiently as possible unravel the mess. I know nothing so damnably annoying as an over-run, and patience cannot always be commanded. Therefore carry a second reel that may be substituted for the one (all loops and ends and dishevelment is it) that has over-run performance. Even if you do not use the substitute the knowledge that you have it by you conduces to calm and method. If use it you must, let your attendant if you have one (a wife or a daughter is better than a hired man) get on with the tangle forthwith and be ready with number one by the time that number two follows a bad example.

If no over-run occurs, and none should if you know your own limitations and use lots of lead weight, then the bait will fall neatly, twenty, thirty, forty yards away. Let it sink while you count six slowly. And now wind it back to you—and what, already?

> Not the knightly rush we know
>   When the sea-bright salmon's ' copped it,'
> But the spoon is checked below
>   Just as if a log had stopped it;

Not the lightning lunge of trout
   Lashing sun-kissed silver whiter,
But, for all that, 'tis the stout
   Onslaught of a yeoman fighter.

And as for playing him ? Well, the first thing is to strike him. It is never necessary to strike a salmon or a trout, but a pike, who takes less energetically, can stand, nay demands, a ' good hard knock.' Give it him, then. And thereafter bustle things up and have him into the boat, or on to the bank, and you be getting on with it. For winter days are short days and with stout spinning tackle you can afford to give a fish short shrift.

And the tackle that I talk of ? We've seen the line, the trace is —— ? Wire, I suppose, is the sensible stuff because it cannot be bitten through. But it is liable to *kink*, that most irritating thing. And though wire is strong it will break at a kink, and also, when it becomes rusty, at the swivel knots, which is its frequent habit.

There is also gut substitute. A friend of mine went, on the last day of the season, to fish for trout at Whitchurch weir. It was a mild, rainy day and, early, he caught a trout of some pounds. *Et preterea nil.* It began to get dusk and he mounted a Thames flight and spun the ' bathing pool ' over. In the fast water a heavy trout had a dash at the bait and missed it. Once again then the bleak came flickering —this time there was no mistake. The trout took close under the sill—ten pounds of trout. He went downstream with a prodigious dash. He came back to the white water, came back so fast that the angler must reel in all he knew to keep in touch with his fish. Into the foam and the bubbles of foam the trout bored, digging and jigging and pulling the rod top down. He sailed into shallower water and now the gut substitute trace showed tautly moving. The angler tells me that he plainly saw one of the knots in it. Very slowly this knot began to slip. It slipped until it parted asunder, for gut substitute is apt so to slip.

And thus the trout was never landed at all and he is probably in Whitchurch weir pools to-day—15 lb. of him by now. But the angler took his scissors and cut his supply of gut substitute into inches and half-inches.

That leaves us with salmon gut. And what's good enough for a salmon is good enough for a pike. You'll not want too long a trace, a swivelled yard-and-a-half is ample. And the odds are that in all your fishing life you'll never lose a pike because it bit through the gut spinning-trace. The reason of this immunity is that the artificial spinning-baits are big and of metal or of wire-mounting and that the hooked pike usually wears them between him and the gut. For the natural baits the flights are of metal and wire and these too are, as a rule, semi-external in application.

A good natural bait is a ' wobbler.' Get some fresh sprats, which will keep a day or two in a cool place and if liberally dusted with salt. Take a tri-angle of size tied to eight inches or more of gimp or wire. Pass the loop of the wire in through the sprat's vent and out of its mouth, and your bait is ready. It will not spin but it will wobble. Its chief disadvantage is that sprats are frail things and fly to bits all too easily. But this you can afford since, with fresh sprats, cheapness and frailty go together. Which is not always the case in a world where one amuses one's self. And watch over your fresh sprats when you bring them home or some busybody will take them and serve them to you fried.

You may, of course, use this tackle with any small fish and, do you want to spin with dead natural bait, the Hardy Crocodile Spinner of the larger sort. is beautifully simple. But make more sure of its ' smiling jaws ' with a turn or two of sewing-thread.

And of artificial baits ? Take any catalogue, such, for instance, as the one I have before me now. There are forty distinct artificial ' minnows ' in this fascinating book. They are coloured and captivating each one, and neither salmon, trout nor pike could resist them. But there is not a ha'porth of difference between the one pattern or the other in killingness, only in price do they vary from, say, 1s. 6d. to 4s. each. Size ? Yes, have a change in size. Big minnows for big, coloury water, small minnows for the small and gin clear. The tints of the artificial minnow I leave to your own artistic taste, for the pike has no preferences.

As a matter of fact, if you use minnow for pike at all, I recommend the metal sorts. And let them wear as few hooks as possible, one triangle at the tail is enough, I think. With the softer materials the pike's seven hundred teeth play havoc—expensive havoc too, at 4s. a time.

But for practical Thames-side use the spoon is really all the artificial bait you'll want. Full many a pike dies with a silver spoon in his mouth. Even in spoons there are colours and shapes, all of which may be disregarded. What does the pike care ? But if *you* like coloured spoons they may be had in variety. Size however may be, triply, attended to. Your biggest spoon should be of the sort that Miss Williams used to catch *you* on in 1883—you will remember that you had been ordered cod-liver oil—' a table-spoonful after meals ' ? And do you not recollect how, on one occasion, and you just taking the spoon, another of your sort blew into your ear with the bellows so that you spluttered and the oil went hither and thither and all down poor little Miss W.'s new dress—dark brown merino and black braid on it ?

And dessert-spoon size and tea-spoon size will make the three spoons needful. Let their hooks also be few. Two triangles on the big spoon, at trace and lip respectively. On the smaller sort, one only—at lip.

On my last birthday, in June, someone who loves me gave me a mother-of-pearl spoon—it was carven on its concavity with scales and fins and it had pink coral eyes. It was like the very young of the dolphins who tumble in the wake of the car of Thetis, ' the darling of Paradise,'

> ' Seas before her rise and break
> Dolphins tumble in her wake
> Along the sapphire courses.'

Just like that it was. Alas, I could not wait till October to try it on the pike that it was meant for but must needs take it to Mapledurham weir forthwith and catch a trout on it. It looked like a magic in the shift of the deep, green, foam-dappled pool. But it hung itself up on that pile in the run by the mill and all my care and willow-wreaths would not move it. I expect that some naiad has found it by now and that she wears it for a trinket about her slippery, ivory neck.

But away with such wild-rose fancies and let's catch another pike. And this we may fail to do if we do not try the likeliest haunts of the fish. Do not try in mid-river, cast under and along towpaths, cast in eddies, potholes and ' caves in the bank where the sly stream steals,' and in all places where you would hopefully try a live-bait.

Indeed it is no bad plan to spin first where you will presently swim a dace. I think that, even if *Esox* does not, without more ado, run at you, a spun spoon puts a potential taker on the *qui vive* and that the live-bait will do business with him anon.

Do not try to throw too long a line, remember that accuracy kills more fish than competition casting. If you want to cast across the Thames remember that you cannot do so to any purpose because, even do you get your bait over, you cannot keep it in the water you want to fish. Better far pull the boat over, drop the weight and, beginning on a short line, lengthen your anchor rope and your throws, in reason, until you have searched the hopeful-looking length of bank to your good content.

In fishing an eddy, or a pothole, by spinning, fish it, if possible, from upstream. Do not cast, with a splash, into the middle of the lie. Cast beyond it and bring the spoon, silverly, to the pike from behind him.

Spin slowly, but not too slow; I recommend a medium between the circumstance of the salmon speed and the helter-skelter that takes the trout.

Spin deeply ; a pike's eyes are placed in his head
so that he may look ever upwards rather than down.
So he lies, as a rule, low in the water and watches,
soulfully, for the passing bait. Yet you will see him,
sometimes, up and sunning himself upon a shallow.
And if you can put a small spoon to him so, without
splashing, he will probably run at it open-mouthed.
For he is there with whitebait in mind as well as the
sunbath that he enjoys.

With regard to the lead weight that carries your
line out so well and truly there is an infinite variety
of such leads. Yet, undoubtedly, the Hardy envelope
lead is a kindly and convenient lead. I use it invariably for all bait-fishing except when I spin. And
there is no reason why I should not then use the
heavier envelopes except that their use, perhaps,
tends to fret the gut. So I use Mr. Geen's boat-shaped
leads of the heaviest pattern that I can buy. They
are painted dark green and they are rather a bother to
mount but they please the eye when up. The Jardine
corkscrew lead is convenient and I notice that ghillies
on salmon rivers seem to use no other.

Pike, trout and perch will, quite frequently, run at
a Geen, or any other, lead, in preference to the bait.
I have never seen a salmon act so, nor, by touch, sus-
pected him of so acting. There was a big trout below
Quarry Woods for a season or so. Some people said
he was one thing, some another, but I think he must
have been twelve pounds. The late Walter Coster
and I used to fish for him regularly and I imagine that
once we very nearly had him. Early one summer
morning we came dropping down to his stance.
While we were yet a hundred yards off, a dace, like

a silver arrow, went splashing here and there until a V-shaped swirl engulfed it. The punt was poled with mighty polings and I was soon within spinning distance of where the dace had died. Once, twice, I cast, and at the third attempt, when the bait was wellnigh recovered, the great trout came *smash* and wide open within five yards of the punt. But it was to Mr. Geen he came and not to the hooks. A pluck, a plunge and he had gone. I never moved that fish again nor do I think that anyone was more fortunate than I.

A general sooth of spinning is that the heavier the weight the further you can throw. Another is that the lighter your bait the heavier may be the lead and *vice versa*. And here is yet a third knowledge, namely, that a light minnow is apt to fly back and catch up on the trace. Some baits seem to do this maddening thing on purpose. I can suggest no cure for it except an envelope lead pinched upon the gut just above the nose swivel. Or, of course, a change to a heavier minnow.

I hope, later in this book, to speak of the cookery of pike. It seems a tempting of providence to say now what you may do commercially with the overplus of the pike, and coarse fishes generally, that you may catch. But there is a market for these fish, for pike especially, in London. They are greatly liked in the Ghetto and good prices are paid. I have never personally sent my pike to market but I know many an honest angler who does so send them. And thus he pays his tackle bill and has a bit over towards a new rod.

If on any day of November, and forward to March,

you should catch a pike of 5 lb. or upwards continue to try in the same eddy, hover or corner, and you will probably catch another of similar size. Pike do not spawn before they are about 5 lb. in weight, and they pair for spawning in mid-season and always with a fish of like size to themselves. And it is a pitiful inhumanity to leave, if it can be avoided, Mr. Pike a widower, to mourn for Mrs. Pike. Or, once again, *vice versa.*

Meanwhile the spoon has ceased to kill and it's getting on for tea-time:

> Home, then, with the rooks that fly
>   Roostward o'er our Happy Valley ;
> Jangling down the Winter sky
>   Sound their voices musically ;
> And we'll vow (if vow one can
>   Eating teas of wide variety)
> ' Jack ' an honest gentleman
>   Though he isn't in Society.

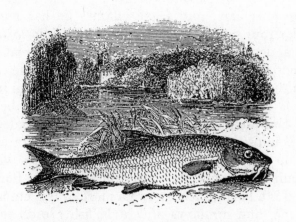

VI. THE BARBEL
(*BARBUS BARBUS*)

The trout his ambush keeps
  Crafty and strong, in Pangbourne's eddying pools,
But patient still in Marlow deeps
  For the shy barbel wait expectant fools.

ANON.

THE barbel is really a carp, or so the experts say. He owes his name, after the Bluebeard mode, to the four minute *feelers*, the little, one inch long, beards which impend two from his upper lip and two from the angles of his rather gross mouth. These four little beards are, so the experts say once more, the most sensitive little indicators in the world. The lurking mollusc, shrimp or water snail, has no chance against them, it is discovered at once and is the barbel's principal *plat* when the silk-weed is not up for him to pasture upon.

The barbel is the most important, the truest and the most stubborn, of the Thames fishes. He is indigenous here, and from Thames he has gone to stock Stour and Avon, who now boast him in quantity and personal bulk. He grows to a great size, fifteen-pound barbel if not common upon the bank, or in the punt, are at least reasonably plentiful in the middle reaches of the river and I do verily believe that this weight may occasionally be exceeded by five pounds or more. These mighty fellows are met with in May by the trout angler who fishes with a live minnow and a little too much weight. For the barbel is a bottom feeder and a more or less omnivorous one, and minnows and little fish are all in the menu. He will not, however, hunt them as a trout or a pike does, yet he will accept them as and when they occur. The trout-angler's minnow will seem just the easy thing. The barbel will take it and, if he does not smash the whole fine outfit, he will in due course be landed and returned carefully to the Thames since he is, till June 15th, unseasonable and sacrosanct.

The biggest barbel that I have ever heard of came about as above. The angler, an expert and knowledgeable angler, was fishing in the open river above Sonning. A very large trout had been located in an eddy between there and Caversham. The state of the weather and the water gave the angler cause to think that the trout would be well down in the deep of the ' lie.' He therefore pinched on another lead or two and presently sat down in the May sunshine, his cork forty yards away, his finger on the undressed silk line. In the angler's boat were two passengers, professional fishermen taking a busman's holiday and studying the methods of the most renowned of Thames amateurs.

Presently a great fish was hooked. It was soon obvious to all that here was no trout but a most prodigious barbel. The angler played it for twenty minutes and then, anxious to return to his legitimate excuse, he broke the fine trace all a-purpose. During the play the fish had been seen, huge, chocolate-brown, white-bellied, and the consensus of sober opinion was that the scale-breaking monster would weigh between twenty and twenty-three pounds. But the trout never materialized and the fisherman regrets to this day that he did not land the barbel and ascertain its actual bulk before returning it to the river. I regret this too but I am satisfied that the poundage would have proved up to estimate.

Barbel spawn in mid-May and it is the most fascinating sight on all Thames to see them, a week or two later, rejoicing that about 25,000 little barbels a-piece have been born to them. Before the Conservancy deepened Goring weir pool and destroyed, with their dredgers and drogues, the first fine rapture of its river beauty, there was no better place to see the barbel in madcap mood than from the old wooden road-bridge. The bridge has gone too but it was a pleasant bridge to lean upon as you went to Streatley. There you would see the shoals of big barbel pushing and rolling on the golden gravels. Golden-brown fish, you would see, in golden-brown water flecked with sunshine and the green shadows of the bulrush beds that thrust up in panoply of green spears out of shallow middle stream. Blue-and-white sky, swifts and swallows to swoop and to soar, speeding wings and speeding water—what summers used to be in Berkshire once !

These Goring barbel always seemed to be, as they porpoise-rolled and leapt and turned over and over, of a lighter shade than the barbel that I first knew in Thames. These were the barbel of Shiplake and Marlow and my memories are of long chocolate-brown backs, bronze-shaded upon and shadowed with jade and olive. But I have no doubt that barbel are as chameleon as trout are, as all fish are, and that they take their colour from their environment and the river-pools in which they swim.

Sometimes enormous shoals of barbel may be seen. Early one morning in the miracle summer of 1911 I looked over a garden wall into the fine water and the fan-out of what the drought had left of Whitchurch weir pool. I saw a dark cloud of backs, backs some so long that I hesitate to speak of them and to compare them in length to dining-room tables. But I saw big backs, medium backs, and backs of mere four-pounders.

I had in my hand a little rod and it was up and baited with a small red worm, for I wanted to catch some gudgeon. The barbel had not seen me and, hidden, I dropped my tackle over the wall. I was rewarded by hooking something like a torpedo that, moving up the pool, smashed me forthwith. Nothing makes a man feel more impotently than to hook a big barbel on a tiny rod. And a barbel is a terrific fighter. His fins are large and strong, his ' streamy ' lines indicate tremendous power and a turn of real speed. Nothing gives you a better idea of this fish's strength than to see, in summer, a shoal of barbel lying, nose against the river, in the very green-and-white rush of Thames as he drives headalong through one of his sluices. There will be eight or nine great fish, shoulder to golden shoulder, sometimes sinking into the mysteries, sometimes ascending till the angles of big forked tails show above the river. Motionless will they be otherwise and, always, keeping their vantage against the full weight of water with splendid ease and power.

I, when first I came to Thames, knew nothing of his coarse fishes and less of his trout, though of the last I had heard rumours. I came from salmon rivers and fly-rods, I came from waters where the ousel and the ring-ousel go from boulder to splashed boulder and where the trout go four to the pound, perhaps, three to the pound if you're lucky.

My father, ' hard by the thundering Spey,' said, when told that I was about to pitch my tent upon Thames-side, ' There are trout in the Thames ; not only that but once I took one out of it.' He said that about 1860 he had been at a tutor's near Boveney. He walked with a contemporary by the river. There was a punt tied to the bank below the weir. In the punt was a rod in readiness for use even to a live bleak that, upon the hook, swam in the cool current. The owner of this punt and its appurtenances had just gone to *The Prince Regent* to get a glass of ginger ale.

The two boys got into the punt and the one, something of a waterman, punted upstream. The other threw the bait out. It was instantly seized and a four-pound trout was landed. A peep into the well showed a supply of bait. So, the rightful angler still absent, a fresh bait was put on and the same cast essayed. Once more it was taken, this time by a trout estimated to be twice, if not thrice, as big as the first. It jumped. It tore the line out in one long run into the white water. Thither the puntsman was not expert enough to follow it. The punt went down-stream, in fact, while the trout went up. The line parted with a *ping* ; the rightful angler stood on the bank gesticulating and scandalously blasphemous.

But he was a good sort, for he presently gave the boys the trout that they had caught and confessed that he himself had been fishing Boveney for a week and had had, during that time, ' never a bloody nibble.'

So I knew a little of Thames trout before I knew Thames by whom I walked for the first time upon a May afternoon. On the footbridge at Marsh I stopped and looked into the clear water. Upon the gravel bottom and only a few yards from where I stood were three large fish, four pounds, five pounds perhaps. ' Trout,' said I.

And as I spoke, from over against the mill, another fish, darkly golden, leapt from bright water into blue air and fell back with a sounding splash. If the three fish on the shallow were big what sort of an outsize in trout was this ? Twelve pounds if he was an ounce. And I marvelled and would have run home for a rod had I had one and known how to use it on a Thames trout.

It took me a month to learn the difference between a trout and a barbel. Where I came from trout were brown fish of a similar brown to the great fellow that had jumped under the mill's wall. So a mistake was excusable, given that a trout *could* be so splendid a fish and prodigious.

But I was soon to be reminded that the caudal fin, or tail, of a trout is square. And that that of the barbel, and of all the coarse fish except the tench, except the eel, is forked like Jove's lightnings or the tongues of asps. And that the trout in Thames is nearly always a silvery fish, silver and blue and dotted on with sable in his prime ; with, possibly, a red spot or so as he ages or goes out of condition. Nearly always is this so. A dark-coloured trout is, it is safe to say, either out of condition or old. Or both these sad things at once. Yet not always, for I once caught a fine, shapely trout that weighed eight pounds and he was as brown as a berry.

And I learnt that, when a trout springs out of the water, which he often does in May and June, he comes out head first, hangs a moment quivering in air, and then drops back tail first. A barbel springs up in similar style but he, at apogee, turns over neatly in air and goes home again as head first as he came.

So now that you know a little of barbel let us try to catch one. The common form of barbelling on the Thames is by bottom fishing, or legering. Your success in the art is the most uncertain thing in all angling. The barbel is the most capricious fish that swims. Carp ? trout ? Oh, don't be ridiculous. In the Thames your trout will not be so many and your carp fewer still. But neither trout nor carp goes flauntingly and in great shoals, schools or congregations. But this is how the barbel goes ; he goes profusely and yet remains the most unfacile of all the fish.

You may leger in a baited or an unbaited swim. If you ask me which way is the more likely to provide sport I will answer that I do not know. But if you ask what a swim is, it is the name given to any particular piece of water where a shoal of barbel may be working.

In the Thames, swims are gravel bottomed almost invariably. The shoals, in early and middle summer, are, as we have seen, on the shallows at the tails of weir-pools and mill-races. As the summer advances they drop back, or push up, into deeper water. But they will not go very far away and may be located easily enough by the splashing brown-and-white, acrobatic turns in which the barbel betrays himself. In the main river the same somersaults may guide you if you will watch for them, dropping quietly downstream at morning or in the swift-haunted dusk.

Having found your swim the next thing is to fish it. If you are going to bait it first, you will require worms. How many ? Five thousand, my lad, five thousand lobworms at, I think, eight shillings a thousand and cheap too considering that these lobs must be hand-caught and cannot be bred in captivity, as if they were lions or meal-worms.

The easiest way of baiting a swim is to engage a professional fisherman to bait it for you. You will pay him for his time and for, of course, the worms which he will get from Nottingham. I do not know why lobworms come from Nottingham but they do. The fisherman will drop the worms into the swim at sunrise and with incantations. He will do this for two days before you fish and he will reserve a thousand of the worms for you to use upon your hook or to throw in, as largesse, if the fun slackens on the morning on which you come out. He will make dumplings of clay and fill them with worms and drop them into the swim. Any fishing book will tell you how these clay worm-puddings are made. Or he may prefer to use weighted, brown paper bags instead of the clay puddings. In this case, before their committal to the deep, he tears off the bottom corners of the bags so that ' the worms they creep in and the worms they creep out,' and the bags fill with Thames water and sink. It is all very expensive and elaborate but the barbel is an expensive and elaborate fish. But he can be done a little cheaper if you use graves from the butcher instead of lobs. I am not quite sure what part of the internal arrangements of a sheep is graves but it is procurable by that name. Worms and graves, then, are the barbel's morbid preferences.

And, as I have said, there are excellent books to tell you how a barbel swim may best be baited and I have nothing new or helpful to add to them. And so, in the grey of a late August morning, you will go to your sport. You will *not* find another fishing the swim that you have baited because Thames fishermen are sportsmen and they understand that a ryepeck, standing like a pinnacle in the wilderness, means that a brother has proprietary rights to the pitch it implies.

You will anchor your boat some twenty yards from where you are to fish. The commonplace rod is the rod that we have up and ready. I use the Nottingham reel on it and, personally, I use the same undressed line with a rub of vaseline thereon. There is no cheerful float to enliven leger-fishing.

The leger I will briefly describe but it can be bought at any tackle-maker's—where, by the way, the worms necessary to it can also be ordered. The leger consists of two foot of salmon gut. Following on the gut is a foot of gimp. To slide upon the gimp is a perforated lead weight. To prevent this lead slipping down to the hook there is at the lower end of the gimp a stop-shot. Next to the stop-shot comes another foot and a half of gut, then a swivel and then the single, fairly big, bait hook. And that's your leger.

Thread now a worm on to the hook ; tail first is the approved fashion. Barbel are said, I do not know by whom, to pick up the worm always by the tail. Swing out the bait gently upon the free reel. When your touch tells you that the lead is upon the bottom, tighten the line until you hold it tautly and in direct communication with the bait. Throw in a few worms as an inducement and now sit down and be as patient as possible, and as wide-awake.

The rod should be held low, the point may almost be on the water. This because it is necessary that the angler should recognize, forthwith, the first symptoms of a bite. When this tiny pull comes to you, let go about six inches of line which you will be holding loose and ready. Then hold tight and strike firmly but not furiously.

I have said that the barbel is a terrific fighter. But he is not a spectacular one. A barbel is not netted after the tenth leap as though he were a Spring grilse below Banchory. A barbel does not take fifty yards fairly off the reel line in his first rush ; neither a trout is he nor a sea-trout. But he is as strong as a cart horse and his are the staying powers of a social bore. He fights deep down and he goes on fighting. The floors of Thames are his home, and if he can rub out your hold of him thereon or break you in his labyrinths of weed and lily stalks, why, he most certainly will. Weight for weight, I do not hesitate to say that a barbel takes a longer time to kill than does a trout or a pike. Or even a salmon.

So strike him firmly but not to the breaking point. It is one of the several extraordinary things about this extraordinary fish that he will continue to use a swim and feed with equanimity upon your worm dumplings the while you fight a dozen or so of his brothers to the death before his very eyes. And yet do one of the brethren beat you—well, a barbel with a foot of fine gut sticking out of his mouth will stampede the shoal like a breakaway of tups.

It is a wonderful thing to see a school treat of barbel enjoying the worm dumplings of their benefactor. If you are fortunate enough to have found and baited a swim in the open river, where some convenience of bank or willow bough allows you to lie secretly and look down into ten feet of clear water, such a show may sometimes be vouchsafed you.

You will see your clay puddings festooned with the pink tails of lobs. You will see the dark cloud of fish. This cloud will taper into a sort of triangle the apex of which is nearest to the treat. The leading barbel will help himself to one worm. He will then go about abruptly to resume his place once more at the base of the triangle while, in rotation, the others duly take their turns.

But the baiting of a swim is a speculation. It is a thing to do once in a lifetime, or twice. If it comes off and you catch 200 lb. weight of barbel in a twelve hours' sitting, you may from henceforth rest on your honours, for so red a letter day will not occur again. If you catch a small perch and one unsizeable barbel you will be equally content to let the experience be your teacher.

To bait a swim and fish it for two days will cost the average angler who must buy his lobs and employ a fisherman between four and five pounds. More than that if travelling and hotels have to be budgeted for.

Once, for the entertainment of a guest, I employed Walter Coster to bait a swim for me at Marlow. No one could have done it better than he. Worms were no object to us, we had lobs by the thousand. Our pitch was the choicest in Marlow's lovely pool and, early and late, we fished it for two days. Our bag was a small eel and a half-pound chub.

To bait then or not to bait ? I think on the whole not to. Go to your swim with a thousand worms. Throw a couple of hundred in, bread upon the waters, before you begin to put your rod together and then another couple of hundred, and possibly they shall return to you, presently, buttered of barbel.

Lobs too are not the barbel's natural food, possibly he never sees a lob throughout the season except one with a catch to it. So his taste in this direction must be cultivated and this may often be a longer task than the two or three days we devote to the baiting up of a swim. Whereas he may succumb at once to the novelty of the occasional and unexpected pinkiness that wriggles upon the golden river-floors.

Another objection that I have to the baited swim, especially the baited swim in the August weir pool, is that it attracts, too often, the trout of the entire neighbourhood. The Conservancy forbids the fishing for trout with worm but it allows the retention of a sizeable trout taken upon the worm intended for his coarser cousins. It is a sorry thing to see an aristocrat killed in such a way. And the more unsizeable the trout the greater is the likelihood that he will defeat the best of intentions and die or ever the extraction of the leger hook is accomplished. I think, with all the fishing books, that when a caught fish is to be returned to the river and the hook has been over well taken, no attempt at extraction should be made. A nip of the scissors to sever the gut, a short holding of the invalid's head to current and a trust in Father Thames that he, and the acids in the patient's own blood, will get rid of the barb in no time, and the trout may hopefully be seen to go.

Were I a Conservator of Thames I think that I would forbid worm fishing of any kind in the weir pools. If barbel swims must be baited within the pools let the method be graves, for of graves, the economical, a trout thinks small beer. And it is in summer that the trout come into the pools after the fry. And it is in high summer and late that the barbel swim is baited.

For in winter the barbel is a slugabed. Under rafts, boat-houses and landing stages, in the seclusion of the deepest holes and river corners that he can find, there, packed like the partridges, he hibernates. But not entirely, for a mild day will bring him out to take, and smash the tackle to smithereens, the roach-poler's hemp seed or his gentle.

So the usual way to catch Thames barbel is on the

leger. But there are other methods, for the barbel is capable of anything from a grain of hemp seed to a fairly large live gudgeon. And many a good fish has been caught on a minnow, especially in late June or early July.

Take the live-bait rod, the ten-foot, thirty-five-year-old, split-cane that I told you of. Put on a three-yard trace of not *too* fine gut, for the barbel is a big fish. A float ? Yes, certainly a float. I use one of the little red pilots of the pike tackle, but any float will do provided it is not *too* corpulent. To the end of the trace attach a single bait hook and such weight (here the envelope leads are in their element) as the water to be fished calls for. But the minnow must be fished fairly deep. Pass the hook through the bait's upper lip and swim it down any, not too heavy, stream, or mill-tail, that you suspect of fish. Be careful to keep a straight line and thus avoid the float reaching the shoal before the bait. I do not think that this question of precedence is an over-alarming one, but it is well to take no risks, and nothing is so slovenly to see as the float-first, Jack before his master, all anyhow style of angling.

Instead of a large minnow, or a small gudgeon, you may fish, by this method, with cheese-paste or gentles, two or three threaded on to the hook, or indeed with any of the usual Thames variants. Oh yes, and if your minnows are all little minnows it is well to use a small triangle instead of the single hook. And to each hook of the triangle a minnow. This rule of three is often extremely successful. If a barbel responds to it, he will take with a nibble, a suck and a little pull. Give him a half-foot of line before you hit him. But if it is a trout that comes, he will probably have you with a tear and a bang and be fifty yards from the punt's till or ever you, white-faced with excitement, are on to your feet.

Thus barbel may be taken with live-bait which is no natural food of theirs. Though, of a dark, blue summer night, and the moon in it as golden as an apricot, you may see a big barbel gourmet come up along the camp sheathing after the minnow shoals. He does not splash and dash among them as do the predatory fishes. But the minnows, to see him, crowd all against the sheathing in a cloud. And the barbel, coming close, opens his mouth and seems to suck into it a tithe of the school. He seems to inhale minnows rather than catch them. And then he lounges upon his way. But you will linger for a min-ute and listen to the nightingale that sings in the vicarage garden.

And that reminds me that a barbel can sing too. I think he is the only fish that can. On such a summer night as that on which he went minnowing just now you may hear him sing. In the quiet comes a croak-ing, then a chorus of small, snoring, puffing grunts. These noises are the barbel singing on the moonlit shallows because of their summer *joie de vivre*. They raise their blunt and bearded noses to the surface and above it. And I suppose that the sound they make is caused by some outblowing of air. But, like the nightingale's, it is a song of summer and the velvet dark.

A big barbel was the subject of a ' fisherman's lie ' story of which I saw the finish. There came a young soldier to the middle Thames in May. He thought that he would catch a trout or two by spinning, a method in which he excelled. But he was infirm of purpose and faint in pursuit. Soon he was finding base recreation in foul-hooking the barbel upon the shallow below the weir. He, of course, returned to the water, most lovingly, any that he landed.

Presently he pulled his blue phantom into a great golden-brown back. His rod was a very small and light rod, his tackle was the most gossamer that credit could procure. He was a good fisherman, but in about twenty minutes the barbel broke him and won free.

The gut had smashed at the swivel ring on the phantom's nose. But some days later the angler was at it again with a new phantom. The Thames is a big river and the barbel in him are many. So it was a wonderful thing that the fisherman should again fall foul of his fish of last Friday. Yet this is just what he did do. And this time he landed the barbel. In fact I netted the fish for him. He was a great lump of a fish and we weighed him before we put him back. He went eleven pounds and some ounces. But the real miracle was that a single hook of the new minnow's triangle had passed through the ring of the swivel of the minnow already in the barbel's back. And without other hold than that the fish was caught and the earlier gear recovered.

If ever you want to ascertain the weight of a fish before restoring it to the river the simplest and safest way is thus. In most fishing punts there is a towel. Lay the fish in it, knot the towel by the four corners and suspend upon the scale. Knock an ounce or so off the result and the nett weight will be that of the fish, who may now be returned to the river with thanks and compliments.

You may also take barbel with the little spinning-rod, the one with the china rings. No float is here required. Only a sea-trout trace, with swivels, and just enough lead pinched on to it to carry out a fair length of undressed line. Attach a Stewart tackle to the gut. Procure a dozen or so brandling worms in moss and a mustard tin. You say that the brightness of the stream behind the mill is, this June evening, brown cloudy with the shapes of the barbel ? Very well.

Row the punt to the tail of the run and anchor her to rock gently out of the current. Put on a brandling and cast it upstream upon a long line to dribble back to you, you winding, slowly, in along the bed of the river, among the big brown shadows. Presently you will get, I hope you will get, a quiet little pull, which, upon the strike which you are now well accomplished to bestow, will develop into the heavy tug of a hooked fish. But before you go to this form of fishing, or any other form of barbel fishing, be sure that you know first where the fish are, for where there are no barbel there will be no sport with them.

I have kept the jolliest way of barbelling for the last. Here is no leger with its lead that is always catching up on the bottom and wanting ' hands ' and patience to coax it forth from the weeds that it lurks among. Here no lobs, lively or languid, are a necessity. Here are no anæmic gentles to malhandle. Nor pastes to manipulate nor living minnow to make, possibly, uncomfortable.

Take the live-bait rod then, the light, old split-cane. No float is necessary above the three yards of gut to which a small lead or so may be attached. Your hook must be a small triangle. This warm August evening the barbel are in the shrunken weir pool. The water that trickles over the moss-grown steps and falls tinkling among the piles is clear and warm. The silk-weed is up and the barbel have been feeding on it for the last few sunny days. But I do not think that they eat the weed *qua* weed. They eat it because it is the overcrowded home, just now, of the water shrimp or snail after his myriad kind. But for whatever reason they eat it, eat it they do, browsing along the sill like a row of brown cows in a byre.

In this clear water the barbel is shy, far shyer than a girl. So creep most cautiously and slink like a shadow until you get to where such stream that remains will carry your light tackle down upon it. There now, you say, the bait has been forgotten? Jump to no conclusions, my son. Rather, stand very, very still; so still that in our suits of sober grey flannel we may be taken for part of the Conservancy's grey painted posts and railings.

The Protean herds are still browsing. So, quietly, drop the bare triangle into that straggle of bright silk-weed. And quietly lift it out again. You see that the hook has baited itself? The little green streamer that now hangs drippingly upon it is lure enough. So float it quietly down upon the lazy current and the first eleven-pounder that it meets with will, I hope, gently inhale it. And then I can assure you that the fun will be furious and prolonged. And when it is over we will steal along, a-tiptoe, to a fresh coign, re-bait the triangle and try again.

And know this. The barbel when caught is a fine meaty fellow and makes, as I hope I may show you later, an excellent kettle of fish. But, and better even than this excellent quality, he is the most stubborn fighter that swims in Thames water and, in cunning and caprice, foxes and Christmas cock pheasants are fools to him. The man who goes out to catch our Thames barbel and comes home with a one or a two after each outing may indeed call himself a fisherman and hold his head high in the Houghton Club or in the tap-room of ' The Perch and Pike.'

But best of all I love the barbels because they roll like big, brown-and-white cats upon golden shallows and sing in the moonlight with the *joie de vivre* of June. And because, so, they are all Thames to me and wild-rose time and the streams running down from the weir.

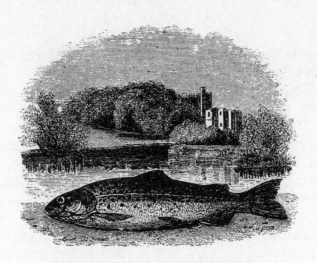

VII. THE THAMES TROUT
(*SALMO FARIO*)

No ! I've never really seen him
But the boatman tells a tale
Of a something (' must 'a been 'im ')
Like a whale,
On the shelving shallows showing
' Where them kingcups is a-growing,'
Only just the other night,
And the frightened fry went leaping from the Presence left and right !

But the skies are smiling bluely,
There is shade along the shore
And the chestnut's litten newly
Lamps a score :
Drop the rod then and be thankful
For the sights that fill the bank full—
Verdant meads and ancient stems
And the broad, paternal bigness and the peace of Father Thames !

P. R. C.

WHO can say if and when Father Thames
will ever again be a salmon river ? Not
I, nor will I venture an opinion among
the prophets.

But I can say that never will Thames
be a trout river within the meaning of the angle.

Never will he be a Test, a Kennet or an Aberdeen-
shire Don. He is not built that way ; he is too big,
he is too deep, he is too placid between his locks, he
is too wild and too turbulent in his weirs. Yet he has
all the flies, indeed his hatches of Mayfly are magni-
ficent ; almost have I seen the expresses that roar
through Pangbourne station held up by the ephemeral
hosts. But only once, as I have told in this book,
have I seen a sizeable and well-worth-while trout on
the job of the ' June bug.' I do not know why Thames
trout despise natural fly, I only know that they do and
that it is a thankless thing to offer a replica to anyone, to anyone who has no use for an original. And
by replica I mean artificial dun, olive, sedge and Tup's
Indispensable. I even mean salmon flies, though what
these are the replicas of I cannot say. But every now
and again a Thames trout may be caught on a salmon
fly which some lazy fellow who has never learned
to spin offers to it. But I have myself only known
one trout to be so taken, one *good* trout. He weighed
something over seven pounds and he was taken by
no lazy fellow at all but by an honest and con-
scientious angler who thought that to offer a bait of
any sort to a fish of the game was an outrage and a
sin. So he fished weir streams with Wilkinsons and
mill-tails with Silver Doctors and was occasionally
rewarded with a swirl at the one or the other but
rarely with aught more tangible. So he sat on the
lock gate and considered.

Then he tied with his own hands (for he was the
sort that made the personal tying of his flies a point
of angling honour) a brown fly, woodcock and so on,
of about an inch and a half in length. He named his

nondescript for himself, So-and-So's Fancy. And it
certainly looked (though its maker denied the resem-
blance) very much like a live and lively minnow when
he worked it, *sink* and *draw*.

And the purist took his tackle to Marlow mill-tail
and there the God of Luck looked upon him. For,
even as he cast his fly, a trout came out of the heavy
water and began to splash on the gravel shallow and
to make a whitebait course of the minnows that
played in shoals against the match boardings. The
angler could see the great fish—a shadow that dashed
hither and thither. He threw the fly to it and almost
as it lit in the water the trout had it, headlong. And
a beautiful trout he was and a well-deserved one and
he weighed, as I've said, seven pounds and a bittock.
But he would as willingly, no doubt, have taken a
brown Devon.

The Thames trout is a cannibal. So are many other
trout. But the Thames trout, as far as my knowledge
goes, is the only trout who is a cannibal born. He
begins on minnows and finishes on one-pound roach.
And as a change he eats shrimps and snails and the
occasional vole, the occasional duckling or young
moorhen.

The trout who go cannibal in other rivers than
Thames are, as a rule, ugly and old. They are fish
who have outgrown themselves, and the insect food
at their command is insufficient for their size. Therefore they live on their smaller fellows when they can
catch them. And this in most rivers is not easy since
the stock of potential nourishment is never so plentiful as it is in Thames.

In Thames a trout has literally only to open his

mouth and get his dinner. And because of this plenty the *fario* of Thames, cannibals though they be, are the most beautiful trout that an angler or a poet (and what's an angler but a poet turned outside in?) could dream. Imagine a big trout, say an eight-pounder, in perfect condition. He is probably a short fish splendidly deep and thick. So short perhaps is he that you will put him at six pounds until the scales flatly contradict you. The broad of his back is tinged with a shade of brown and water-green that melts, upon the flanks, into blended cream and silver. He is dotted with black spots, never a crimson, brook-trout spot has he unless he ages or is out of condition. His big square tail and his dorsal fin are blue-black. His head is small and game and aristocratic. He is indeed a comely fish and a gallant one to look at and did you lay him beside a sea-silver Spring salmon or a clean run sea-trout it is not he who would lose by comparison.

If you ask some Thames residents they will tell you that there are fewer of trout in the river than of any other fish. Of this I am not so sure. The Thames trout do not rise to a fly and therefore they are not so continually seen as are the trout in other rivers. Watch a Test four-pounder feeding, he will continue to show himself for half an hour on end unless somebody catches him. And not only he but a dozen like him must be taking advantage of the same hatch at the same time. It takes a lot of olives to fill a four-pound trout. When a Thames trout of size feeds there is a swirl, perhaps two swirls, there is a roach, or a half-pound dace, that splashes and is gone, engulfed in a third swirl. All this happens in some fifteen seconds. If you have seen, you have seen. If you have not you will not see again for twenty-four hours maybe. For a trout when he has fed has finished and will return to his stance, probably some deep hole in the neighbourhood, and there he'll stay till he is hungry again. He makes one mouthful of his meal, his Test brother must make a hundred or ever he is satisfied.

And so a Thames trout, never so greatly in the limelight as other trout are, escapes casual observation or is mistaken for a jack or a dabchick by the uninitiated. But how is it, if indeed the trout in Thames are few, that there is not a ferry, a lock, a human habitation on the green banks where, if you ask, you will not be told of a trout that feeds, or two or three that feed, ' just opposite the garden ' ? I cannot suppose that Thames trout haunt the homes of men of a purpose as the cock sparrows do, I can only think that they are there naturally and because they are distributed throughout the river reaches in a fair profusion.

As to spawning, another matter of Thames controversy, I am sure, while the trout will, where possible, work up into tributaries, such as the Pang, to spawn, that many spawn in the river. On a December day, given suitable conditions of water, you may see the big spawners working on the redds at the tail of most weirs. But all too often the flood water of winter will interfere with these peeps into nursery life. If I were a trout I'd spawn in the safety of the big river every time ; for a big fish in a little water, in season or out, is never safe. And there's many a fine trout who leaves Whitchurch pool in November for the Pang, that drops downstream again never to his, or her, Father Thames.   And yet, season after season, I take out little trout, eight inches, six inches, either on chub fly or spinning-bait, and a heartening sight they are, these babies of an ancient race, who scuttle off again into the amber places to grow to as many pounds as they are ounces to-day.

In the drought of 1921 I counted a shoal of eleven trout in Marsh weir, each one being under half a pound in weight.   There was no scintilla of doubt as to their nobility for the water was clear enough for a counting of spots on fat little flanks.

I have seen Thames trout chasing almost every species of fish who swim in the river, but I have never seen a trout, or a jack, after a perch.   Folks say that the spikes worn by the perch make him an impossible meal and an unpalatable.   But both trout and pike swallow their dinners head first and a perch's spines lie down when stroked head to tail.   Yet both trout and pike take their quarry across the back in the first instance and, possibly, they have learned thus not to mell with anything so porcupine as a perch.

The loch trout in the North are hardier fellows—or hungrier.   I must tell you of one of them even in this book of Thames.   I must tell my story for two reasons, one because I like to talk about big fish and another because a perch as the potential food of trout comes most apropos into it.   So then : When I got out of the 2.25 from Waverley it was 3.45 or thereabouts and the sun of a wet summer was shining.   Now I like going to places where I have never been before, especially if I find the sun there.   And to be received by strangers as an old friend is pleasant too. And I like a chauffeur who loves his car, his employer, the country he lives in, and the art of angling—and who will talk about all these with enthusiasm the while he takes you 'where the sun and the wind are flying' and where tea is ready as soon as you are. I have heard the medically minded inveigh against tea as a meal—especially the Scotch tea. But baps, fruit-gingerbread, jams and jeels, and all that go with them, remain my delight and my undoing. And now would I care to go down to the Loch ? And the Loch that I am about to be free of is no popular resort, competitive and cosmopolitan. It is the resort, red-lettered, of the guests of its proprietor. These guests do not talk of their liberty overmuch lest they be deaved by their kin and acquaintance for a word to Himself. But if you mention a name in a tackle shop then, whether in Princes, Buchanan or any other street, the head of the firm will come out of the inner office and serve you personally.

At some time or another I imagine that the Loch was the labour of Mother Ice or else the crater of a volcano—if in Tweedside volcanoes were. Anyhow there she is now, a mile of Loch maybe, and the pale, whale-backed bents that rise up from her, they slope gently to a pale sky. But do you, unbreathed, stroll up the eastward eminence you will get the surprise of your life. For, of a sudden, you will be standing a-top of five hundred foot of rock, and below you will be the sea crawling and rumbling in her terrible places down under, just to show you, this summer day, that she watches and she waits.

But you will spit upon her for luck, as I did (and

just missed a rocketing blue-rock pigeon), and return
to the Loch and be rowed out among the water-lilies
in a miniature whale-boat. To fish most lochs is
monotony, every cast the same cast and the maximum result of any one of them the possible pounder.
But where your loch is a place of piscine milk and
honey, a Canaan where a pounder becomes a five-
pounder and a five-pounder—but, as of old they said,
' we anticipate.'

Anyhow, there is no monotony in loch fishing *this*
August afternoon. What flies did I use ? I can only
remember that I fished three wet flies, little tiny ones,
a-row. And that one of them was a March Brown.
For the trout here are gentlemanly fellows who prefer
a wee fly on light tackle to worm, wobbler, blue phantom or Silver Doctor, all of which, trusting to the
good taste of his trout, the laird allows, even en-
courages. The afternoon was *lown*, here and there a
dimple on the flat water, here and there a pucker.
But never touch of a fish for me, and at seven I
walked up the hill to dinner, encouraged by the notes
of a pibroch blown, as ' Neil himsel' ' might have
blown it, by amateur lungs. There was hare soup to
eat with a potato in it ; there was a three-pound
trout for the pair of us, a notable *plat* and of a deeper
pink and a nobler delicacy than are those of any
salmon. There was a young grouse. There was a
white wine, chilly to a charm, and a port to sit over.
There was coffee strong as brandy and brandy soft as
milk. I make these mercies my excuse for not being
on the water again before nine.

The light was going and the air alive with bats.
' I mind that one took my fly,' said the keeper. ' And

what did you do with it ? ' ' Oh, I just put it in my pocket and told my daughter (it's her that's parlour-maid) that she'd find a sweetie there—you'd have heard her scream here.' ' And what became of the bat ? ' ' It wasna hurt and we just let it away again.' Our boat drifts on. The glow of a cigar in the second boat waxes and wanes. ' The moon is up and yet it is not night,' and something close to the lily-beds takes me with a bang. He is among the stalks and out again, an acrobatic beggar, but presently the net is under him and, short and thick and golden and nearer three pounds than two, a trout is mine. And his twin brother joins him not ten minutes afterwards. And then, within a few casts, I get what the gods have been leading up to—a fish that takes resolutely and then goes headlong into deep water and ' sounds ' like a whale. A quarter of an hour later his weight is found to be five pounds and four ounces, and he is, I am told, the heaviest fish of the season—so far. And because of him I go home very happy and, full of the pride that apes humility, to bed.

Next morning, the laurels thick upon me, I am fishing by 10.30. A grey day it is, a cold day, a day of leaden waves and rocking lilies, a day of the *haar* that is blown in smoking squadrons. Likewise a day that wears to evening without a rise. An evening when a tired man might, and did, waver between port and sport, the ingle and the angle. But the angle had it. At 8.30 a pound trout repaid the angler and encouraged him to cast on and on and on——

It chapped ten o'clock and a sickly moon came struggling through. Near the landing stage the angler cast mechanically into shallow water. The trout that took the point fly went seventy yards before the rower could dip his oars and follow.

Now am I a peacock to display myself further ? Why yes, of course I am, and only lack the words wherein to be loud speaking and lyrical. But I remember how, at long last, a great shape, symmetrical, thick, thickly dotted upon, and golden as honey, was in the net and a voice in the dark, a voice that sounded out of its ordnar', was speaking to me. ' I've netted many a *salmon* that was smaller than this,' it yammered.

This was a trout of eight pounds and eight ounces. And within him was a half-pound perch, spikes and all, and what he wanted with my wee March Brown I do not know.

And dear me, how I haver ; but having mentioned a March Brown I must tell you more of this very identical fly and its further meritorious service to me if not with Thames trout at least with trout of a tributary of Thames. For when we had given the big trout his *coup de grâce*, when we had sat awhile to admire him as he lay, shakily striking matches I knelt and, with hands that trembled still, I removed the brave March Brown from him, and, vowing that no fingerling of eight ounces should dim the memory of what the little Death had done, I put it into that small portion of a biggish fly-book that I call Valhalla. And I came away South with it, and there for a year it leant, like the soldier in the song, upon its sword. And on a summer day I was taken to fish a certain dry-fly water in Berkshire. I will tell you of that day.

It was the hottest, so far, of an incandescent July. The trout, the grayling too, were for nothing whatever. The sky was blue unalterable. The distances danced in the heat. The grasses were scorched and pale, the beechwoods languid. We sat, my host, a lady and I, under the cedar outside the fishing hut. We ate our lunches, smoked, and told each other, first, sheer improbabilities and then downright lies. A hot wind, a sirocco, arose and made the day hotter. And still the sun shone in a changless and brazen blue. My host, a spare man, a man of iron resolution and the energies of an elderly flea, presently, unable to cap one of my adventures with a better one of his own, arose, took his rod and wandered upstream. The lady and I sat where we were. Four Alderneys in the middle distance stood knee deep in the river and flicked at the flies with their tails. And these four cows, after I had watched them for a ten minutes or so, suggested, in some vague back-hand manner, that I ought, since I had come out to fish, to be flicking a fly myself.

There is (in the teeth of pundits and cavillers) a fearful fascination about the unorthodox. Impossible days demand impossible deeds. And one fish taken with a *bend sinister* to make his capture kenspeckle will be remembered when a dozen just-so fellows who need no memorial are become as the snow-broos of last March. The river that I felt it my duty to be fishing ran through private grounds and the park of a manor house. In the park it spread out and became a wide shallow just below where an avenue bridge spanned it. Below the bridge both banks were thickly timbered. These banks were the home of

about a dozen large trout, cunning and specialized
brutes, who coming out on to the shallow to feed and
display, had been fished for so often from the bridge
that a footfall upon it, or a shadow over the arch,
sent them scuttling to cover like so many rabbits.
The sirocco to which I have referred was blowing
straight downstream.   The bridge was a wide and
handsome one, and its walls were of fretted stone.
Walls they were with a lattice of lozenge-shaped open-
ings to them.

The lady tiptoed on to the bridge and peeped
over, and a dozen trout went all ways at once.

' A wet fly,' said she, ' a wet fly cast downstream
and worked subaqueously has no drag.'

' This is a dry-fly water,' I said.

' He won't be back till tea-time,' said she.

' I haven't got one,' said I ; ' only,' I said, turning
pages, ' Gnats and Quills and Spinners and Tup's Indispensable and something that Skues—Ah ! ' I said.
I had got to Valhalla and found there a salmon fly or
so ; also a faded little March Brown from Reston
Loch.   And this little warrior was brought forth, like
Achilles, from its seclusion.   It was mounted upon a
trace not so fine as all that.   The trout were biggish
ones, and a trout who does not suspect is nearly as
big a fool as a salmon.   And a salmon is a very
foolish fish, indeed.

The lady and I walked openly on to the bridge, and
bent over and looked downstream at the troutless
water.   The sirocco continued to blow.   I went to the
upstream side of the bridge and leant my shoulders
against the wall just above the keystone of the arch.
Opposite to me the lady lay flat upon the ground,

and keeked through a convenient lozenge on the downstream side.

Nothing happened for quite five minutes. Then she said in a whisper, ' One's coming upstream now.'

My rod was a tiny affair, no shadow of its line— lengthening to and fro—got further than the middle of the road. ' To the right,' said the recumbent rangefinder. To the right, upon the sirocco, I cast. ' A little more line,' said she. A little more line was paid out. ' Walk a yard or two left,' she said, ' He's coming—stri——'

I struck and the reel screamed. The lady jumped up. I made two steps of it across the road, the little rod kicking like a live thing in my hands. Forty yards downstream a two-pound trout leapt once and leapt again.

Presently the lady said, ' There's a place where you can get down at this end, and where I think that I can net him.'

In both particulars she was right. And a plump and shapely trout he was. And with mutual con- gratulations we went a-top of the bridge again. Once more I leaned upon the upstream coping. I could feel the heat of the stone through my grey flannels. Once more the lady laid her down upon the gravel. This time it was a quarter of an hour before she spoke, before she had news for me.

A long time later I heard, upon the golden afternoon, a stable clock chap five. We had, by then, two brace and a half of trout, the biggest getting along for three pounds. The lady decided that the rise was probably over. So she rose herself. And the little March Brown, having tasted blood, went back to

Valhalla. And we, the lady and I, went to the hut
and made us tea.

Presently our host came disconsolately downstream. He had caught a small grayling and trodden
upon a wasp's nest the while he landed it. We did
not mention the March Brown. Our host was, is, a
great artist of the dry-fly method. He looked at our
trout. It almost seemed that seeing them he dis-
approved of our fortune. If he sees this, I feel that
he will still more disapprove of it.

But, you say, may we not now catch a Thames
trout ? Why, of course you can when I have pointed
out to you another jewel in the crown of Thames.
There is, then, no other river who is an adjective to
his trout. What man speaks of a Kennet trout, a
Test trout, a Don trout ? A man will say of the
stuffed six-pounder with the Drake in the angle of his
jaw, ' Yes, isn't he a topper ? I caught him at Kint-
bury, the Kennet, you know, last June.' But when
you exclaim at the ten-pounder, glazed and immor-
talized on the opposite wall, your host will say simply,
modestly, proudly, ' A Thames trout.' Just that he'll
say and no more. But, as he tells, he'll be hearing the
cuckoos in Quarry Woods and seeing the streams that
tumble off the weir, white water and green, streams
to take a big trout in such as no other river may show
you but the Father of Streams.

So come along ; we will go down to the water this
May morning and see what we shall see.

There are but two methods of fishing for Thames
trout—spinning and live-baiting. There can be no
question which is the better sport, but little result lies
in spinning except in the earlier part of the season or

when a summer flood puts a stain of colour into the late June river.

The Thames trouting season lasts from the 1st of April to the 11th of September. In practice it is a much shorter one than five months and ten days. For the river is usually too winter big to be fishable before the end of April and too summer small after the first fortnight in June. In July the shrimp hatch out and the trout, gorging themselves thereon, go off their natural food till the middle of August. Given a not too droughty summer, the last month of the season may supply another good fish or two out of the weir pools. Weed makes the main river impossible for spinning and, in many places, for live-baiting after the mid-June. The cream of the season, the days during which your season's bag will mostly be made, are the last fortnight in May and the first fortnight in June.

When I began to fish the Thames there existed a legend that the bigger trout fed, approximately, at the same time daily. 'You can set your watch by him,' was the invariable ending of the story of the big fish opposite the boat-house who fed at 5.8 p.m. But a long series of disappointments convinced me at last that these regular meal times are purely apocryphal.

You may say what does it matter when a trout feeds ? The answer is that when a Thames trout is not on the move, when he is not hungry, he is practically uncatchable. He is only hungry, thanks to his food supply, about once in twenty-four hours and then only for a minute and a half. If you happen to be out during those ninety rampageous seconds and if you are still fortunate in that he sees your phantom before he catches his dace, you will probably make a trophy of him. But if he gets the dace before you get him he will see you damned first. For a trout does not, as a man does, chase things for the sport of chasing them. And this apathy of his, which arises from a plentiful commissariat and a slow digestion, is counted to him for sagacity and cunning above other trouts. Whereas he is no more intelligent really than a potted salmon. On the other hand a pricked fish will rarely come again, and a pricked, or a much fished for, monster soon suffers from gut shyness. And that's all there is to him except beauty, delicacy at table, and fine, occasionally terrific, fighting qualities.

When I began to fish for him a long time ago I practically shared the whole river, so far as trout went, with one other enthusiast. I lived at Marlow during the summer of 1912 and I can remember seeing, May to September, never another angler out but myself on that quarter mile of lovely weir, except, maybe, a grey heron, statue still, in the summer dawning.

I began my career when the great sportsmen-anglers of Thames, Mr. Englefield, Mr. Francis, and others, had left off. Since then a new race of trout fishers has appeared and to-day most weirs have, on a May Saturday, on a June Sunday, a trout angler or so who fish without professional aid or personal knowledge. And without particular enthusiasm or success. These, for the most part, *danglers* rather than *anglers*, are content to trail, on coarse tackle, a half-dead minnow in the run and to hope for the best. And so Thames trouting, Thames spinning, becomes a lost art.

But let us try to revive it here and now. Let us suppose that it is a May morning and that under a blue and white sky with a dozen swifts to it, the punt glides quietly through the lock gates and drops downstream. To left and right the meadows are cloth of buttercup gold, in the lock garden the lilacs, purple and white, are in full flower and fragrance ; a waft of them follows us down river. It is trouting weather and old Thames is at his most perfect, his most green pulse of England moment.

In the punt is the twelve-foot split-cane complete with Nottingham reel, undressed silk line and all. The swivelled trace is two yards of medium salmon gut and the weight it carries, half-way along of it, is the largest pattern made in Mr. Geen's boat-shaped leads. The leads that are painted dark green. And— the bait ?

The bait to use, Mr. Francis said so years ago, is the bait that you can best make to spin. And beyond any doubt if you, or your boatman, can mount a dead bleak on a Thames flight so that it will spin like a flash of diamonds there is no bait to approach it. I can tell you how to mount it, of course, but I cannot tell you how to make it spin for I have not the magic of the finger tips. Which is, to-day, almost a lost magic and only known to one amateur of Thames and one of the few remaining professionals. And here, before I talk further of Thames trout fishing, I am going to quote Mr. Sheringham who has written, 'There is only one man alive who has any business to mention a Thames trout in print—and he is Mr. A. E. Hobbs.' The above in self-extenuation.

Here is how to mount a Thames flight—the easiest

thing in the world. The flight itself is, on gut, a sliding lip-hook a-top of three triangles. Take a dead bleak, one that is already stiff is to be preferred, and impale it on the flight, beginning at the tail, to which you impart a cute little curl which is the crux of the matter. And that's the third triangle disposed of. You now attach triangles numbers two and one to the convex flank of the bleak. And you finish the performance by passing the lip-hook through both the lips of the bait that you employ. It sounds simple, does it not ? And now it *ought* to spin like a sparkle of gems. But, in everyday practice, it will only wobble. But even then it is a goodish trout-catcher and an excellent taker of Dee salmon who prefer a wobble to a true spin.

On a salmon river an average jog-along skill will catch you as many salmon on a spinning-bait as the artist catches. On the Thames the artist beats the average angler always. For his artistry depends not so much on long distance casting but in *accuracy*. The artist must be a Jack Horner fellow, expert in corners and in putting his bait, at a range of forty yards, into any of them. The angler who can do this is the one to pull the plums out. I will give you an instance of what I mean. It was high summer, the river was low, the weeds were up. As the boat glided by a trout fed, thirty weedy yards away, splashing in an open space, half a yard wide and a couple of yards long. The oarsman steadied the boat, the angler picked up his rod and, casting a quill minnow to an eighth of an inch, hooked and caught a four-and-a-half-pound trout. No one but a consummate artist could have taken that fish—no one. And how can this accuracy be obtained? It cannot be. Practice will make an apprentice proficient. But the artist of the spinning-rod, like the super game shot, like the championship billiard player, or the poet, is born and not made.

However, you can have a lot of fun as a mere disciple and honest angler. And no weeds are up on this May morning to discomfort us, and since we cannot coax a spin out of our Thames flight, we will put on an artificial minnow and start in. And the bait shall be, for the sake of greater accuracy and length in casting, a three-inch blue Devon, a metal affair with a single triangle only, for the fewer hooks to a bait the better I like it. If it were not that I hold accuracy before all I would use an unweighted blue phantom, but such is too light to throw far and, on account of its lightness, it is apt also to fly back and hook up, its loose triangle to help it, in the gut or the lead. A weighted phantom without a loose flying triangle is equally as good as the metal Devon that I recommended. These two I prefer to a dead natural bait fished on a ' crocodile ' or any similar mount. They spin well, and though their unnatural hardness may occasionally give a fish, who seizes them, a tenth of a second's warning to spit them out or ever the hook has him, they can be shown to a trout attractively where a lighter bait would, flying back, probably fail you.

Besides Devon and phantom a small silver spoon is a useful change bait—especially in a water that is slightly coloured.

In spinning the open river it is wise not to waste your energies in the broadcast manner of a salmon stream. Rather go idling along, stopping here, stopping there, to throw a bait at the end of an eyot, to work one flashing athwart the shelter of the bridge's arch and buttress, to cast one in any bay or eddy that may strike you as a likely place to hold a trout. And all the time be looking for evidence. Do you, for instance, see, a hundred yards off, a shoal of terrified bleak leap and splash, hasten thither and it may be that you will be in time and that their tyrant, their ten-pound tyrant, shall—well,

> Glide on ye stately swans with grace,
> Ye ne'er again shall see
> His headlong dash among the dace
> Beneath the willow tree,
> Ye little bleak lift up your heads,
> Ye gudgeon skip at score—
> The run between the lily beds
> Shall know its lord no more !

And if you land and walk upon the bank remember to cast under and along it rather than out into the river unless, of course, you have reason to think that a trout is feeding in mid-stream. And look for evidence still.

For instance, if under your feet you see a cloud of ' bait,' or minnows, huddled close in shore, spin carefully beyond and around them, for something big has lately frightened these little ones. And remember that little fish have no fear of big fish who are not hungry, who show as yet never a sign of wanting to dine.

Listen to evidence too. A young lady came to me last summer and said, ' I know that you fish ; what fish in the Thames is as big as a salmon and has spots on it?' I told her. Said she, 'Oh *no*, it wasn't a trout, I've often seen trout at Bridge of Allan.' But the event proved that it *was* a trout she had seen sunning itself.

When you spin in a weir pool another good bait is a wagtail. And, as a *wobble* bait, here is a good one. Take a dead bleak or gudgeon. Thread through it, vent to mouth, on a baiting needle, a single triangle which draw close against the vent. If this is cast out among piles and broken water and reeled in again it is a likely, a very likely, fate for a heavy trout. It will not spin but it will wobble tipsily and, quite often, do the trick for you where your true spinner will not. Try it in holes and corners and in the ' slacks ' between the piles and at the angles of sluices.

When spinning, spin *fast* and, in the main river, throw your rod point upstream when your bait is within a foot or so of the bank; this will cause it to swerve, coquettishly, aside. A trout, if he happens to be following it, will make his dash at it now or never.

In a weir the bait may be held for a similar moment or so in the fast water where it will continue to revolve for as long as you choose. Trout are very apt to take advantage of these last chances.

This summer I saw a very large trout, sixteen pounds perhaps, run at a three-pound jack which a lady had hooked and was holding in the white water under the weir's sill while her attendant hastened for the landing-net. The trout seized the pike and turned with it. Then he let go. I tried to catch him for a week but he never showed again.

Pike I have no doubt kill many small trout, but this is the only time that I have seen a tit-for-tat attempted. There are prodigious trout in the Thames, but they take prodigious bait and, night feeders, are seldom seen.

I once lost a very handsome trout who took the small red worm on which I was catching perch upon the shallow below Cleeve pool. He got among the piles and broke the light tackle. I was particularly sorry to see him go for he would have made a bonny tailpiece to as pretty a mixed kettle of Thames fish that ever I caught. I had in the punt that August day (and a flood clearing) barbel, pike, chub, perch, roach and an eel ; the trout, he *was* a dazzling fish and all of six lively pounds, would have made it a memorable basket.

But the bulk of Thames trout taken are taken on live-bait in the weir pools. Most men use minnows, not because they are the best bait but because they are the easiest to come by. In the old days the professional fisherman could supply his customers with gudgeon and bleak by the help of the ' cast ' net for the use of which the Conservancy issue licences to river keepers and trustworthy men. And to-day, as I have said, few such exist. Albert Wells is one, Bob Young, of Medmenham, is another.

Live-bait fishing requires patience without apathy. Which means, don't go to sleep, don't lose touch of your bait, don't stop *fishing* it, and don't fail to be expecting a *knock* in the next three seconds.

I have told you of the rod you will use, I have told you of the reel, the line—the greased line, and the landing-net. You will want three yards of fine gut trace which you will weight as required with the small and convenient ' envelope ' leads. These leads should be a yard above the bait. And, once more, you will require (a yard and a half above the weight to suit the deep water) the little red pilot float. Its duty is, however, *not* to indicate an offer, your hands will give you news of that, but to mark, in this fine and far-off method, where your bait has travelled to on the stream.

Your hook will be a lip-hook and a flying triangle, which you will allow to fly. Remember that a big trout takes a big bait. So take from the can a large and lively gudgeon, put the lip-hook through his upper lip and drop him into the river. The run will take him gently downstream for fifty yards. Let him, however, travel on the fringed edges of the current rather than in the fiercest of the foam. *Very slowly* reel him back to you and, when once more under the sill, hold him just below the surface of the water for some thirty seconds. For last chances, as I've said, are often indeed a trout's last chance.

In a weir stream a trout who means business will usually take like a tiger—one tremendous tug and forty yards of line out in four seconds. A headlong moment which is sometimes prefaced by a rapping *rat-tat* as though the trout had ' had at you,' his mouth shut and in preliminary play. In the open river a trout's methods are sometimes (but by no means always) more leisurely. Here, especially in the case of a big fish, he will take the bait quietly and swim off with it. This will mean that he holds it across the body and that, by the time he has gone ten yards, he will have turned the bait in his mouth to swallow it, as is his custom, head first. He should now be struck, firmly. And he will respond, I hope, by almost tearing the rod from your hands. When live-baiting from an anchored boat, have some line pulled off the reel and laid on the seat for your eight-pounder to sail away with. When playing a big trout, or a big anything, from a boat stand in the stern. If the fish makes a dash and a dive under the punt with you, you can, by merely swinging the rod's point, keep the line clear. If you are in the middle of the boat this, especially with a passenger on board, is not always an easy thing to do.

Live minnows are best fished two at a time, a point minnow and a dropper on a good length of gut. This last should be arranged so as to be within a foot of the point minnow. Put each minnow on a small single bait hook. Impale through the upper lip and not in the back.

And, once more, I beg you to treat your live-bait with consideration and to give freedom to any one who looks tired or who, even if still lively, has tempted his fortune on your behalf for any length of time. If you must take live-bait by train or car an old bicycle pump is a useful thing to take along with you. By its help you may keep the water aerated and the little fish in good trim. In hot weather a lump of ice laid *on top* of the can is likewise of benefit. Bait cans are the best cans when they have an inner envelope of perforated zinc to contain the gudgeon. For this envelope may be lifted bodily out and sunk in the stream attached to a string the while you fish. At the end of the day let your surplus baits go. They will *not* keep till next Saturday. The best bait for a big trout is a big gudgeon.

It is against the bye-laws for one angler to fish *two*

rods on a weir. This means that no one may live-bait and have a leger out at the same time. You may of course alternately spin with a spinning-rod and live-bait with another. To keep your place at a sluice, your rod, leaning on the railing, will always be respected. Without this precaution you may go to tea and find, on your return, that a newcomer is in your place.

If ever a trout looks like going through the sluices of a weir with you *slacken line and let him go*. Last year I hooked a big trout above Mapledurham weir. I could not hold him on my light tackle and he went through the sluice. I tried to stop him and he smashed me in the fall. This year I hooked another trout in the same place. He served me in almost the same spritely manner. But this time, when I saw that go he must, I let him have a slack line. Thereon he shot through the sluice like a bullet. He took seventy, eighty yards off the reel and stopped. I let him settle. I got on to the weir and, with the help of the lock-keeper and a long boat-hook, recovered the loose line where it trailed in the spouting green of the sluice. I cut the silk (for of course my rod was on the wrong side of the railings) and attached it to the reel line of another rod which a lady on the weir was using. I wound in and presently felt that the fish was still on. Ten minutes later he was in the net, six pounds eleven ounces and my best trout of this past season.

VIII. THE BREAM
(*ABRAMIS BRAMA*)

In a morning up we rise
Ere Aurora's peeping ;
Drink a cup to wash our eyes ;
Leave the sluggard sleeping.
  Then we go
  To and fro
  With our knacks
  At our backs
  To such streams
  As the Thames
If we have the leisure.
     JO. CHALKHILL.

N the Thames the bream just occurs. I mean that, only occasionally will an angler say, 'I am going, to-morrow, to fish for bream.' I think the reasons for this abstemiousness, this lack of enterprise, are three. Thames is a long river and though the bream in him are, here and there, reasonably plentiful these swims of plenty are widely apart. Therefore who is going to travel from Marlow to Sonning reach or from Goring to above Benson pool to catch, perhaps, a bream when he might catch a barbel to more advantage nearer home ?

Again, the Thames is a deep river. In lesser waters the bream angler may locate his prey, even follow it, by the mud that it stirs up, the bubbles that it blows, as it hog-rootles for water snails and larvæ along the bottom. It would take a lot of bream to make a show of this sort in the summer Thames. And the bream, like the barbel, is a summer fish. And except upon occasions of unseasonable warmth, the bream lies snugly in the mud under the boat-house from November until, almost, the cuckoo comes.

But perhaps the best reason of all why the bream is not a popular fish in London's river is because the Conservancy prohibit night fishing and the bream is as nocturnal a feeder as is the owl.

Izaak Walton spoke kindly of the bream as a table fish. I have never proved his words, but I should say that a dish of bream properly prepared might be excellent. Anyhow, bream was a *plat* that had the approval of the Church and a weekly bream was Man Friday to many a fat Abbot of the Middle Age.

If the T.C.C. allowed night fishing I think that I might become an enthusiastic breamer. Not that the methods of breaming are exhilarating at all. But the use of a luminous float would be delightful—a little Jack-o'-Lantern upon the waters, a Will-o'-the-Wisp to dance among the lily-beds when, at last, I got a run. A float too whose luminosity may be made more luminous by the addition of a white and decorative swan feather.

But since we may not catch Thames bream by

night we must turn, if we want a dish of bream, day into night. And how we do so I will presently say. But first we must know where we are likely to meet with the bream. And this is not so difficult as perhaps I have implied.

The bream is a gregarious fish and a most sociable. When his spawning is over, in late May or early June, he goes a-roving in companies. He is a restless fellow then for a month or more and an Ishmael of up the reaches and down again. But towards midsummer he, in a general way of business, will return to certain old-established haunts, vicinities and swims. And Thames is a river of tradition and any Thames fisherman will know, for instance, where Mr. Splitshott filled his boat half-full of bream between 5 a.m. and breakfast time on the August bank holiday of 1921. I'll tell you of one of these bream haunts here and now.

Pole the punt into Hennerton Backwater, below Wargrave, and rejoin the main river at Beggat's Hole Ferry. On the Berkshire bank, just where the backwater ends, is a lawn shady with elms. Also there is, or was, an ancient willow who leans out, mopping and mowing, to the Oxfordshire shore. Just up river of that willow (yes, I see bubbles) you will find bream of a midsummer morning. Or else you will not, for, of course, I cannot be positive. But you will get an appetite for breakfast even if your float bobs not at all, and a memory or so, perhaps,

> ' Of days when we drifted down lily-starred streams,
> Green willows, pink parasols, gold water-gleams,
> When life was a sunny procession of dreams
>   With Nina, Christina and all.'

And now that I have hinted to you where bream may be found, I will tell you, as well as I can, how they may be caught. The bream will take every sort of bait in the world except live-bait or the likes of a dry Wickham. He will even take a spinning flight if you spin deep enough and meet with him in good quantity. And if he happens to be hooked in the tail, as was the bream that I took lately upon a Thames flight, you will put him back again to be caught, on cheese, next Tuesday.

I have never heard of a Thames angler seriously baiting up a bream swim, though on lesser rivers than ours it is a common proceeding. But it would do no harm to have the gardener's lad go, on his way home, and throw into the river, where you bid him throw them, certain, cricket-ball size, globes of barley meal, boiled potatoes and gentles. If he does this for a night or so you will feel that you have done as much to advertise yourself and secure the appreciative attendance of bream as good sportsmanship requires. Bream fishing too is the most leisurely of all the angler's easy ways, so why make a toil of it even by proxy ?

Bream may be caught from the boat, anchored well above the swim about to be fished, or, as here, from the bank. In the latter case go cannily, for the bream is the most susceptible of all fish to the repercussion of a boot upon a bank. So approach him delicately and walk like a cat in his presence. And remember that if a noisy noise annoys an oyster a whisper is a scream to a bream.

Set the alarm clock for 2 a.m. and curse it not too

much when, at 2 a.m., it alarms you. At 2.15 you
may get up and make tea upon the waiting spirit
stove, whistling, under your breath, the while Sir
Harry Lauder's *It's Nice to get up in the Morning*.
Shaving you can postpone until to-morrow and a
bath until you come in to breakfast. So hurry a suit
of dark grey flannel over your pyjamas, drink a cup
of tea and step, quietly, along the corridor and down
stairs. The bream angler must ' study to be quiet '
not only upon the banks of Thames but in his
own sleeping home. So move about delicately and
pick up rod and tackle (placed ready overnight
upon the hall sofa) as though you committed a
felony. I am afraid that with the best will in the
world you cannot open the hall door without noise.
There is no hall door in all Thames side whose
lock, when turned at 2.30 a.m., does not go off like
a pistol shot. I know for I have had, from Lechlade to Ditton, experience of many early Thames
doors.

Do you ever slip out of a sleeping house on a fine
morning without thinking how truant Persephone
leaves the slumbering Palace of Pluto—early, early ?
No, I daresay that you never give a thought to her.
But *I* do, something in this wise :

> The winds on earth pipe bugle free,
> They've wakened sweet Persephone ;
> She's stretched her ivory arms, has she,
>   Her sea-blue eyes she's blinked ;
> And ' Oh ! ' she's said, and ' Oh ! ' she's said,
> ' 'Tis time that I was out o' bed,
> The rooks are building overhead,
>   I dreamt 'em most distinct.'

She doesn't wake her serving-maids,
Neat-fingered Phoebes of the Shades ;
She's brushed her hair in shining braids
    Bright gleaming as king-cup ;
She's laid her chiton out to don,
She's warmed her bath with Phlegethon ;
She's found her sandals, slipped them on,
    And hooked her own self up.

And now a-down the palace stair,
O'er coal-black marble huge and bare,
Behold her run, so rosy rare,
    And white as mayflowers fall ;
Low laughing in a roguish dread,
Down echoing corridors she's fled,
And ' Hey for holidays ahead ! '
    Says she, and o'er the hall.

And now she stands on tip-toe's tip,
The big door's upper bolt to slip ;
And now, a finger laid to lip,
    The lower back she's shot ;
She's turned the great key, clanking clean,
And out she steps, our little Queen,
Who wonders just how bold she's been,
    And rather hopes a lot.

Now in the nether morning mute
She stands half shy, half imp acute,
To take the grim guards' clashed salute
    With most becoming mien ;
Then, prettier than I can tell,
She trips across the asphodel ;
While early ghosts she meets say, ' *Well*,
    Of all things, there's the Queen ! '

And here she's come to Styx's flow,
Where an old puntsman (whom you'll know)
Says, ' Goin' over, Miss ?   Why so,
    Just do 'ee step right in ! '

And adds, good-willed as boatmen are,
' So Missy, found the door a-jar
Once more ?   My service to your Ma ;
    You'm lookin' peart's a pin.'

Then o'er that rayless flood they glide,
And out she hops the homeward side,
And, ' Thank you, Charon dear ! ' she's cried,
    ' You'm welcome, Miss ! ' bawls he,
As off, like swallow, see her fly,
And, as those little feet flit by
The crocus flames, a thrush on high
    Shouts, ' Here's Persephone ! '

*   *   *   *   *   *

Child goddess of the daisy-chain,
If thus I've brought you home again
By Fancy led in Folly's train,
    With liberty undue,
Forgive these vanities of song,
Poor dreams that to the bard belong ;
For, dream he right or dream he wrong,
    Who cares if come you do ?

And now we stand on the dew-drenched gravel outside the hall door. The day is making fast, blue above
it is and the beechwoods showing green and dark
green in the muffle of the mist. The river mist that
implies another hot day for later on. But, as yet, it
is delightfully cool ; and quiet, quiet, except for a
dove in the sycamore. For the thrush that welcomed
Persephone stopped singing three weeks ago. However, step round to the tool-shed and get the
worms in their bag of damp moss and we'll be getting
along.

The tackle we have with us is the ' live-bait ' rod
and I wish, I must say, I wish that it was a foot or two

longer. But it will serve. Nottingham reel as before,
undressed line as before, also the pilot float though a
quill would, I fancy, be the occasional float of the
angler from the Ouse. However, behold, the breamer
cometh.

And among his outfit this morning is a little fold-up
stool upon whose striped seat of canvas he will sit,
for though there is much grass in the place there is
also much dew. And here we are at the swim which
is gravel bottomed and about eight-foot deep. Walk
and talk quietly. Attach to the reel line two yards of
fine, but not too fine, gut and then a single bait-hook.
Arrange the light lead on the line as when legering,
which indeed we are. Then why the float ? Well,
Thames bream fishing is mainly a game of patience
at which you cannot cheat. Were we legering for
barbel we should sit continually our finger on the line
and as hopeful as a heron. When we fish for Thames
bream we are hopeful too but rather with the hope-
fulness of the man with a ticket in the Calcutta sweep.
However, optimistically toss in another globe or so of
ground bait—you remember, barley meal, boiled
potatoes and gentles, with a stone to be the sinking
weight and the kernel of each globe ?

And now see that the float is adjusted so as it may
sit cheerfully on the surface while the shot lies upon
the floor of the swim and the two feet of gut bottom-
line moves freely beyond it. An easy matter this since
we know the depth of the eight-foot swim to an inch.
Did we not know it we should have to mess about
with a plummet. But as we *do* know we will at once
begin to fish.

And this is the way of a Thames breamer. He

cuts a rod-rest from a tree not too near the bank.
And a rod-rest is an equilateral of twig upon an
eighteen-inch branch whose end is sharpened and
driven into the green bank. Why is the bank above
a gravel swim greener than a bank that goes sheerly
into soft mud ? I do not know but it seems to me
that it is so.

The rod-rest erected the angler places his camp
stool within an arm's length thereof. He casts his
tackle into the swim, he feels the lead touch bottom
and he sees the float comfortably cocking. He now
adjusts the rod in the rest and sits down to wait.

And he may wait a very long time and he may
change from lob to brandling worm, from brandling
worm to gentle, or gentles, from gentles to cheese-
paste, a biggish piece of it, and still be waiting. I
cannot say why one waits for barbel rod in hand and
for bream with rod in rest. It is a matter of fashion
and good form I suppose, like drinking ' more blood '
with the stalker when you shoot a stag and never with
the gamekeeper when you shoot a rabbit.

At intervals, however, throw in, hopefully, a little
more ground bait. And presently it may be that,
should you be looking and not just enjoying the grey-
and-green coolth, you will see the float first wobble
and then sink, surely in the most deliberate and un-
emotional manner in all angling. But would you
know a bream if you saw one ?

Well, the bream is rather a handsome fish although
his shape, somewhat in the style of the drawing-room
bellows, does not suggest speed or much fighting
power. He is, in fact, slab-sided and his tail is nearly
as long and as forked as the rod-rest we cut just now.

Though his flanks are deep the bream's back is not broad and his weight, when he has it, goes in length and depth and not in great thickness. He has a small rather well-bred head and a red-gold eye which he rolls ravenously when he is in feeding mood. My impression of the bream when I am playing him is that he is dark blue of back and silver of side. But when he is on the bank his back is jade and his sides a very beautiful bronze.

You will get a somewhat similar optical delusion along with the driven grouse who looks to be a black-and-white bird as he comes to the butt. And yet, when shot and gathered, he is red-and-brown. But the bream's fins are blue-black as the sloes in the hedge. And, as we can see, he is a methodical taker.

If the float continues to wobble and move about upon the surface without going under, this probably means that the bream has taken the bait and has risen with it in his mouth as far as the gut length below the lead permits. So whether the float goes under, as ours has, or remains agitated only, let us strike at once, strike gently.

The bream will probably be hooked and, if he is, he will resent you and prevent you (rather than fight you) deep down and boring. His breadth of beam helps him to be stubborn but he will, with a plunge or so, quickly succumb.

No Thames angler has a right to talk of bream when a man from Nottinghamshire is present. But I will say that, as far as my Thames experience teaches me, the bream sorts himself into sizes much in the manner approved by the perch and the salmon schools. But the large bream that are taken in

Thames seem to be solitary fish. And we have some mighty fine specimens to our credit, for the bream grows to be big. I have read that there has been a Trent bream of 17 lb. But a four-pound bream is no bad bream for the Thames where half that size is the shoal size, though I have heard of fish twice four pounds, twice and more, and have actually seen a seven-pounder taken.

But these bigger fish, I think, play a lone hand and are caught in baited barbel swims. I think that they are solitary because they will occur in a day's barbelling where no other bream is taken, whereas were bream present in the shoal, I think that more than one would be taken and the punt with two rods out and all. Also I think that the big bream are solitary because a shoal of seven-pounders would be too good to be true.

If you hook a bream of size in a weir stream he is a difficult fish. The big fish that I saw taken at Whitchurch was as awkward in play as an empty bucket might have been. He turned his great side to the current and, drifting, he took out line and more line. He turned his nose to stream and came like a kite that has missed stays. He turned his flank and went, with Father Thames again, like an indolent dish-cover. Eventually he was beached on the eyot-shallow, for come to the net he would not. He is now in a glass case as he deserves to be.

Last summer I saw a big bream above Benson weir; I think he might have weighed more than seven pounds. I was trout fishing on the weir and the bream, spent with the labours of spawning, came drifting against the sluice gates. And upon his side

he lay among the flotsam. I lifted him out in the
landing-net and propped him, head to river and right
side uppermost, among the green bulrushes through
which the mill-stream pours its lively waters. I do
not know if this weary giant recovered, but I hope he
did and that he will yet make a specimen fish for
some honest angler.

But the man who fishes for bream in the Thames
has little better chance of filling a pillow-case with his
spoils than the man who fishes for something else and
looks on bream as catch crop.

But always for the bream fisher is the quiet water,
the quiet green bank and another summer day just
coming.

There is also the bream angler's breakfast when
the summer day has well come. Fresh eggs there will
be for the bream angler, fried bacon, a kidney or so,
toast and butter, honey, the hottest coffee, and strawberries, innumerable strawberries. And then a cigar
among the roses and possibly a tankard of cool, brown
ale about eleven o'clock.

IX. THE TENCH
(*TINCA TINCA*)

'Tight lines,' says brother unto brother,
  At morn 'tight lines', at eve's decline,
'Tight lines', again each answers other,
  For, Tay to Tweed and Thames to Tyne,
  Tension's the angler's tribal sign,
And though the trouts that most they mention
  Supply them tenseness trebly tense
Yet that no line can have its tench on
  Without a tench is only sense.

THE POP-GUNROOM POETRY BOOK.

THE tench has been called the pike's chirurgeon, possibly because he is covered with a fine golden varnish, which some people call slime, and which is supposed to have a healing quality should a tench rub himself affectionately upon the flanks of a pike who has just been quarrelsome with an otter or with another pike. But the likelier reason for this pet name is, as has been pointed out by someone, Mr. Sheringham I expect, that the tench quite frequently fortifies the pike from inside.

The tench prefers, so it is said, a pond to a river, and the smaller the pond the bigger are the tench that may be expected of it. The record tench in this country is twelve pounds and I simply don't believe it. Half the weight would be a prodigious fellow, and I should be surprised if Father Thames could show me a five-pounder. He has, however, an occasional three-pound tench as I know, and I fancy that Mr. A. E. Hobbs could introduce you to a four-pounder if you were to ask him to let you see his collection of personally captured Thames fish. And a tyro of Thames could hardly do better than see so wonderful a temple of inspiration. Think of a wall covered, floor to ceiling, with ten-pound trout, think of yards and yards of barbel, think of bream as big as an intimate tea-table, think of me as a liar and then see for yourself and say that I am, after all, conservative in my envy and enthusiasm.

The tench is a handsome fish, he is dusky golden in colour and his scales are so minute as to give you for a moment the impression that he has none at all. His shape is somewhat that of a stocky and high-conditioned trout, square tail and all, but his large single dorsal bewrayeth him.

Tench, like bream and barbel, hibernate; the tench, in fact, is a summer fish, a summer fish above the barbel and beyond the bream. Mr. Sheringham, who loved him, has written of him that the word 'tench' has within it all the splendid pageantry of July.

Thames tenching is not specialised in because, like the bream, the tench feeds at night when no man may fish in Thames. So to catch tench we get up with the summer bream-fisher and his song before sunrise. Or else we just wait for the tench to occur, which he will do occasionally on a grey, cool day when we are fishing for perch with a small red worm and it upon the floor of the river.

But let us not be lymphatic about the tench and casually await his occasional convenience. And so 3 a.m. shall, once more, see us, tackle-laden, crossing the stile (its top bar wet, dusky wet, with the dew), and striding, in our high boots, among the haycocks and down to the misty river. And while we walk we will talk tench, and the habitats of tench.

The fact that tench are in the Thames makes me think that, some day or another, a Thames angler will catch a really fine carp in the river. For carp and tench go as surely together as June and July. And tench are not unplentiful in the Thames. I think that the well-known Medmenham professional Young had eight (or was it ten?) fine tench in the Henley Regatta reach, one after the other just as the sun rose and the shadows of the elms lay across the sleeping meadows like slumbering giants.

I forget the weight of this goodly basket if ever I heard it, but it was no doubt an important weight to carry home if an unimportant one to remember. And, talking of weights, the male tench weighs more than the female tench, say the copybooks. But not (like myself) to know which tench is which, makes this knowledge of the pedants a pointless one.

But, you say, an open regatta reach is a strange place wherein to find tench from what you have heard, from what you have read?

You are right and I expect these fish were taken in some weedy bay or backwater and that Rumour who said regatta reach was as ignorant, or untruthful, in her statement as she usually is. For tench love weeds and floors of mud and the quiet lumber-rooms of the river, corners where débris of all kind collects and disintegrates beneath a surface carpet of green weed and vegetation. And tench, who hate the heat of incandescent noon, have appetite at prime, a prime that goes hand-in-hand with the promise of heat that lies under the heavy blanket of the summer mists.

And what, he having appetite, will a tench eat ? If left to himself, my son, he will eat larvæ, shrimps, salads, water-snails, all the minute animalcul——

You don't care a curse about natural history ? Well, why didn't you say then that your question was prompted by a mere selfish desire for, what you call, bites ? The tench, when he will take at all, will take any bait that you like to offer him. Any bait that is useable in Thames—crust, gentle, paste, wasp-grub—anything except weed and a live minnow and the likes of a live minnow.

' Do you drink anything ? ' asked the curt employer of the candidate for the post.

' *Anything*, Sir,' huskily replied the applicant.

The tench is something like that, but it is upon worm, lob or brandling, that you will catch him this morning.

And the rod ? The live-bait rod, the light, little live-bait rod, will do nicely since we shall be fishing from the punt. And had we been fishing from the bank it would have done well enough too. Though in this case I might have wished it, as I wished it when we went a-breaming, a little bit longer.

And here we are at the river, and the swim that we shall presently be fishing looks an ideal tench water. It is, in fact, the tail of the mill-cutting at Mapledur-ham. And yesterday afternoon we borrowed the lock-keeper's long rake, the river-rake with which he keeps his chuckling sluices weed-free and open, and made with it a swim for tench, raking the ruffle away and clearing a space as large as a circular dining-room table to seat ten people. And, while we were about it, we took, yesterday, our swim's soundings, dropping our plummet and making our plans and measurements. For the tench is a coy and cloistered fish and it is not wise to intrude on his privacy too closely just before we fish for him.

If few Thames anglers bait up a bream swim I should think none at all paid this attention to the tench. Nevertheless, yesterday, when I had done with the rake, I dropped into the swim a few of those jolly globes of meal and maggots that we employed to entice the bream. And now that we have got the punt, softly, within casting distance I will throw in another one or two of the weighted balls.

The tench, like the bream, has a sensitive ear. A step on the bank, the splash of a paddle, the vibrations of the *vox humana* all affect him acutely. So slip the punt's anchor overboard as if you were in church and put the rod together without boast of words.

And the tackle ? The tackle that will catch a bream will catch a tench. But for tench in this shallow water I like a finer gut, a smaller bait hook, and a bullet a little less than was the lead we used last week when we caught the bream. The pilot float, as before, suits well and looks pretty. We will now bait the hook, yes, with one of the brandlings, and cast our angle into the river.

The float cocks nicely, the bullet touches bottom, just enough and no more. We can now, in obedience to the ancient superstition and custom of the tench and the bream, which provides that no baited rod be handled prior to the strike, pull a hopeful foot of line off the reel, prop the old split-cane against the thwart and forget about it until the float goes pop.

Men who fish usually smoke. And some smokers can smoke with impunity before breakfast, even big, swarthy cigars, that wear gold-and-scarlet cymars, can some men smoke at 4 a.m. Can smoke not only as they stroll home to Grosvenor Square through the pearl-grey romances of Mayfair at sunrise, but when they get up and dress and go to fish for salmon or, as Mr. Kingsley has said, to climb Alps, they walk also behind the same bright-girdled, ell-long Muria.

Men who can smoke thus betimes, even if their tastes and banking accounts confine them to the smoking of pipes and cigarettes, say that this early tobacco is the most pleasurable of all. But I who am only amateur of the habit cannot smoke before breakfast either with enjoyment or without trepidation. So here in the punt while we wait on the tench's times and seasons I must employ myself with the scenery and the greenery and make my Lady Nature substitute for my Lady Nicotine.

At the moment, however, the white mists are so thick that scenery scarcely is and greenery consists in the bending river bulrushes (' little green fishing rods,' they have been aptly called) and the looming, glooming umbrage of the fog-bound elms on the eyot hard by.

But if we will sit quiet, as indeed we must sit if we would presently catch a brace of tench, there are sights to be seen, there are sounds to be heard. We shall for instance see the otter, even the otter and his family, coming home from frog hunting along the top of the weir. Home to the eyot they go where I imagine that they have their holt. I should like to entice one of the cubs into the punt to occupy me but this I cannot do, yet, if I am lucky, I may, in the landing-net, catch this velvet-brown, unsuspecting vole as she comes paddling by. Missed her, by all the virtues of Diana whose protégée she is ! I believe the silly little prude thought that my intentions were unkindly whereas I only wanted to fondle her a spell and put her out board again. But she dived like a dabchick.

I can hear two doves somewhere and the croak of a water-hen. What was it that Fair Haired Duncan of the Songs—ah, yes :

And sweet it was when the white sun glimmered,
    Listening under the crag to stand—
And hear the moor-hen so hoarsely croaking,
    And the red grouse murmuring close at hand ;
While the little wren blew his tiny trumpet,
    And threw his steam off blithe and strong,
While the speckled thrush and the redbreast gaily
    Lilted together a pleasant song !

Not a singer but join'd the chorus,
    Not a bird in the leaves was still :
First the laverock, that famous singer,
    Led the music with throat so shrill ;
From tall tree-branches the blackbird whistled,
    And the grey bird joined with his sweet ' coo-coo ';
Everywhere was the blithesome chorus,
    Till the glen was murmuring thro' and thro'.

But in midsummer woods no birds sing. There is, however, the ceaseless lull and lapse of old Thames as he takes the lasher, a lasher shrunken of July to a splashing spoonful or so. And into the murmur of him, since we can neither smoke before breakfast nor catch a vole in a landing-net, let us read the river legend of Ægle until the tench take.

Naiads they were called, those good little sisters of the Golden Age who were part and parcel of the waters of Cephissus and his hundred blue and kindred streams, and who played, tumbling over each other as pretty and slippery as so many otter cubs, in his pools and golden shallows, or hid pale as Lodden lilies among the green rushes.

And Ægle was the prettiest of them all. Her eyes were as blue as rivers seen through beechwoods on a blue May morning and, all amber shadows, her bright hair poured about her gleaming little body. So pretty was she indeed that when the early Sun saw her as she sat on a stone to dry herself, he of a sudden fell in love with her; and I for one can but admire his very good taste.

But Ægle, smoothly as an otter, slipped off her stone into the river again and was gone. Not because she wasn't rather flattered but because she didn't want to have to make up her mind about anything before breakfast. At least let us think so. But the Sun was inconsolable and kept looking for Ægle from different angles all the day long; and all the next day and the day after that. And Ægle kept peeping at him from under a lily-pad, and she thought what fun it was to be loved by so fine and splendid a young gentleman, ' *and*,' she added to herself in a little, small voice, ' to love him back again.' But still she didn't want to make up her mind about anything before breakfast, and, if you think in that way, you can put off the making up of your mind for ever so long, for you can always pretend that you mean *to-morrow's* breakfast. Besides Ægle, you see, only had water-melon and water-biscuits for breakfast anyhow, and perhaps that isn't having breakfast at all. So don't let's blame her a bit.

But the Sun—he was young then and impetuously impatient—said fiercely, ' I'll show her,' and then he added fatuously, ' the darling ! ' And show her he did, for he was both powerful and a personage and precious inconsiderate of others when he wanted anything. But there—so are lots of good people, people too who have not got the excuse *he* had of wanting so lovely a thing as Ægle. So he shone—for days he shone, till the skies were hot and blue and hazy and never a raindrop fell. And Ægle said to herself, ' I see what he's up to,' and she was frightfully frightened but frightfully happy at the same time.

But the trout and the chub and the caddises and all the funny little creatures that live in rivers were not happy a bit. How could they be when they saw their home gradually getting littler and littler ? And so they gathered, huddled in a dark cloud, under the shrunken splash of the falls, just as you saw the barbel huddle in that drought of a few years back ; and there they held a council, all their tails and fins fanning at once, faintly but in the most agitated fashion.

' It is all Ægle's fault,' they said, for gossip on her affairs had of course been quite unavoidable ; ' how *can* she put us in a position of so much discomfort and danger ? '

' And yet,' said a handsome old trout whom Ægle had guided out of a fisherman's drag-net only recently, 'Ægle has a heart of gold ; why not appeal to it ? '

' You wish to make a *sacrifice* of me ? ' said Ægle, trying hard not to dance about and clap her hands ; for can anything be more satisfactory than to be implored to do just what you are simply dying to do and then be hailed as a heroine for saying ' Yes ' ?

For, of course, ' Yes ' is just what Ægle did say.

' I told you that the child had a heart of gold,' said the old trout importantly.

And so the next morning, when the Sun, who had got up earlier than ever because it was Midsummer Day, came tiptoe and golden through the big oaks and down to the river, there sat little Ægle on the rock under the fall, her blue eyes dancey and her bright hair glancey, and a nibbled little bit of watermelon beside her to show that she'd had her breakfast at last.

And the Sun took her in both his burning arms, and together they stood a minute, he and she, one with the joyful dazzle of water before he caught her up with him into the morning.

And did Ægle never come back to her fishes at all, at all ? Why, of course she did, and every day when the Sun shines you'll see her and her lover in any Thames weir pool ; for, when Sun and Water were blent all those years ago, they, with the dancing blue eyes of Ægle and with the brightness of her gleaming hair to help them, made, in their moment, a rainbow in the whiteness of the fall—the same little occasional rainbow that you may see any sunny afternoon under the weir at Mapledurham. And when the great arc of glory stands across our valley and we know that it stands for The Promise of the continual kindness of Sun and Water, may we not still say that therein little Ægle and her lover go riding down to the river again with the sunny showers—the singing showers which make the running rivers which were, and are, her home?

But look at the float. The float which has stood still for so long has got a move on it at last. It is rocking gently from side to side, it is sailing gently across the swim. Fishermen will tell you that a tench stands on his head to take the bait and that having done so he rises towards the surface. Thus, and his movements being leisurely movements, he does not pull the float under water with the cheerful gusto of, say, a perch. So count ten slowly and then strike precisely.

A tench is no great fighter and though this one tries for the weeds several times he is soon controlled and allows himself to be towed to the net down the yard-wide channel that we made with the rake yesterday, just such a tow as this in mind.

It is 5 a.m. now and the mist is lifting. Another brandling we will put on and we will cast it out and, sitting down once more, we will be as patient as possible. We have not so long to wait this time. In less than half an hour the pilot trembles and resumes its travels. Once more the rod is picked up, the strike given, and another tench is taught to be a tench.

Now even if we get no other knock (for on Thames a bite, a nibble, a pull, a touch, a pluck, a 'rug,' and

a tug are, one and all, called ' knocks ') we shall have
two very pretty bronze-and-gold fish to take home,
and if a brace are no great number, they are tench
and two tench are twice as many, let me say, as you
will catch on most of the midsummer mornings on
which you go down to Thames with a tench-rod.

And the returning tench-fisher may breakfast in
the manner of one who has fished for bream and never
in the anæmic water-melon mode which was good
enough for Ægle.

X. THE CHUB
(*LEUCISCUS CEPHALUS*)

The chub he is of worthy sort
Benevolent and bulky,
And doth afford a stately sport
When trout are dour and sulky,
For even if it is July
Man still must out and throw a fly
Or surely find himself, say I,
Blue-devilled and in dull key.

THE POP-GUNROOM POETRY BOOK.

THE chub has a hundred good qualities to recommend him to the Thames angler. But he has one outstanding merit. He is the only important fish in the river who will take a fly ; it is for the chub only that the visitor from the Test, the Itchen or the Kennet may angle, without a subsequent feeling of *gêne* when he must confess, in The Fly-fishers' Club, that he has been fishing in the Thames.

It is a pitiable sight to see a purist from Stockbridge beside a weir pool. Some years ago one such professor came to stay with us for Whitsuntide. We took him to fish for trout. He was a deplorable calamity. It was raining a little. He could not spin.

Huddled up in a mackintosh he sat in a punt and watched a float with a resigned expression and an earthenware firkin of ale beside him which belonged to the professional fisherman in attendance. I wished that some of his clubmates from the Houghton would happen along but none did. He still talks of Thames trouting (so I am told) as 'meathook and window cord.' All this is said because, had Whitsun fallen subsequent to the 16th of June, my friend might have caught chub on a dry fly and had a jolly bank holiday after all. The chub too, besides being the fly-fisher's fish, is a hearty chap who does not hibernate but, ware and waking the season through, is in his finest fighting form during the cold weather. The two best chub that ever I caught I took off the towpath below Cleeve weir one November day. I was spinning for jack with a medium spoon and I caught the chub, each an ounce or so under five pounds, in almost consecutive casts. And, a moment or so later, the same spoon took a seven-pound pike.

But, for enjoyment, give me chub in July; in this sort :

> When silent is the blackbird's trill
>   That made the May-month tuneful
> And when the lasher's shrunk until
>   'Tis but a single spoonful,
> When cattle stand on shallows bright
>   Among the water-lilies
> And noonday dazzles diamond white
> And other fish lose appetite,
>   The chub my refuge still is.

And a very good refuge too, for the hotter the day and the clearer the water the readier is the chub and, withal, at his most difficult. And what could the angler sportsman ask more than that ?

The chub will take literally everything you like to offer him from a dry Wickham to a live gudgeon and his dietary includes strawberries and cherries and small red pilot floats. But in summer, when one fishes for chub, the fly is the method. The fly-rod anyhow.

Bits of worm about as large as a bumble-bee, portions of snail of similar size, these upon a small bait hook and fine unweighted gut will, cast like a fly, kill as well as (or better than) a fly. But this is a messy method and I think that a fly does as successfully.

A summer bait too that has accounted for big chub is a small frog, and many honest anglers and good sportsmen use it. The frog is killed first of course. A large bait-hook is placed through the reptile's body so that the angle of the hook is out of the mouth, the shank protruding from the tail ; the hind legs are tied to the gut. This latter may be weighted with a small envelope lead, or a shot. This bait is fished on a fly-rod in the ' sink and draw ' style of the salmon fisher. I have never used a frog for bait because I am sentimental about frogs, who are pretty and yellow and hop-in-the-grass, and I scunner at killing them to amuse myself when an artificial fly is equally entertaining. And despondent frog prisoners in a bait-box nearly break my heart.

Chub are gregarious and, in assorted sizes, haunt the same summer places year after year—places of gravel bottom and shady bough from whence the caterpillar occurs, places where the sunshine filters through green leaves and where the grey, cruising shadows sail in the leisurely amber. But I think that the very big chub, and we have some whoppers, are solitary fellows something like the big bream. The biggest chub I ever saw landed out of Thames, or any other river, was taken by Mr. Eric Parker, as it ought to have been, and—but he shall tell you about that chub himself. This is what Mr. Parker says of that Dead Sea Apple ; and from *English Wild Life* I quote him :

' These Thames weirs hold great chub. Once at Mapledurham, fishing for trout, I hooked a fish which I knew was not a trout, for there was nothing tigerish in the pull, but a sullen weight, an inertia which threatened tackle but which belonged to no shape that would show itself. At last the fish came up and into the net, rolling broad and brown and silver-yellow, and at last the attendant fisherman lifted it to the stone coping, and he and I and my host stared at each other without words to say. For it weighed seven pounds, the largest chub that I or any of us had ever seen or .will see again, and I had caught it in the close season. In lilac-time, trout may be taken, but not chub, and that yellow tub of a fish went back to the Thames.'

I personally put that chub at nearer eight than seven pounds. The lock-keeper's estimate was nine ! Albert Wells, the professional from Wallingford, who netted the fish, guessed its bulk to be seven-and-a-half pounds, and Wells has seen more chub in a landing-net than I, or you, have seen in Thames water.

But, seven, eight, or nine pounds, I have seen bigger chub in the river than was Mr. Parker's chub. They have never been weighed. And if ever I do catch a ten-pound chub it will be, like Mr. Parker, in Maytime and when I am fishing for trout in a Thames weir pool. And I shall pat his big bronze flank, say that he is a noble fellow and a twelve-pounder at least, hope to meet him again in July and slide him back, as the bye-laws bid me, into the broken water below the sill.

I will tell you about one of those big chub. I went to fish at Mapledurham one summer day. As I crossed the footbridge above the tumbling river I looked down and saw, upon the 'apron,' nose to current and bronze back almost out of the water, the biggest chub that ever I saw. He was enormous, he really was. I put my waders on and approached him, delicately, along fifty yards of splashing sill. I got within reach of him, I got so as I could look down upon him, peeping through a green up-thrust of reeds, from a height of eight feet or so. There I increased my estimate of his weight from ten pounds to thirteen. I dapped a fly in front of his blunt nose.

He *was* a huge chub and his mouth was as big as a cheese plate. He came wide open to the fly—a large red Palmer. Then he saw, I fancy, a wink of my Judas gut in the sun. He turned away with a heavy flounder and slid, tail first, off the 'apron.' The river picked him up, a long grey shadow, and he was gone.

As I splashed back to whence I came, I signified the chub's size to a lady who waited with a landing-net. I signified it in the usual manner, that is by an, in no way exaggerated, extension of the arms. I noticed as I did so that an onlooker, an amateur photographer, was snap-shotting the weir ; but I thought nothing of that for on a summer day the kodak is common on the river, and a weir pool, with or without an angler, makes the pretty picture indeed.

Months later, in the lounge of a country hotel, I turned over the pages of a ' snap-shot ' album. Pictures were within it of Athens, Florence, Rome, Edinburgh Toun, the Tiber and the middle Thames. ' Hullo ! ' I said, ' *What* a strange chance, here am I walking along the weir with a fishing-rod ; why, that must have been taken (yes, indeed it must, because I'm showing how big he was) the day we saw that enormous chub ! *What* a funny thing ! '

Then I glanced at the caption, inscribed in a clerkly hand, beneath the picture. It was a title in two words. The two words were, *The Liar*.

Chub on the summer Thames must usually be sought betimes and in a boat. The reason for the boat is that Thames, most of him, is too big to fish from the bank while lark-earliness is necessary because if the angler postpones his sport till after twelve on a fine Saturday the holiday craft and the cacophony of the Gods of Tin will have shifted the chub out of the shallows. And it is useless to fish with a fly in deep water, in fact it may be said to be nearly useless to fish with a fly, a wet fly or a dry one, unless you first see the chub that you are to offer it to. And so when the boats come let the afternoon chub angler go from the main river to the weir pool. But he will want a weir ticket to admit him to the bridges and sluice bridges.

Standing on these, he may look down into the runs and see the chub, nose to stream, quietly rising and falling in the fast water or cruising, in little companies, along the sills and aprons. And now if the angler is tired of the fly let him lay down his fly-rod and take up the ten-foot split-cane that I have called my live-bait rod. Only to-day no live-bait is required of it, nor float nor too much lead.

Put on a fine trace with a small triangle at the end of it, put on a shot or so, or one small envelope lead. Get the bag of cheap cherries purchased, *ad hoc*, in Pangbourne as we drove through there this morning. Cut one or two into pieces and scatter them into the stream to float, a scarlet flotsam, to the interested shoals. Watch them as they go. One by one they disappear as the portly chevin suck them in. Now take your knife and a cherry, and make an insertion in the latter through which you may remove the stone. In the place of the stone insert the triangle and close the pink juicy edges cunningly about it. Throw in ground bait anew and now drop your tackle over and let cherry-*cum*-triangle go gently upon the current.

Plainly you can see the venturer and now a three-pound chub has seen it too. A chub is never in a hurry. A trout that means business comes headlong. A pike who wants the wobbling spoon rushes upon it, olive and gold and a capacity of cavernous jaws. A chub lounges up to the morsel, considers it, opens his pale lips (which have been well likened to a large rubber umbrella ring) and absorbs the bait.

And now that we have seen him do so we can strike him firmly and hook him. A chub is a good beginner, he pulls good and hard and in this fast water he is a worthy antagonist. But he comes presently, like many a well-hooked fish before him, to the long-handled landing-net. And a goodlooker he is, bronze and olive and belly-fins of gules, and his name chub suits his bluff, portly and highly respectable appearance far better than do the alternatives, ' chevin,' ' chavender ' and contemptuous ' loggerhead.'

Yes, a chub in fast water is a brave fighter. I remember that I hooked one on a live minnow that I intended for a five-pound trout that lay in Temple weir—the little Temple below Cleeve. This chub played with such spritely exercise that, for three minutes at least, I was paying him the supreme compliment of thinking that it was surely with Himself that I had engaged.

So put on another cherry and try again. And if you prefer, and have the choice, you may use, instead of the cherry, a strawberry (but it comes off easily), paste, cheese paste, macaroni, bits of banana, wasp grubs, gentles, crust—anything, anything that will give the goodly mouthful that the chub enjoys. But a red cherry looks prettily in the clear bubble of the run and suggests summer time and old Thames songs like *Twickenham Ferry*, and it's all one to the chub what you float down to him. For if a chub wants you he wants you and if he don't he don't. And if he happens to see you or suspicion your presence on the weir he certainly does not want you.

You have seen a trout ' put down ' often enough I fear. He leaves his stance with a scandalized flip. He darts over the gravel between the lily-beds, he dashes upstream and downstream, he hides in the slow movement of the weed, he runs in under green and daisied banks. But a chub is no such temperamental fellow. Take the fly-rod, walk this way and I'll show you what I mean.

Nose against the sill in the quiet water between the two sluices, see, there lies a large and solitary chevin. This fish is waiting for what may occur. His poise is an upward poise, that is to say his tail is in streamline with the nose of him. Should he decide that your fly is not an occurrence within the meaning of the act, that your Coachman, contrary to all good taste, wears spurs, he will not dash off like the trout that you have given similar cause to distrust you. No, the chub will merely drop his head by half an inch and, in corresponding measure, hoist his great forked tail. And now you may continue to cast over him till the cows come home and he will not budge from his aloof contemptuousness without you throw a brick at him—or foul-hook the clown and drag him out and box his ears.

I have said that mostly the Thames chub are taken in summer and early in the day. And also that the chubist must nearly always fish from a boat. He will know where to find his fish, for chub, like bream, return yearly to the same localities.

These chubbing grounds are frequently the gravel shallows thrown up by weir pools. Chub also work into mill-tails and lively waters of all sorts. But it is worth while casting under any bank or eyot that is wooded to the water and boughed about. For here chub haunt to batten on wasps and bumble-bees and all the fat things of July.

There is a choice of chub flies, but one is as good as another. I use a Zulu, summer day in and summer day out, a Zulu with a half-inch tag of white kid glove

on the barb of it. I do not know what the kid is for,
but I was brought up to think that the chub liked a
Zulu better so than in the entire Ethiopian. I use
a red Palmer as a change and with these two flies I
take as many chub, and as big ones, as my brethren
do.

But I think the biggest chub are found well up in
the weirs. And that they are solitary fish, though
sometimes it may be that their solitude is a solitude
à deux. And I think that they have beats, as have,
so I am told, the big trout of Blagdon. These big
cruising fish seem to pass certain places at regular
intervals. I have spent many hours, sometimes with
a rod and sometimes without one, sitting on the stone
steps on the lock side of Mapledurham and I have
seen the chub swim by, sculling slowly and sluggardly. They pass and occur again at intervals a
morning through.

Unless he is a finished oarsman the early chub
fisher will be better of an attendant who is expert in
a boat. For the boat must move silently as the boat
of Charon and stealthily as goes the first lieutenant's
pinnace on one of Captain Marryat's cutting-out
expeditions.

Slinking upstream in the daw'ing you will come
presently to the chub waters. Ahead of you is the
great horseshoe of the weir, its mighty voices muffled
down to a tinkling summer symphony. The spawning redds at the entrance to the wide-open of the pool
are fringed with willow boughs, the movement of the
water runs here in shallow ripples over an acre of
amber shingle.

Upon this acre is a grey-blue cloud in slow but

perpetual flux. This is what we have risen so early to see. This is the shoal of the chub. But it is unlikely that you will see therein any of the fathers of their people, yet three-pounders are not unplentiful, possibly an ounce or two over three pounds are some of those present.

Therefore let the boatman approach with care, and, at a range of twenty-five yards, let him rest upon his oars. Now, if you are young and unskilful at the chub you will yield to excitement and cast a random fly into the middle of the shifting cloud. And such ' browning ' tactics will forthwith be rewarded by the hooking of a half-pounder whose too public plight will cause his companions to ignore your next effort and, anon, to drop back into deep water where no fly will avail.

But the proved angler will, on approaching his quarry, when it is there in bulk, wait a bit before he attempts a cast. Soon a worthy fish will become separate from the bevy. To drop the fly a foot or so from his blunt features is easy. The chub will stroll up to it, consider it, and then he will open his mouth. And, as he closes it again, you will strike. There is a kick, a plunge, and your little rod bends prodigiously, for you have hooked him. The boat backs away behind the eyot and the chub—three pounds of broad-scaled bronze—is shortly yours. And, look, the shoal is still on the shallow and we may have, if we are leisurely and lucky, another of its members, even two, before it decides that this particular shallow is unhealthy for chub.

And then we will row off softly and cast under the willow boughs and fill the boat's well with a dozen

fat chevin most of whom we will return to their
Thames when, as the day grows hot, we ourselves
return, in excellent appetite, to our eggs and bacon.

I do not know what might be called an outstanding
morning's sport. I have taken in the neighbourhood
of two dozen chub between six o'clock and eight a.m.
But this is not notable. Albert Wells tells me that
he has kept, after returning many to the river, a
basket of ten chub weighing thirty-three pounds.
And a very pretty basket too. I think that must
have been a sort of gala occasion for chub because
Wells tells me that he saw that morning fifty grey
yards of chavender below Day's weir. I have never
seen so many as that but I once saw a vast concourse
of chub, and some big fish among them, lying off
Lord Shrewsbury's island in Cleeve reach. But these
fish were keeping a fast, for never one would make me
an offer for anything of mine with a hook to it.

I am reminded by summer chubbing of the danger
to dogs that lies in leaving them tied up in punts or
boats. Anyhow most dogs loathe fishing and they
are dreadful fidgets in any sort of pleasure craft. But
it is a dangerous thing to leave a dog tied up in a
moored boat on too short a chain. If he become bored
he will try to jump out and, falling into the river, will
presently drown, since he can neither climb into the
boat again nor reach the bank.

I have seen this exemplified almost to the point of
death. The owners of the dog had left it in the punt
while they walked in the woods at the season when
pheasants sit on eggs. The dog had tried to follow
and had fallen into the water. We, foot passengers
upon the opposite bank, saw a something that

splashed and struggled feebly. Wells, stripping, swam over and rescued the dog, whose ladies returned as he did so. They found a wet and very naked man indeed in their punt. Delicacy forbade their demanding an immediate explanation, delicacy forbade Wells from offering one before he had regained his garments. But the scene ended in blushes, laughter and much mutual goodwill.

Up and down Thames I do not suppose that one angler in a hundred fishes for chub in winter. Then the chub occurs on the occasional leger of the bank fisherman, the occasional spoon of the spinner for jack, the occasional anything of any angler for other than he. I think that if I went to try to catch a Thames chub in winter that I should fail in the attempt. But if try I must I would paternoster with a large live minnow wherever I could find a suitable spot; I should catch perch and jack and perhaps a chub thus. The places that I should choose would be slacks and deep eddies, the sluices of mills, indeed all bits of winter water that looked deep and quiet and secret. And I do not think that I should want a sack to carry my chub home in. I have never heard of a Thames chub swim being baited up in preparation to a day's fishing, but I have baited a swim for barbel and caught one small chub there instead of the barbel that I had hoped for.

Dapping for chub on the Thames, on the middle and lower reaches anyhow, is never practical except from a-top of a weir bridge or in some exceptional circumstance of cast. Dapping is a morning's fun on little and thickly wooded rivers, and great pull-devil-pull-baker fun it is. I love the chub, a lusty

fellow who takes a float under with a will, and if he
ceased to swim in Thames water he would carry a
lot of good sport away with him, ay, and also no small
tithe of the joy of an angler's summer.

And before I leave him I will quote one of the most
famous, yet one of the least known in its entirety, of
fishing poems. I will quote Mr. W. St. Leger's verses
on the chavender or chub, the first four lines of
which, in some form or another, all men have heard :

> There is a fine stuffed chavender,
>   A chavender, or chub
> That decks the rural pavender,
>   The pavender, or pub,
> Wherein I eat my gravender,
>   My gravender, or grub.
>
> How good the honest gravender !
> How snug the rustic pavender !
> From sheets as sweet as lavender,
>   As lavender, or lub,
> I jump into my tavender,
>   My tavender, or tub.
>
> Alas ! for town and clavender,
>   For business and for club !
> They call me from my pavender
> To-night ; ay, there's the ravender,
>   Ay, there comes in the rub !
> To leave each blooming shravender,
>   Each Spring-bedizened shrub,
> And meet the horsy savender,
>   The very forward sub,
> At dinner at the clavender,
> And then at billiards dravender,
>   At billiards soundly drub
> The self-sufficient cavender,
>   The not ill-meaning cub,

Who me a bear will davender,
   A bear unduly dub,
Because I sometimes snavender,
   Not too severely snub
His setting right the clavender,
   His teaching all the club !

Farewell to peaceful pavender,
   My river-dreaming pub,
To sheets as sweet as lavender,
To homely, wholesome gravender,
And you, inspiring chavender,
   Stuff'd chavender, or chub.[1]

Ave, then, and farewell.

[1] This poem is printed here by the courteous permission of the Proprietors of *Punch*

XI. THE ROACH
(*RUTILUS RUTILUS*)

But if I'm content with a little,
Enough is as good as a feast.
ISAAC BICKERSTAFF.

THE roach is a small fish, a man may go through a long angling life and never see a two-pound roach at all, probably never a one-pound roach. Therefore there can be no romance about a roach in the point of view of *size*, for it is in their fighting weight that the angler finds the poetry of the actual fish that he captures. He of course finds other poetry in the angle than the fighting powers of fishes, even than the fishes themselves—is there not, ' all a green willow,' the sunshine on the broken waters, the first swift, the April cuckoo in Hart's Lock woods, the pretty girl in the dinghy whom the angler could have sworn smiled at him, the golden reed beds of a jewelled January and Thames crisping among them, the ale at the inn ? Of course there are all these things for music and more, much more.

And yet the roach occupies a niche by himself among the fishes and before him the lesser candle unceasingly burns. If the salmon is ' the fish ' the roach is the roach, and where the salmon is, and has been, the enkindling joy of hundreds, the roach has been, and is, the recreation of tens of thousands, which is perhaps the better part after all.

Men claim to have caught, in other waters than Thames, roach of three pounds. Men say that the roaches of Father Thames wear the two-pound look at the very outside. But are you, Sir, who say so, so sure of your ground ? Would you know a three-pound roach, did you see one, from a chub of a similar size ? The anal fin of a chub, you say, is convex ? Well, the anal fin of a roach is not so concave as all that—look at the next two-pounder that happens to you. Look even at the three-pound chub ; if you have any sort of imagination, even if you have a pair of scissors, you can refuse to see convexity here and ' shout ' on a three-pound Thames roach forthwith.

And what ought a roach to look like otherwise ? I cannot answer your question better than by quoting Mr. Yarrell who says : ' The roach is a handsome fish. It has more colours than the rainbow, dusky green on the back with blue reflections that become lighter on its sides, passing into silvery white on the belly, the irides yellow, gill-covers silvery white, tail and dorsal fin tinged with red, pectoral fins, ventral and anal fins bright red.'

A handsome fish indeed but, even at two pounds, only a little one.

And let the roach fisher, whose ideas run large and riotously and who refuses to have any truck with my chub notion, comfort himself in that if he never achieves his ambition, which is a two-and-a-half-pound roach, that possibly, quite possibly, such a fish, such a true roach, does not exist. For many wise men hold (not of course the wise men who have glass cases marked in gold letters ' Roach 2 lb. 10 oz.' and, underneath, a caption which says, in gold letters too, ' Taken at Goring-on-Thames, 10th February 1921 ') that any roach that exceeds 1 lb. 10 oz., which was the weight of the roach that they themselves took at Hambledon in 1912, is a hybrid, a bastard with the gross, plebeian blood of this or that in him to dropsically enlarge the royal blue blood of roaches.

The roach, small and insignificant, can yet exercise over some angling natures a charm and a balm that even the trout fails of. When I first fell in love with the Thames it was at Shiplake, and it was not long before I was noticing that a stout man, dressed entirely in black and topped by a black billycock hat, sat upon a camp stool every Sunday above Marsh Lock and fished, reaching with a roach pole out and over the rushes, for roach. I learned that he was a Londoner, an attendant during the week in a lavatory on the underground railway. And that he locked up on Saturday night and caught the theatre train to Henley. That, arrived there, he walked up to Marsh and sat down and waited till the bye-laws bade him begin to fish. And that there he sat fishing till it was night and time to catch the nine something up to London again.

I did not learn all this from the angler himself, nor do I know if he caught many roaches, for he had a gloomy and taciturn soul (a depression of spirits I daresay, engendered by his dismal calling), and he disliked to be talked to. And I cannot find it in my heart to blame him. For I myself hate the chatty person who asks a total stranger, ' Had any sport, Sir ? ' Years and years ago I walked beside the Wey on a warm summer Sunday. My companion was a wag ; and he was not my companion by choice but by force of circumstance. There were many roach-anglers out, some on the bank and some in boats. To all of them my acquaintance addressed the above maddening enquiry. And some gave him civil answer, some no answer at all.

Now before I here point a moral, I am reminded to tell you a tale of the late Mr. Toole. It was Sunday afternoon, he and Mr. Beerbohm Tree (as he then was) were in Brighton and bored, badly bored. They left the crowded front and wandered into the empty, sleepy town. They came to a mile long street of houses. Above it the hot sky was blue and cloudless and, save for a dog asleep in the middle of the dusty white road, not a living thing was in sight.

Mr. Toole rang the front door bell of No. 1 and, following thereon, he rang the front door bell of every house in that long, dreary street. Afar the bell must jangle in every one. And replete domestics or drowsy householders, eventually, must come to doors. And of each the great actor enquired in agonized tones, ' *Could* you oblige me with a bit of groundsel for a sick bird ? '

And now to come back to the Wey and to the roach-anglers of Wey. I have said that some of these gave civil answer to the jester's enquiry and that others did not reply. Presently we came upon a punt moored to the bank beneath a willow bough. In the punt were a young man and a pretty girl who were not fishing for roach. Nevertheless this playboy of mine could not let them be. Peeping round the tree trunk he asked,

'Had any sport, Sir?'

'Not yet,' said the young man, and a hefty young man he was; 'but I am going to have some now.'

Whereupon he stepped swiftly ashore and, gathering the wag up, he dropped him into the water.

And here we are coffee-housing when we ought to be roaching. Let us, for a start, presume two things, firstly that you know nothing of the roach at all, and secondly that you are not content in your ignorance, that you, really and truly, *want* to know something about the fish that you are going to catch.

To begin at the beginning of things, the roach is of the carp family and, spawning in May, he lays, so says Mr. Marston, whose opinion certainly ought to be respected, a hundred thousand eggs which hatch out quickly given warm weather. These little fish are born to a hard life in which everyone's hand, or mouth, is against them. However, they are not eaten by their own parents, for the roach is never a trout, is never a cannibal. After spawning roach are the most dwamly of all fish and so weak and foolish that they may, almost, be taken by hand. It is for this perhaps that the roach has been called the river-sheep. He cannot be called silly-sheeplike at any other time, though in herds he goes and in companies he feeds, indeed an October roach is, next to the barbel, the cunningest commoner in the Thames. And if I were my Conservancy lords I'd have no line wetted for a Thames roach till the first of August; let the roach come in with the mallard, say I, when he is as fit to eat as he ever is and to catch as he can be.

Early in the season the roach seem to be more on the shallows than in the deeper river ; as the year advances the herds appear to haunt the deeps rather than the shoal water. But as a rule perennial, the roach may be found everywhere and always. And men woo him in more modes and styles than ever they employ with a maid. In salmon catching there is the cast and the Spey cast. These only. Take any fishing book you will and you will find that the roach has, at least, six distinct manners and methods. One might almost say that to every roach river is its roach's own fate.

But it is with the Thames roach that we are principally concerned. When I want to catch a roach I get into the boat and row along till I find a nice streamy bit of water with, if possible, a gravel bottom. If you do not know where gravel is your patent range-finding plummet will tell you. You will feel the clean knock of it when it takes the floor. If it is the mud that it finds, the sensation you will get is that of a cow who walks through a poached gateway. If your fingers are insensitive fingers and can feel nothing for you but the cold, look at the cork insertion on the returning plummet. In spite of the six foot of water in between, the cork retains symptoms of either a striking of grey gravel or of a wallowing in the mire. Roach, like most other fish, prefer gravel to mire, though at the same time they are fairly tolerant of the last.

Well, having found my gravel and my depth I arrange matters so that the baited hook shall swim at, say, six inches above Thames floor and, for once, I use a quill float instead of the little red pilot. At least I say that I do, but in practice I have found small difference in their respective merits. I now throw in some ground-bait, bread, bran and gentles, anything does so long as it, rolled up upon a kernel of stone into cricket-ball size, sinks seductively. I use my fly-rod or my ten-foot split-cane and, with either, a Nottingham reel and a fine undressed (except for an application of vaseline) silk line. My trace is a yard and a half of fine gut weighted, according to water, with four small envelope leads placed a foot or so above the small hook. A gentle is the easiest bait. Pass the hook, with a single in-and-out, through the outer skin and leave the barb to protrude and the maggot with a lot of tail to wag.

Now drop the tackle outboard and let it, the quill cocking, sail down the swim which is usually fifteen to twenty yards in length. When it has made the journey, which it should do on a taut line and with a quill which gives precedence to the gentle, winch it back to you sharply and make it repeat the movement. And remember that, on the Thames, we do not say ' wind up,' like they do on Deeside, but ' winch in.'

The roach is a delicate biter and therefore the travelling quill must be watched with a hawk's eye. If it moves but a hair's-breadth, a tremble, you must strike and you will probably have hooked a fish. Throw in occasional ground-bait, avoid splashing of oars or paddles, and you will catch, I venture to say, all the roach that you require. But you will not be a roach-fisher.

And I have seen, in September, big catches of roach made on weed, on silk weed, fished upon a tiny triangle. Fished off the weir (where you have located the companies of the roach) in exactly the same way as that to which the barbel succumb. But, even with a big bag of roach so taken, you will still not be a roach-fisher.

Who then *is* a roach-fisher ? Why, Walter Coster used to tell me that the London roach-fishers who, in pre-war days, sat of a fine Sunday from Quarry Hole to Stone House were, many of them, swell mobsmen taking their leisure in the most delightfully lazy way in the world. And if you come to think of it you will agree that nothing is so sedative as a roach-angler's Sabbath and that no man's nerves are more important to him than the nerves of the cracker of swell cribs.

But of course there are many men who fish for roach who have never robbed a duchess of her diamonds in all their unenterprising lives. These are the dull fellows like myself. But there is another class of roach-fishers who may be called the professors of the art, the supermen, the men to whom there are but two sorts of fish, the roach and the rest.

These men are not common on the Thames, they are generally the sons of lesser rivers, Ouse, Arun, Colne and Lea, and a score more provincial waters, where *Rutilus Rutilus* is Caesar. But your Thames enthusiast exists and he is invariably the artist of the roach pole. And a very good artist he is, even though that loved cliché of our kind, ' the merry music of the reel,' means nothing to him. For of course the roach pole has no reel attachment—but

I have described this really beautiful form of fishing-rod already.

Our expert of the roach, however, knows not only how to use a roach pole. He is the very Mrs. Beeton of ground-baits and holds that ground-baiting is the essence of the game. He is a past master in these essential preparations, 'cloud' or 'solid', he has nothing to learn either in recipe or application. On a rough estimate I think that there are fourteen kinds of 'solid' and the 'clouds'—how innumerable they are ! But what, you ask, is a cloud ground-bait ?

It is a bait prepared by grinding a solid, such as a stale loaf of bread, which has been previously oven-baked to a brick, into powder. Into this powder mix some sifted sugar (half a teacupful to the loaf) and, if you like, a spoonful of salad oil, cream, or condensed milk. Mix thoroughly till all is smooth and small as fine sand. This, at the river side, may be watered to taste and rolled up into globes of the size of a walnut. These globes, when thrown into the stream, will dissipate and precipitate exactly like the 'snow-storm' toys one used to see once and never see now. The roach are ravished by the pretty effect of all this in the clear water and they hasten from near and far to the expert's swim.

And then the expert proceeds—I feel here a little unworthy for I have never in my life tried to fish with one of the professor's twenty-footers, and anything that I know of them is the result not of practice but of peeping. But I will do my best to be practical, and before I begin I will try to give you a picture of the expert himself as he steps out of the train and on to the Goring platform this October Sunday morning.

He is a lean, elderly fellow and he is dressed in dark clothes. His face is lined and a little weatherbeaten but not with the tan of the countryman. He has not shaved since yesterday and his cheeks show the dark grizzle of a strongly growing beard. His moustache is a drooping straggle of grey and brown, his eyes are mild and grey and melancholy. He will put his steel-rimmed spectacles on before he begins to fish. He has neglected the razor because he has been up since 5 a.m. putting the last touches to his Captain Biscuit ' cloud.'

And here I will stop to say that this early habit of the roach-fisherman was once an asset of high legal importance to Mr. Marshall Hall in one of his forensic triumphs. Anyone interested in criminology will remember a trial for murder of twenty years ago— more than twenty years ago, maybe. It created, at the time, a nine days' wonder, and a two se'nnights' sensation. The prisoner's acquittal depended on his being able to prove to the satisfaction of my lord and the gentlemen of the jury that he was within doors at four-thirty of a September morning when, in the grey light of dawn, a beat constable had seen a man leave a house in a mean street where, even then, in an upper room, lay the naked body of a young woman murdered by means of a razor ' or some sharp instrument.' It was not disputed that the young artist in the dock had been in the dead girl's company till after midnight, it was not disputed that he had the habit of associating with the flotsam of pavements and public-houses. He went into the box and swore that he had left the deceased alive and well at 1.30 a.m. and that he was at home by 2.30. But he was a bachelor in lodgings. Who was to prove his return at 2.30 a.m. of a Sunday morning and all the world asleep ?

In the room above the prisoner's room lodged an elderly man who came forward and swore that he was out o' bed and dressed at 2.30 and that he had heard the prisoner come in, seat himself on a creaking bedstead, remove his boots and drop them, first one and then the other, on to the floor.

'Why,' asked his lordship from the bench, 'were you up and dressed at two o'clock of a Sunday morning ? '

' I am a roach-fisher, my lord,' explained the witness with simple dignity. What could be more satisfactory ? But even then I fancy it must have been, as the Duke of Wellington is reported to have said of the Battle of Waterloo, ' a damned near thing.'

The judge was a deeply religious man and, perhaps, a little out of sympathy with Youth and its follies, perhaps even out of sympathy with roach-fishing on Sunday. He commenced his summing up and it seemed that his weight was to be thrown against the prisoner. The latter listened entirely unmoved. But not so his counsel. For it was obvious that Mr. Marshall Hall's nerves were in tatters and he himself on tenterhooks. He sat forward, his eyes on the judge, his lips twitching. Gravely my lord continued his terrible indictment of immorality and to what immorality inevitably led. Solemnly he paused. But when he spoke again it was in lighter tone. ' But after all we are not here to try immorality,' he said.

Mr. Marshall Hall relaxed in his seat with a sort of sob. He pushed his wig back in the most positive relief and he mopped his forehead with his hand. The prisoner remained unmoved and, half an hour later, he was, thanks to Mr. Marshall Hall and to roach-fishing, a free man.

And so we will go back to our roach-angler. He wears black leather gaiters and thick Government boots. He is a policeman in his public life ? You are not far out, only no policemen fish for roach. Policemen, as Mr. Gilbert has sung, 'love to hear the little brook a-gurgling, brook a-gurgling' and the roach does not live in such a little brook as this of Mr. Gilbert's. No, our angler is a Battersea postman and, take it full and bye, all the best roach-fishermen are postmen. There is, I imagine, something in a quick *rat-tat* that teaches a quick strike when the quill curtseys. And to drop loving letters into letter-boxes is akin to dropping ground-bait into swims :

> And so shall I awaken
> In days of daffodil
> To peace and eggs and bacon
> And sunshine on the sill,
> And there the early postman he
> A whistling Mercury shall be,
> And bring from those I love to me
> Word that they love me still.

That's the sort of postman I mean, and he is a roach-fisher I'm sure. And I'm sure that our friend here is just such another and that he has never delivered a legal blister or the insolence of an editor in all his life.

He wears a black, blanket-lined ' oily ' and a scarf of red tartan. His pole and folding net are packed compactly in a waterproof cover. These he carries over his shoulders at, what a rifleman calls, ' the slope.'

But his gait is not soldierly, for, slung upon his packed pole, he bears over his shoulder the box without which there would be no roaching. The box is of wood and it is painted black. It has a strap of leather athwart it, side to side, for handle and support. It stands two foot and some inches high and its beam is one foot. It contains tackle of all kinds, but its real use and excuse is to be the throne of the bank angler. It is as much a symbol of roach-fishing as is the pole itself. It contains, besides tackle, the bank angler's keep-net which is a collapsible cage of fine mesh in which, sunk in the river, roach can be kept alive. I cannot see much point in keep-nets. Undersized fish should be returned forthwith, and sizeable, unless of course it is intended only to take a percentage of the catch home (which, by the way, is rarely the intention of the bank roacher), are better tapped on the head at once and put into the canvas bag. Once more I say that I cannot understand the mentality of the angler who does not, forthwith, kill a fish if he does not mean to return it. The roach is tenacious of life and most captured roach are allowed to linger for hours by their captors who are naturally, no doubt, men of the kindliest sort.

And presently our angler is by the swim that he intends to fish. He walks quietly, he puts his pole together with discretion. No threading of the reel line through the rod's rings for him. And for that I pity the pole angler, for to hear the short, *staccato* sounds of the reel, ' like the call of a corncrake,' Mr. Bromley-Davenport says that they are, prior to a day's fishing is a jolly and a hopeful thing.

Now he makes his depth-soundings without splash

or hurry. He attaches to the ring at the end of his cane top-joint a short length of fine line. Then the gut, the quill, a shot or so, and then the small hook. This whole attachment equals the length of the pole. The angler throws in ground-bait. He puts his long-handled net where he hopes that it may be handy presently. The actual net, like the net of other roachers, is made just big enough to take a two-pound roach. The true roachman declines to admit that fish other than roach are in the river and that even if there *are* others he does not want to have any ado with them.

And so, conservatively, he sits down on his box and, baiting his angle, makes his cast upstream. The line is weighted so as to allow the quill float to ride deeply in the water. The hook must trip daintily along on the floor of Thames.

The pole is laid upon the open palm of the left hand as lovingly as though it were a Christmas box. With the angler's right hand it is guided and controlled. The rod point follows the bait until the quill dips ever so slightly. The angler strikes. The roach is hooked. The roach-angler is not as other anglers are. He shows no emotion, he makes no sign. He remains *in situ*. He unships the pole from its butt. Left-handed he reaches out his net; right-handed he draws the roach over it. There is no splashing, there is no hurry.

And so the October day wears to evensong and to the train to town. Methodically the fisherman packs up and trudges stationwards. Over Streatley Hill the west is clear and golden, low to the hilltop leans the silver sickle of the young moon.

XII. THE EEL
(*ANGUILLA VULGARIS*)

'WHAT have you caught?' asked the elder person of the little boy who had been worming for trout.

'A good deal,' answered the child.

'Let's have a look at them, son ... oh, don't try to be funny, you silly little fool.'

For of course what was the basket but an eel and not a particularly good eel either since it measured only about a foot and a half when it might have been five feet? For I see that the record eel, recorded in Mr. Green-Drake's valuable *By Mere and River* and elsewhere, has a length of ' over five feet.'

And I wish that I had known as much a year or so ago, for I must myself have caught an eel that would have about tied with the record. It was in Scotland and I was spinning for salmon with a pickled gudgeon. The bait had just gone to bits. I threw it into the deep river and put on a fresh one. Just as I had done so I saw a great eel. I had never seen such an eel outside of Reading Museum where there is a Kennet eel of—well, it looks like an Anaconda in its glass case. But this eel was alive and in the river where, undeterred by the flavour of formalin, it was eating the remnants of my late gudgeon.

I offered it, with a shudder, my new bait. I do not mean that I offered it spinning. I dropped it in and let it lie on a big, brown boulder. The eel came sinuously to it. It looked an evil fish and I began to believe all the sinister things that had been told to me about eels. It nosed the bait, it opened a yellow and reptilian mouth and took hold of the gudgeon. I struck and hooked it, lightly, but enough to haul it on to the bank where, happily for my tackle, the hold pulled out.

The ghillie came with a whitish face. He looked at the eel as though it was the Accuser of the Brethren. Then he beat it to death with the handle of the clip. It was never weighed. For one thing because Gourlay would not touch it and for another because we had no spring-balance with us. But I held it up by the tip of its tail. And the length of it fell from my shoulder to the sole of my brogues.

Gourlay kicked the corpse into a whin bush and I forgot it until just now when I read, in the printed word, that the record eel was five feet long and thereupon they fetched me the yard measure. And from my shoulder to the ground is just under five feet. And I daresay that the eel, eels usually have, had a kink in her somewhere—' her ' she must have been, the limmer, for the male eel is a manikin. And so I should not wonder if I was the rightful holder of the record for eels in the British Isles. A proud title.

The eel is the most mysterious of all fishes of Thames and not of Thames. The mysteries of the eel are more than the mysteries of the salmon. The eel is a miracle ; God has made it the most wonderful of all creatures of the waters. *What* instinct sends the eel up Thames to the mill-cutting at Mapledurham where we caught those two tench the other day ? The mill-cutting where the river débris collects and disintegrates and, in flood time, tumbles over the lasher and away to Caversham on the big waters ? And *why* comes the eel ?

We know why the salmon comes back to Balathie on Tay and passes up the Troughs at Makerstoun on Tweed. We recognize the call of the head-waters and the springs and the spawning redds below Braeriach who bears the infant Dee. We guess at the urge, the impulse, that moves the winged legion of birds southward to follow the sun and, perhaps, to draw therefrom some element necessary to life and hedgesparrows' eggs in an April hazel copse at home. But the eel ?

But the eel one morning, an October morning when the days go by like a flight of macaws and the woods above the weir pool are heathen palaces and *teocallis* of gold, comes to the shallow water on the lasher's lip where the bulrush grows and whither that big trout followed your spinning-bait last May. And there the eel sees the heathen goldenness of things and perhaps remembers. Anyhow he says ' hey, for the Gulf of Mexico ' and he wriggles through the reed bed, pitches over the lasher and into the pool, crosses the shallows under the mill eyot, picks up the stream, turns the corner into the main river and has gone.

And, like the young Lochinvar, he ' stays not for stock and he stops not for stone.' I mean that just because he has turned the above corner on the current it does not say that such dilly-dally travelling is his usual style.

Now did ever you hear that a running salmon, in a deuce of a hurry to get over the loup and away up to Glen Clova, came out of the water below Maulsden and short-cutted it, over the dry gravel and meadow grass, into the river again at Tail of the Leat ? Or that a kelt, March mended, and called by the song of the white rollers on the lean black rocks at Ferryden and the healing, blue water beyond Rossie Island, reversed the route of the running fish as it stepped east again ? No ! And no more did I and I know the South Esk river as well and better than I know Father Thames.

But an eel in a hurry lands and takes short-cuts to the Gulf of Mexico and makes nothing of so doing. Mr. Eric Parker tells me of how a correspondent of his met two hundred eels marching down a dry, gritty road at ten-thirty of a summer night. The watcher rubbed his eyes, a white owl hooted, the moon winked at the waking Stour, and the procession moved on for Mexico via the Sargasso Sea.

I have never seen two hundred eels on the turnpike but, by the mercy of Pan, I have met one who walked across a Thames meadow. It was above Hambledon where a friend and I fished for trout in June. There the Thames swings right-handed in a wide bend. Obviously the nearest way to Atlantis, and beyond Atlantis, is to land below Regatta Island on the Bucks bank, cross the meadow and rejoin the river below Hambledon lock.

We continued to fish, spinning from the punt that dropped slowly downstream. There was reported to be an enormous trout haunting off the green lawns of his lordship's garden. But we did not catch it, possibly because a lady sketching in the meadow screamed aloud. There was an adder about to attack her, an adder of venomous appearance and horrid *swingyness* of tail. And what was it after all but an eel making an early start of it, early because, as I've said, all this was on a June day and three months before the excursions begin ? My friend reassured the artist and gave the eel a lift (or a *hurl* as we say in Angus) in his landing-net as far as the lock and away it went again downstream.

And when the eel goes to sea it travels fast. But first it changes its dress from yellow-belly to ' silver.' I do not mean that it becomes a creature of pure and unsullied argent, for all it does is to change the tint of its mustard-coloured underneath for a shade of white which is by courtesy called silver. And even then it is not a bonny fish or a beautiful and so the eel can, for all its mystery and romance, never be quite the same to the angler as the salmon is. For anglers, and most other men and women, judge by

appearances, and personal beauty goes a long way
with us all.   And

> The salmon's the fish
>> Among all fish and always
> May he flourish let's wish
>> In his great and his small ways,
> The salmon is mighty
>> And silvery shiny,
> And, like Aphrodite,
>> He comes from the briny ;
>
> His looks are supreme
>> Among fish that are catchable ;
> The lady we deem
>> To be likewise unmatchable ;
> And, charmed by their features,
>> We cry with emotion
> ' Two beautiful creatures
>> And each out of Ocean.'

And I cannot think that the author of that excellent little work *The Pop-Gunroom Poetry Book* could
write like that of the eel—not he, nor anyone else.
And of course the salmon is a bonny fighter.   And
the eel is not ?

Well, there again, really, I cannot say.   For his
weight the eel pulls hardly and stubbornly and I
daresay that on light tackle he could put up a worthy
resistance.   But the eel only begins to fight where
the salmon takes the count.   The salmon, when once
Sandy Faa has the clip into his silver ribs, is over and
done with.   But the eel *before* you have caught him is
never truly troublesome.

Let us suppose that fresh-water eels grow great as
congers.   And I think that congers of a hundred

pounds, and more, are possible fishes. Let us be modest and suppose that we hooked a mere fifty-pound eel where we hooked the salmon just now. And that Sandy, knee-deep in the water, had the clip into it at last. Why, of course (you'll say) it's only *then* that the fun would begin. And can't you imagine it ? Can't you imagine it, you who've had a fleabite of a two-pounder eel tied up in your trout gut like true-lovers' knots at the court of King Solomon ?

And so I think that in all fairness we must admit that the eel is a fighter and worthy of our respect as such. And before we think of him on his journeyings I'll tell you the quickest way to kill him if you've caught him before he starts. Pick him up in a cloth, a dock leaf or a bit of newspaper, and dash him to the ground, to the shingle or the towpath preferably, and he's dead and done with forthwith. And, once dead, you must eat him, for all your prejudices, and is he not the most delicious and delicate of the coarse fishes ? But you must skin him before you cook him. And this is the easy way.

Nail him up on the kennel door, a nail through the head of him. He'll hang like a dead stoat in a gamekeeper's larder. Now take a sharp knife and make a circular incision just below the pectoral fin. And so take you hold of the severed edges of his pelt, holding them in a dry cloth, and you'll peel his skin off him as easy as you'll pull off your own wet stocking. And now you can behead, clean and cook the eel according to one or other of the recipes. And the kitten can have his head to play with. But if he escapes this end ?

Why then, as I have said, he goes to sea and when he gets there he travels fast. And he would need to, this little brown-and-white traveller. For he has three thousand miles to go and five months to go them in. It is to the Dane, Mr. E. J. Schmidt, that we owe such knowledge of the eel as is ours. We know that the temperature of a tiger, tropic sea and the pressure of a thousand fathoms of salt water are the essentials of the mating and reproduction of eels. We know that the eel leaves our rivers in autumn and that, in the spring of the ensuing year, the eel's fancy, like man's own, lightly turns to thoughts of love. The spawning proceeds into the June month and by the ensuing June the resulting alevins are two inches long. These little creatures live for a year, for two years, in the upper storeys of Ocean and then they are three inches long, elvers and full grown, and must be coming slowly home to Thames, to Tweed, to Severn and to the rest of the rivers. And, about their fifth birthday, the elvers run the rivers which are to be their homes.

And their parents ? Some men say that when the eel has spawned that then he, and she, die. Others hold that, like the bee, the male eel alone dies while the female survives him. This theory is advanced in the Swedish school-book, *Naturkunnighet*. On the other hand I can find no evidence of the mature eel coming up from the sea again. Nor do we know *why* the eel must mate in the great waters and at the great depths or why the elver must come back to the river to become an eel and, having come back, how long it takes him to become one. The Romans said that the eel lived to sixty years and that he grew slowly.

So when next you catch an eel by accident and he ties true-lovers' knots in your 3x gut do not just call him a bloody eel and wish that he had never left the Atlantic. Think of him rather as one of the most interesting and romantic creatures that God has made, remove the hook from him gently and, if you really do not want him, put him into the river again or else send him to me who love stewed eel and parsley sauce better any night than boiled salmon and cucumber.

There is, to-day, no elver run in the Thames. Which means that the elvers do not come up and under Shillingford bridge, 'shoulderin' ache other out av the water an' ye'd but the luck to see thim,' but that they come in the modest quantities that befit the truthful anglers who fish for eels in the Thames. And most bank anglers have a leger out, fishing itself, while they ply the roach pole. And all is fish that comes to the bank-angler's leger no doubt, but he keeps hoping ever that the fish to come will be an eel. And I myself, when I fish a weir pool for trout, as often as not ask my attendant, if I have one, to throw a coarse leger-tackle out up-river and see if he can catch me an eel the while I catch myself a trout.

I do not think that anybody rod fishes for eels in the Thames except in this catch-crop style. The river does not lend itself to the eel-catching that one used to practice in Angus long ago. No hook was required, nor gut, nor much reel line. One procured the inside of a rabbit. One wound Aunt Caroline's worsted about and about it until it looked like a skein of knitting wool from which obtruded gruesome things. This morsel was tied to a bit of brown sea-line and lowered, attached to a stiff rod or even a staff, into mill leats and dams. The eels flung themselves upon it ravening, the rod was lifted swiftly and smoothly and, or ever they could clear their teeth from the worsted, they were on the bank. This form of eel fishing has a name but I cannot remember it. It has the further advantage that the chances of eel entanglement are reduced to nil. But I fear that we have not enough eels in the Thames to make this mode practical. It requires a small river and the same paved with eels.

So, in the Thames, we rod-catch eels on legers or achieve them when we are fishing for perch with a small red worm. But the best way for the amateur to take eels in the river is by the method of the basket. These eel baskets are made of close-woven withy, they are torpedo-shaped and about a yard and a half long and, in their thickest circumference, about a yard. They stand, say, sixteen inches high. They have a tunnel-shaped way in at one end whereby entrance, if you are an eel, is easy and exit impossible. The sort of entry that makes a lobster pot what it is. There is a trap door at the end of the basket whereby bait may be put in and eels taken out. There are three suitable weights tied by wire, two on to the basket's shoulders and one at the base. The weights must rest on the ground and be sufficiently heavy to keep the basket steady, flat and level, on the river's floor. There is, or ought to be, a handle running end to end—in the reverse direction, that is, to the handle of a garden-basket. These traps I used to buy for a few shillings from Walter Coster at Marlow and I fancy that they can be got from such Thames-side professional fishermen as remain or from local tackle shops. Some folk call them grig-wheels or gig-wheels.

But having bought a trap the next thing is to bait and set it. In spite of what I said about offal and worsted, the eel prefers live-bait, or freshly killed bait, to any other. Coster used to bait his traps with gudgeon, alive or dead. But I think lobworms are attractive too. Coster used to set these traps either in Marlow Pool or in the weedy and rather lively water that runs down to Quarry Woods. He would set them in, perhaps, five or six feet of water. The traps were arranged so as the weed covered them and their entrances faced upstream. And, occasionally, they would be marked with a float or a big bit of cork. The traps should be set at evening and lifted early in the morning. For one reason because the eel is supposed to be nocturnal and a roamer by the light of the moon, and for another, and a more important, the eel is a summer fish and the Thames is a public river and a playground stream. And you don't want an iron-shod punt-pole driven, smash, through your property by the brown and dripping right arm of that active lad, young Aubrey Fitz-Lennox, who comes up from Bourne End, with a pretty girl in the bows, at eight miles an hour ? Moreover it is possible that some inquisitive or dishonest person may, by noonlight, notice your daymarks and haul up your trap and away with it and its contents. So set the traps late and lift them early ; at Marlow the professional hour was 3 a.m., but that is perhaps a counsel of perfection. And, when you have them up and out, clean and sun-dry them. An eel, it used to be said, will scunner at a trap tainted by other captives and foul with dead bait. And, when cleaned and dried, the traps may be set again in any quiet bit of Thames, under banks, in mill-tails and river coigns where the green weed wavers, in any water, deep or shallow, where the eel haunts. And though you will seldom catch aught but an eel in your eel-basket I have, to my regret, found a trout wedged into the entry of my trap and dead as a door nail.

But Mr. Englefield, who wrote so lovingly of the river he loved and lived by all his long life, tells of a most astounding mixed bag made by one of his baskets. A summer flood had been running and ' Red Quill ' had laid down his grig-wheel in a shallow, close under the bank. These are what he found when he lifted it at daybreak. A vole (drowned), five eels, three crayfish, a coot (dead), countless minnows, a bull-head, and three pike, the largest being one pound and a half ! This trap had been baited with lobworms.

The traps are lifted with a long-handled boat-hook, so do not you forget to put one into the punt before you drop downstream in the green morning and the sun just drinking the mists up.

I think that eels on the feed take quite large fish. Last summer I found a big eel dying against the reed-bed above Mapledurham. It was an eel of, I should judge, two-and-a-half pounds. It had in its gullet a roach of at least a quarter of a pound that had, in its own dying, choked its adversary and done him (or her, more probably) to an equal death.

Fifty years ago eels were caught at certain Thames weirs, mills and similar places, by those picturesque ' fixed engines ' known as eel-bucks. Few of Mr. John Leech's river sketches are complete without eel-bucks. As far as I remember the only eel-bucks left to-day are at Hedsor, upon Lord Boston's private weir.

These ' bucks ' were on the principal of the basket trap. They were great torpedo-shaped engines of withy, and my recollection of them is that they were eight or ten feet long with a circumference in proportion. They stood across a likely water, tackle supported, six, perhaps, a-row. They were not traps quite in the manner of the basket trap because the eel-buck is not baited. Its mission is to stand, in company, across some passage or river narrow into which its tackle may lower it when required. A line of bucks reminds one of the old-fashioned ' holed ' mouse-trap that killed the captive at once. Only of course 'bucks' are catch 'em alive-o's. And the eels, pressing on, come to the row of round entries in the current and, ' Here,' say the eels, ' is slack water for a yard or so.' And in they wriggle and there they are— eel-pie and done for. For there is no Gulf of Mexico for the silver eel who goes in by the eel-buck door.

I think these eel-bucks represented certain old-time Thames fishing rights, rights of Lords Abbots and others with whom they have expired. Anyhow I, who know my middle Thames, know never a ' buck ' upon him to-day save the ' bucks ' of my Lord Boston.

And here I'll wish the eel that the Water Babies may see him safe past eel-buck and basket and the leger's lob. And that he may make the pleasant journey and that, in the mysteries of the deep sea, he will not forget the mill-cutting at Mapledurham and all the green shadows and the peaceful places of Father Thames.

XIII. THE PERCH
(*PERCA FLUVIATILIS*)

The Perch, though striped like any tiger,
Wears spikes upon his back the while,
So no young lady of the Niger
(You'll recollect she rode a tiger ?)
May sit on him and wear a smile :
Yet should she do so, and should you,
Addressing her, ask, ' How do you do ? '
And still for information search,
I fancy that the damosel
Would of her saddle truly tell,
' A most uncomfortable perch.'

THE POP-GUNROOM POETRY BOOK.

HEN I write the word ' perch ' I go back to the beginning. And so I expect do other men. For whether we caught him in England or in Scotland, in Thames or in some char-haunted lochan of the hills and the Ice Age, the perch has been the initial fish to ever so many of us.

It seems to me now, that triumph, that first fish of all, is the triumph of someone else in another life than mine. I see a mile of grey water, blue-ruffled by the August wind that comes up easterly out of the far shining North Sea. But it's a dour land this that lies

at the gate of the Highlands. The loch lies among
stone dykes and fields of anæmic oats. There is a
low, green hill, pale grass and black rock, that cocks
up in the middle of the landscape. On the skyline
lift the fingers of factory chimneys. The shores of the
loch are fringed with reed-beds and there the coots
sit, rocking, rocking on the leaden ripples. Well out
on the water rocks a big green coble. In the same
are elder persons ; and their rods, that are outboard,
make the coble look like to a water-spider whose legs
they are. There are two frocked children in the boat,
a pug dog, and a big maroon-coloured hot-water can—
spout, handle and all. This can is full of live minnows. And the party are perch fishing, for with perch
this great water is alive. A hot-water can seems a
strange place to put minnows. But is there not the
story of the proud parent who came to the verger to
arrange for the christening of his first-born on Sunday
next ?

' Thee can't have 'un christened Sunday,' said the
verger.

' An' why can't us ? '

' Cos paarson's goin' fishin' come Monday an' he's
got his minners in t'font.'

A man with reddish whiskers takes a minnow out
of the can, he baits a hook, he hands a rod to one of
the children, he hands it to myself, I suppose. There
is a makeshift float, the cork of a soda-water bottle.
The boy clutches the rod till his knuckles show white,
pop-eyed he gazes at the float. There is a tug at the
brown line, the cork bobs and goes resolutely under.
' Yon's him,' says the man with the whiskers. The
rod is jerked in air. Upon the hook kicks a striped,

green fish of eight ounces with a silver belly and red fins. It is a perch and I am an angler blooded and made perfect. And that was the long time ago.

It must have been thirty years later that I saw my first Thames perch, and I saw him in bulk. I had walked from Shiplake to Caversham on a cold March day. I went up the hill and under the quarry on the right where the nightingales sing in May. I went down the hill to Sonning and over the field footpath and the two plank bridges and there I heard Caversham weir before I saw it. But presently I crossed the stile and came to the tail of the long pool.

I think that the beds of weir pools alter in much the same way as the beds of salmon pools respond to spate water and the shifting of the shingles. For I have been to Caversham since then and sought there for what I saw, on the March day that I tell of, and found it not.

I found that day a deep ' pot,' or what we should call a ' pot ' did we talk of a hill river. It lay under a willow bush ; I remember the catkins on the thrust of the sap and that a kingfisher sat among them, intensely blue in the keen, blue morning. He went like the striking of a match—blue and orange. I looked between the boughs where he had been, I looked down and I saw a sight.

The little pool was ten yards in circumference and four across. It was bottomed in gravel and brown silt. It had a deepness of six or eight feet of clear, wine-brown water. An under-tow kept this clarity in perpetual movement, the brown water, circling gently, crept out and stole away and a smooth new swirl took its place.

In this natural aquarium swam specimens of nearly all the Thames fishes. Except the barbel, the trout and the Great Panjandrum himself who is the twenty-pound carp that, some day, I am going to take out of Thames. And I shall probably catch him in the same season that I catch the fifteen-pound trout who haunts under the chestnut candles above Hurley weir pool and the fifty-two pound salmon, the sea lice on the roots of his great tail, that I mean to hook below Dalmally, some September afternoon, and see gaffed at Inverawe two hours later.

Well, in that Caversham water I saw such a diversity of pretty fishes as never I saw before. Dace and roach, bleak and minnow, and many another. But the perch swam there like parrot fishes. And indeed the perch is a pretty fish and I think the Thames perch is the prettiest perch of all. He is a darker fish than other perch, he is olive and green and brown. His golden flanks are more golden than the flanks of the perch of lesser rivers. His stripes are tiger stripes, and tropical. He is rough scaled and splendid. His fins are as scarlet. Frank Buckland says of him, ' No lady's dress was ever made so beautiful as that of the perch's.' And Mr. Englefield, in a more practical approbation, cries, ' He is in edible qualities second only to the trout.'

The perch is gregarious and, more than other gregarious fish, he sorts himself into carefully matched shoals. The bigger the perch, of course, the smaller the shoal. The perch is swift and predatory and were he a bigger fish he would be a most murderous fellow. But in the Thames a one-pound perch is a good one, and a two-pounder taxidermal. The biggest perch

that I have personally taken was from a lake at
Aldermaston which is close to Thames and yet is not
Thames. This perch weighed one ounce under three
pounds and I have him in a glass case and, since I live
on the banks of the river, I do not say, unless asked,
that he is not a Thames perch. He took a small dead
roach with which I was spinning for jack along a
rusty bed of bulrushes, and when I had him in the
net I shouted, being uplift by the occasion, that he
was five pounds.

'Red Spinner' has told how he took a marvellous
brace of Thames perch on a two-hooked paternoster.
It was, I imagine, a day of St Martin's summer. I
think that the river was flowing at July level and
that the golden leaf fell upon it and, golden and jade,
that Thames came idly lipping the punt where sat
the sage. From whom I will now quote direct.

'I tied the boat to the bushes and, throwing out
my baited hooks into the middle of the river, I laid
the rod down but with the instinct of a true angler
raised up its point to make the line taut. Then, soon
lost in the music of Shelley's immortal verse, I forgot
all sublunary things. Suddenly the rod shifted and
its point was drawn under water. My book dropped !
A peculiar struggle and a moving weight told me that
a fish was on. I had only a small net with me '—(you
will remember what I have said about the *size* of
Thames landing-nets, I hope ? If not, let 'Red
Spinner's' words remind you)—' therefore I had to
be extra careful. At length I saw, in trembling excitement, a monster perch hanging on the upper hook
and the gleam of another lower down in the water.
Both were ultimately lifted out safely. They were

exactly alike in shape and condition, splendidly marked with five greenish-brown bars, a sheen of gold. And in the scales, some hours after, they balanced each other to a nicety weighing two-and-a-quarter pounds each.'

But ' it ain't the hen that cackles the most that lays the largest egg.' And it is not the angler who throws out a bait and, leaving it to fish itself, declaims :

> Liquid Peneus was flowing
> And all dark Tempe lay
> In Pelion's shadow outgrowing
> The light of the dying day
> Speeded by my sweet pipings,

who, as a rule, catches the biggest Thames perches. And so we will forthwith set about seeing who *does* catch them and how he does it.

He is probably the man who knows his river well. And the haunts of the perch. Which are generally near the works of men, camp sheathings, the piles about the weir, mill-tails, the buttresses of the bridge. Also the eddy below the eyot, the end of the reed-bed, the lee of the trunk of the submerged elm that's lain off the lawn since 1914, the cave in the bank below the railway and before you come to the ferry at Gate-hampton—all these are likely places for the painted shoals to be cruising and picking and choosing. But in summer the perch are more likely to be in the shallower places than in the deeps where December finds them.

And do not look for perch *anywhere* after the end of January until August is here and, sickle-winged, the departing swifts assemble and the wasp grub may be dug by the man who dares. And why ? Because the perch spawns early in March when he is still, legally, in season and who wants spawners and mil-ters ?

When I want a perch or so I take my ten-foot cane and set about it in the same way as I set about the roach. Float, hook and shot are much the same as then. A red worm, or better a live minnow, is my bait and I fish this tackle swimming it in any likely swim and, anon, paddling the punt quietly down to the next one. Always paddle a fishing punt while you are actually fishing. The Thames fishes do not pay much attention to oars and paddles, but a punt-pole, in among the lily roots and the glimmery places, gets on their nerves.

There is no bait for a Thames perch to beat a live minnow. And it is often fished on a paternoster that wears two hooks. Two hooks are a mistake I'm sure, in spite of the brace of big fish, simultaneously taken, that ' Red Quill ' has told us of. Wait till you have your record perch in play. Here he comes to the net fighting like four pounds of painted rainbow ! How gorgeous he looks in the dark water, how gorgeous he'll—oh hell ! oh hell ! oh *hell* ! The second hook has fouled the pile, the great perch has broken your trace and your heart. So one hook is enough for a perch-pater.

And you will fish it just as though you patered for pike. You will, when you get a bite, lower the point for a second or so before you strike. It is, you'll see, just like jack fishing. Only you will be using light gut and a small hook ; and a minnow instead of a dace.

Personally I prefer the float method to that of the

paternoster, the method of the little red float. But the perch must not be struck with the rapidity required by the roach, with whom speed is everything. The roach has an upper lip that he can elongate like an elephant's trunk. Thus he can savour a bait and eject it with the lightning haste of a llama who spits and expectorates. The perch has not this physical advantage.

The perch begins by making the float bob. Let him. A second later he'll do it again—*tug tug* and under. This done he will move off with you and *now's* the time to hit him.

Perch, as I have said, go in shoals and, like the barbel, they do not seem to care how many of their schoolmates are hooked, played and netted out under their own eyes. But do you lose a perch he'll stampede the whole party.

If your luck is in and if *you have ample bait and then some over*, you may kill big baskets of perch in the Thames. The two best days of which I have personal knowledge were a November Saturday and Sunday. The bag, made with Albert Wells at Wallingford, was ' about ' seventy dozen perch, thirty dozen one day and forty dozen the next. There were two rods out on each day and the bait was live minnow and dead, for the perch took the dead bait as readily as the living.

I am sorry for the ' about ' but many of the perch were returned forthwith, and the counts, though approximately, I hope, correct, are estimates. Of this total about four dozen fish were kept, the rest were returned to the river. The largest weighed one pound eleven ounces.

So I did not see these fish in the brilliant bulk, but they would have been, surely, a remarkable sight. The biggest ' basket ' of Thames fish I ever saw was a creel of roach. I walked one September afternoon across the footbridge above the second prettiest weir on Thames. And that that is Hambledon weir I, after long consideration, am almost sure. The run on the mill side was being fished by a picturesque figure. This angler was a leonine-looking man with aquiline features and a head of hair. A handsome fellow and, as I learnt later, a well-known actor. He excels in sock and buskin as all men know ; though, perhaps, few know his powers in a roach-fishing part. He wore waders and he stood on the flat of the weir, which was summer-small. He had a light rod and was, with the lightest tackle and a single hook, catching roach on silk-weed in the same manner as you and I caught the barbel at Mapledurham. Each time that he dropped his hook in a roach had it. And he kept all that he caught, handing them up to two little boys on the footbridge above him. These two had a sack and it was almost full of roach. I have often heard of anglers ' wanting a sack to carry 'em home in,' the ' 'em ' being the particular fish that the angler is out for. But till then I had never seen either the sack or the catch that required it. Nor have I seen them since. I admired the sack and complimented the fisherman. In that beautifully modulated voice of his he told me that he had filled two sacks already. I have wondered what he did with all those roach when he returned to town—gave them to duchesses most likely. But speculation is futile and we must return to the perch.

I think that, best of all, I like to take perch by spinning. You will not fill a sack with the spinning-rod ; you will not even fill the average bag. But with any luck you'll get a dish of perch, and what, on a winter day, could be more delightful than the getting of it ?

Take the small spinning-rod, and attach to the light line a light gut trace, a light weight (you will not want to make any long casts) and a small spoon— ¾ inch, or one inch, is usually large enough. You may use indeed any small spinning trifle you choose instead of the spoon, but you will not better the latter. Men who despise spinning (because they cannot spin and are too indolent to learn) may catch perch with a wet Alexandra fly, fishing it *sink and draw, sink and draw.* But they will only catch thus an occasional Thames perch and when they do catch him they will be surprised at their success.

Choose a mild winter day and go on foot to your fishing. Take along with you a bag, a landing-net and a contented heart. You know the familiar haunts of the perch ? Thither go, then.

You will find yourself beginning the day at the mill-tail and the mill-cutting. Keep out of sight and draw the spoon discreetly along the masonry, under the beams and betwixt the black piles. You will have seven good perch here and a splashing, five-pound jack or ever you cross by the ferry and try under the wall and off the sill of the weir before strolling on to the big eddy by the stile below the lock. The day will pass joyfully enough I fancy and your bag shall be reasonably heavy to carry upstream at tea-time to

Pangbourne Bridge and the station. But the way shall be musical for, as you go, the South Berks shall be hunting a fox in the big woods above Hardwick across the river. And there is no such music as that of foxhounds who run in a big woodland. It is one of the *sounds*. The voices of wild geese is another. And the wings of wood-pigeons, either in thunderclap of lifting or in the high and rhythmic cadences of flight, is a third. And, once, eleven whooper swans (like the brothers of little Elisa) went seaward in the big West Wind. Upon purple clouds they went over a dark green, white-capped bay. A small boy who heard the wild trumpets of them swell and die said, ' They sound like hounds in cover.' And that was the highest compliment that he could pay and it brings us back to Pangbourne and the perch.

Now sometimes I think I'd rather see a big perch miss a spinning-bait, or turn aside from it a-purpose, than I would catch him. In winter the deep Thames is the colour of jade and, in it, the bright and bristling perch in his rainbow indignation looks as bold as a Samurai of old Japan, a Samurai in *gusoko*—chiselled, inlaid, repoussé—armoured in green and scarlet and gold. And you only see him to perfection when you see him suspect a spoon upon a December day.

And just how big a perch may we expect to catch ? I've said that, in Thames, a two-pound perch is a bonny fish. And that surprises me for the perch has in Thames, where he exists in bulk and quantity, everything he wants to make him great—room to expand, food of all sorts in plethora, convenient spawning grounds (and how beautiful and lace-fine is perch spawn !), all the blessings, you would say, are his in the river. But the Severn perch remains the bigger fish and the perches of Broadland are bigger still.

And another aspect of the perch surprises me. In Continental countries, in Sweden anyhow, there exists a fish called a *gös*. This creature I believe to be a cross between a pike and a perch. It is coloured, striped and armoured like the latter and it has the head and rather the shape of a pike. It grows big, a ten-pound *gös* is not uncommon. And it is an excellent, a truly excellent, table fish. Now if this fish is a genuine hybrid why do not our Thames perch and pike, intermarrying, produce göslings ? And if the *gös* is a distinct species of fish and capable of reproduction (of which a hybrid is incapable) why do we not introduce him into home waters ? But perhaps he would be a most troublesome fellow to old Thames, ogre, cannibal and devil-fish ?

So we will e'en leave him where he is with the *lax* and the *stor lax*, the midnight sun and the aurora borealis, and remain contented with our native and uncontaminated 'Stripes,' than whom 'no lady ever dressed more beautifully' and whose edible qualities are 'second only to those of the trout.'

XIV. THE CARP AND SOME OF HIS
SMALL RELATIONS
(CYPRINIS CARPIO)

*And there were present the Picninnies and the
Joblillies and the Garyulies and the Great Panjandrum
himself.*

SAMUEL FOOTE.

IN a great river like ours there must be
both little fish and big, as was ordained
in Eden. Many of the big ones we have
seen already—barbel, pike and trout, and
very fine fish they are—but they do not
take a fly except by accident. Indeed in the Thames,
the middle and the upper anyhow, the chub is the
fly-fisher's only refuge because the beautiful and tasty
little dace who is, in smaller rivers, so typical a *fly*
fish is not worth the flick of a dry Black Gnat or the
flop of a wet Wickham. But I sometimes catch a
dace when I am fly-fishing for chub ; he is generally a

fish of about a pound weight, and I never can remember how to tell the difference between a fine dace and an inferior chub. The one (but *which* one ?) wears its anal fin concave and the other convex. I have, at the time of writing, had a 'look see' in a fishing book and for the moment I know that the chub is convex and the dace concave. But I shall have forgotten again by the middle of June when I daresay I shall return an important dace of one pound five ounces to the water considering him to be an unimportant chub. It is of advantage sometimes to a celebrity thus to resemble a man of no importance. I myself have a personal likeness to a well-known author. On one occasion we were both present at a semi-public dinner. The celebrity slipped away early but I was late in taking the road. When at length I went out into Piccadilly and the chill fog of a December night, a lady was waiting to upbraid the famous gentleman who had gone before. I had, for half a minute, a difficulty in dissuading her from making a whipping boy of *me*. But the dace shall go unsuspected.

And a pound dace is a good fish. It is not a very unusual one either, though anything over the pound mark is rare. For summers past there has been a shoal of dace on the up-river side of Mapledurham weir. There is a shallow there between a green weed-bed and the lasher's lip, a small shallow. But the dace are big dace, there must be several over a pound present. They are accustomed to see people go to and fro on the footbridge and they are entirely tame. But quite uncatchable.

I never put up a fly-rod and go out for the chub below the pool without having a shy at the dace first.

The procedure is always the same. I kneel on the stone step of the bridge and, unobserved, flick a fly into the clear movement of the water. I flick it so that it falls wide of the shoal. It sits on the surface most naturally. My gut is gossamer. A large dace swims up to it. He looks at it attentively and calls up another pounder. They both look at it. I can imagine that the one says to the other, ' Dear me, the optimist again,' ' Dear me,' replies dace number two. And that is all. But I, on one occasion, stung by the indifference of these dace, threw a spinning-bait beyond them and bringing it fast through the shoal foul-hooked a member of it. I landed and returned him, a little, I hope, humbled.

The middle Thames is too big and deep a river to make dace fishing with fly an individual sport, but as I have shown, the dace occurs occasionally to the chub fisher and is mistaken for a chub. Like most Thames fish he will take anything you offer him if you will but offer it unostentatiously. The prettiest dace-bait is a red currant, the ugliest a maggot. Fine gut, a quill float, a small single hook, a weight smaller still—these will catch you dace if you will ' study to be quiet.' The mission of the dace in the middle Thames is to provide live-bait for the pike angler. Therefore during the summer months he goes un-fished for. Lock cuttings and like quiet places are his homes in October and there men catch him on crust and red worm against Sunday next. He pulls a float under with decision and should be struck as he does so. When the mayfly is up the dace rise gluttonously throughout the first ten days of June. Sunshine and chestnut blossom, swifts and swallows and the hatch coming down, down—these are the dace days and the fortnight of the fly-rod. These are also the days when the Thames dace is protected by bye-law.

It is only on tidal water that the dace is taken seriously and for the sport of him. Below Richmond, walking down river, you will come to Isleworth, 'sleepy,' 'riparian' and 'hamlet' Mr. Binstead calls Isleworth. Somewhere about here are long shoals of gravel over which, at low water, the stream runs briskly. The river then looks unfamiliar. I do not know why except that it is shallow and that it runs fast. It is unfamiliar too to see Thames anglers who wear waders except upon the weirs of the upper river. But here we have anglers who wade and fish two wet flies a-row as though they fished the Whaupie and not the Thames.

These men are fishing for dace and catching them by the dozen and by the five dozen. It is only at low water that this is possible and the anglers keep their stances without much movement and make hay while the sun shines. The dace down here are smaller fish than in the upper river but they provide a sport that, while it lasts, is often fast and furious. I do not think it much matters to the dace what fly you offer them, the sort that catches 'brownies' in Whaupie in the late 'Aprile' will catch dace at Chiswick, and at Isleworth, in July. And sometimes something more than dace.

One day I watched these dace specialists at work, for, indeed, I have never fished Thames in his tidal waters myself. Suddenly I heard an exclamation and I saw that one of the anglers was in something worth while. Something that made the reel sing and the rod kick and nose dive, and something that took twenty yards of line headlong and then threw itself in air with a splash. ' *That's* no dace,' said I.

And it wasn't, for the angler presently beached a three-pound trout. I asked him if he often saw trout in the tidal water. ' Never before,' said he.

An hour later I met the same fisherman. The tide had turned, the rise was done. We recognized each other and nodded. He said, ' I hooked another trout after you'd gone. Twice as big as the first——' ' Yes ? ' said I eagerly. ' Smashed me to hell,' said he.

I asked an expert about these tidal trout of the dace waters. He could not tell me much but he did say that, some years before, a dredger at work had struck and killed a fish, reported to be a trout, which was supposed to have weighed ' about thirteen pounds.' It would be worth, maybe, the while of some London angler to take a spinning-rod and phantom and go to these urban waters some June evening when the tide suits. He would want a boat I think, and I should not be a bit surprised did he want, in the result, a landing-net too.

The gudgeon is another of Thames's little grandsons whose popularity as a sporting fish has passed with the passing of a fashion. When our grandfathers were young fellows in whiskers and wideawakes what was more modish than a gudgeon party ? You required a dozen or so young men and a dozen or so pretty girls in Balmorals and crinolines. And then, chaperoned by Aunt Lavinia or Mamma, hey for Taplow or Maidenhead all of a summer day ! Arrived, the party assorted itself into pairs, to each couple a

punt, a fisherman, two rods and a rake. Imagine the
innuendos of that agreeable rattle, Fred Hieover,
anent the last ! But the rake was the gudgeon rake
and not Mr. Hogarth's kind at all.

And so they all went out on the water and fished
for gudgeon in the manner that we employ to-day
when we catch gudgeon for trouting purposes—the
only use that 1932 has for this nice little relation of
the barbel.

This is what happened in 1852. When the punt
came to a good gravel bottom, such as Maidenhead
reach is famous for, Fisherman Andrews would push
his rypecks home and moor up to them. He would
take the rake and rake the floor of the river, just as
we do to-day. From far and near the gudgeon would
come to feast on the flotsam that the rake threw up.
Andrews would bait the two rods with small red
worms, bits of small red worms. Cousin Lucy would
look the other way while he did so.

This done Lucy and Fred would fish for gudgeon
just as we do now. They would let the bait swim
down about an inch above the bottom of the river.
The two or three shot on the trace made this easy.
The quill bobbed. ' I've got a bite,' says Lucy.
' Strike 'im gentle, Miss,' says Andrews, ' *Ooh*, I've
caught one ! '

And so the sport would continue till three o'clock.
Then the punts poled up to the landing stage, Cousin
Lucy trailing her pretty fingers in the water and wanting to pick the lilies. At the landing stage the catches
were counted. Twenty dozen gudgeon to a punt was
no uncommon basket. Our party then ' repaired '
to Skindles Hotel below Bray Lock and ' partook '

of a gudgeon fry, the champagne that the occasion demanded being the privilege of the punt with the fewest gudgeon. But it never cost more than seven-and-sixpence a bottle and Charlie Mallowby's purse is well lined even for that of a Grenadier Guardsman. And Charles and Miss Amelia Haycocks have bagged but a hundred and eleven gudgeon between them. A miserable total for which Charlie blames the pope (another opening here for Fred) who invaded his swim.

And indeed the pope, or as Andrews calls him, the ruff, is a greedy and pugnacious little bottom fish of four brown inches long and spined on the back like a perch. He is frequent in swims and prompt, and successful, in disputing them with the pretty little grey-and-moon-coloured gudgeon. The pope ceased being a sportsman's fish long ago. He belongs to the brutal old times when he was caught by the gentle anglers of the period and, a small cork impaled upon his spiny dorsal, thrown in again a dozen or so at a time. It was highly diverting then to see these little depth-loving fish try to go home and the corks preventing them.

The bullhead or miller's thumb is another spiky and pugnacious creature. He lives on the floor always and alone. And, largely, he takes his colour from the floor he lives on. If he was three foot long instead of three inches or so he would be the ugliest and most dangerous fish in the Thames. For he is as fast as a flicker of light when he moves upon his gravels and he has gone with the jerk of a cube in a kaleidoscope. So too has the loach gone who lives in the same gravel deeps.

But the loach is a gentle little fish, mottled and grey and with the beards of a barbel whom he resembles in shape reduced a hundredfold. It is said that if you see a stone loach restlessly shifting about on a clear shallow that thunder is imminent.

But come, the prettiest of all the little fish is surely the bleak, the river-swallow, old Izaak has called him. The bleak is of no use to any angler except as an ornament to his summer day and as a bait for a big trout. He may best be caught for this purpose on the smallest of flies, say a Tup's Indispensable, say a Red Tag, dapped down to him where he swims on the surface. Or else upon a tiny hook made tempting to him by the tail of a tiny red worm.

I never think of bleak without remembering how I used to lean on Marlow bridge on my road to Coster's fishing-punt that waited at the hotel steps. Always the sun was warm on my back and, below me, warm on the green and myriad backs of the bleak who darted here and there, into the shadow and out again, just like the silver swallows that Master Walton would be calling them. 'The bleak are up,' said Coster when at length I came; 'we'll see a trout move to-day.'

As if I did not know that the bleak, the green and very silver bleak, were up !

Another worthy little fish of Thames is the stickleback; and handsome is he too, which many worthy people are not. I call him ' of Thames ' thus glibly but I cannot remember him in the actual river. There is, though, at Ewelme, Ewelme old as Britain, old as Time, a cress bed of slow crystal and emerald which is the nursery ground of the stickleback. And this makes him a Thames fish, for is not Ewelme a Thames village and famous even in our valley of History and of England ? And, in his May spawning dress, the stickleback is the smartest little soldier ever you saw. Steel blue his back and thrice armoured ; scarlet, orange-scarlet, his throat and front. He looks finely. He is as balanced as a hunt terrier. He builds his nest of weed and between the bulrushes he hangs it to rock in the golden current. It is as large as a sherry glass and in it is room for the stickleback's two wives. The male guards the home ferociously and, when his children come, these he guards too from, alas, their worst enemies, their mammas who, the amazons, would eat them were it not for their plucky little, handsome little sire. *What* a sportsman a stickleback would make did he grow to twenty pounds and take a Jock Scott on light tackle swinging to him in the tail of a weir pool !

So we will think of something that *does* weigh twenty pounds and not half a pennyweight. And that is the carp, the best worth catching, perhaps, of all British fish. But perhaps as a Thames fish he hardly ranks. And yet in Thames he is and occasionally he is caught by some absolutely unworthy angler who has a leger out for an eel. This honest fellow will not appreciate the carp, he will not know what the gods have sent him, he will not even care. He will exhibit his trophy in the bar parlour and accept the verdict of the *cognoscenti* assembled that what he has caught is, in spite of its ell-long dorsal, a particularly fine chub. He will take the carp home, he will eat and forget it. There was a carp caught thus in Shiplake Hole not so long ago. There was a twenty-pound carp caught at Benson—unappreciated both.

Walton has called the carp the water-fox and its brain is, I believe, greater than the brain of other fish. A hundred years is no age at all for a carp, and as he lives he learns. He is not indigenous to the Thames or to any English water. He is, like the rose and the pheasant (so English both and so alien), a foreigner. But he came to Thames in 1490 so he may be said to be, by now, well established. Indeed he is not worth fishing for in the river. Better forget the carp entirely and some day you will catch him on a lobworm when you are fishing for barbel or bream. He is called the Golden Carp but his mail is bronze. He is a noble antagonist when hooked—or so I am told. And if fish for a Thames carp you must, in spite of what I've said, this is how I would go about it.

I would first find a bit of water that looks like holding a carp. I would find a shallow backwater or mill-cutting with here and there a deep and mysterious-looking hiding place. The shallows would be shady with the broad leaves of lilies. I should devote a summer to this place when I had found it. But I should not take a rod there at first. Only a camp stool and a book. I should get there when the light came and wait, and wait till twilight smudged out the opposite, the Berkshire, shore.

There, if you are lucky, some morning, just after the clock on the grey church behind the mill has sounded a solemn four, a huge bronze fish will leap in elephantine playfulness, will wallow like a bathing alderman.

Or else you may find your carp at noonday. The

leaves of the lilies will tremble and part ; a thick, golden-brown back will heave among them like a fat man who turns over in his sleep ; and then it will sink again into the shadows, the lily stalks and the bronze-green water.

And next day you will bring a rod. The ten-foot split-cane for me. The Nottingham reel also, the undressed silk line, three yards of fine gut and a small triangle. The weight (one medium-size envelope lead) may be applied to the trace about a yard above the hook. You may bait with a *small* new potato, about as big as two hazel nuts. This potato should be boiled first and in a solution of brown sugar. See now that a tiny float is adjusted to match the deepness of the water. And now pitch the potato out so that it falls into that yard or so of clear space that lies between the two lily-beds. Well thrown !

Next, as the August day widens, see that the line is taut, rest the rod on the tall reeds that hide you (*hide* you, remember) and sit down beside it on your small striped canvas stool. But look to it that some fifteen yards of line are first pulled off the reel and coiled neatly upon a sheet of newspaper or cardboard. Do not move the bait, do not touch the rod till you go home to-night at eight-thirty.

When these instructions have been daily carried out till the middle of a warm September, then at 6.40 a.m. you shall notice that the patient little float is rocking ever so slightly. And your heart will bounce, and your face, under the sunburn, will go, I warrant, the colour of butter.

And see, oh see, the line on the cardboard—coil by coil it moves as the tiny float swims of a sudden from its stance and wanders gently away down the lane between the lily-starred stalks and shadows. Twelve yards, thirteen, fourteen—pick up the rod and strike firmly. A terrific tug shall respond to you, off the little rod, in half-ellipse, a hurricane of line shall be torn.

In this way, then, you will, I hope, hook your carp, hook the centenarian of the lily-beds, and may the luck of the big landing-net be yours. I have, however, only once seen a carp in the Thames. I and the lady with me saw, twice in one summer day of 1928, an enormous fish who sunned himself with a shoal of barbel in the weir pool at Mapledurham. He looked almost golden in comparison with the barbel. I will not say how big he was, only that his girth, as he lay in the warm water, was like, the lady said, ' a child's balloon.' Some day, perhaps ?

The carp is not golden, but a golden tench is as redly gold as a ripe orange. I have never seen one in the river, but that such a prodigy is possible the specimen in Mr. Hobbs's collection of Thames fish testifies. But I suppose that such a tench is but an aquarium curiosity gone feral and *fanti* ?

It is in this way that the occasional huge goldfish is met with. There comes the rain in winter time. The river wakes and stretches its arms. It rises, it crosses the road below the church which it has not crossed since 1917. It invades the gardens of Sir Dudworth Ducat's summer residence. His riparian lawns are under acres of wild, white water. Miss Daisy Ducat's goldfish are washed out of the fountain and down the ditch into the river. They are a handsome lot of about half a pound each. Arrived in the Thames some go to feed the pike. Others feed themselves and grow prodigiously and, once in a way, you will see one and say that he is six pounds of flaming, golden fire and the most heathen thing that ever swam in a Christian river.

Golden orfe are not indigenous. And neither are they gold. They are lemon-coloured fish and as handsome as paint. Mr. Frank Buckland stocked golden orfe of old into the Kennet, whence they have reached the Thames, either on flood water or else carried thither as spawn in the crop of a hungry mallard and then, for some reason or other, ejected to fertilise in Cleeve reach. For it was in Cleeve reach that I saw two golden orfe when I was fly-fishing for chub not so long ago. They were on the shallow by Lord Shrewsbury's island and I tried to get them to take a fly—frantically I tried. But they were obdurate. I last heard of these pretty fish in Cleeve weir pool. And of some more on the redds at Mapledurham. But, apart from the specimens in Mr. Hobbs's museum, I have never seen an orfe out of the water.

To many people all little fish with fins are minnows —minnow is synonym of the minute, the infinite small thing. But the Thames minnows who swim in clouds against camp sheathings are, some of them, fine three-inchers and able to hold their own with any other light-weight—so they say. The biggest minnow that I remember was a four-inch fish with which Walter Coster, one evening, baited my hook to catch the big trout in the hotel corner of Marlow pool. This minnow was not a success with the trout who, of course, may have been scared of him. Anyhow, after he had been fished with for an hour, I let him go and, for all I have heard to the contrary, he may swim in Marlow weir pool to this day.

I enjoy to see a summer shoal of minnows pushing and frisking, the males splendid in their mating scarlet and moon-pearl. I am lying on warm grass and looking into idle Thames water and the minnows are to me as much a part of the pageant of a June day as Thames himself is.

XV. AN EXERCISE IN THE OBSOLETE:
A WEIR ALSO A WERE-WOLF

Let them that list these pastimes still pursue
And on such pleasing fancies feed their fill;
JOHN DENNYS.

THE professional Thames fisherman as Mr. Briggs knew him has gone, or practically gone. I do not mean to deny that here and there between Richmond and Rushey is a man who makes the major part of his income by taking his fellow men and women out fishing, but I say that this sort becomes rarer every April. Nevertheless an angler who comes for the first time to Thames in the hopes of catching Thames fish can usually find some longshoreman who fishes and can manage a boat to attend him and tell him how to fish and where.

But these good fellows, Thames anglers themselves, rarely know anything of angling except how to catch jack with a live-bait and where a leger might account for an eel. The trout is a sealed book to them, the barbel a come-by-chance to the leger's lob, the tench unattainable, the bream undreamt of. And therefore the 'Mr. Briggs days' are done and with them have died the tales of professional and client that must have existed once in the same profusion as the fables and legends that bind the Scots and Irish ghillie to one's imagination. Possibly the fashion will change again and a new race of Thames anglers will create a new supply of knowledgeable Mentors to attend upon them. And it is not the salmon who has taken the old-time angler with him. For I do not suppose that a salmon was ever taken in the Thames on rod and line. All were taken in traps at the weir gates and the last authentic salmon was a Boveney fish got in June 1855. I say authentic for there is the Chertsey salmon of not so very long ago. For the sake of any who do not know about the Chertsey fish I will, at the risk of being tedious, repeat the tale anew.

A roach angler, on a summer day, saw floating down his swim an enormous fish. It was dead and he raked it out with his net. An inquest, held forthwith by the club assembled, pronounced that the deceased was a trout of twenty-five pounds, a record trout even for old Thames. And the fish was presently acquired by a local inn much frequented by anglers. It was sent to a taxidermist. It was returned in a glass case. It was exalted in the entrance hall, a trophy for the world to see. Below the case a caption said, ' Thames Trout, 24 lb. 10 oz., taken

opposite this hotel.' Presently rumours of the ' trout'
reached Breams Buildings, and Mr. Sheringham, I
think, came personally to investigate. That the exhibit was no trout a glance told him, but how infinitely more intriguing was the splendid reality—a
Thames salmon, at last ! But urgent enquiries re-
sulted in pathos and her brother bathos.

A young married couple occupying a house-boat
below the weir had had a gift from Aboyne. It was
a salmon. Now in the giving of a salmon *bis dat qui
cito dat* is the motto to remember. And Uncle George,
on Deeside, had omitted to be mindful of it. In fact

> The way was long, the way was hot,
> The salmon was infirm a lot,

indeed such a ' rocketer ' was it that while Angelina,
holding her pretty nose with one hand opened a tin
of sardines with the other, Edwin, defying T.C.C.
bye-laws, tipped the nuisance out of its mat and into
the river as the quickest way to be quit of it. Even
then it hung about in home waters for some hours
and eventually had to be pushed into middle stream
with the punt-pole.

There have been many attempts made, besides
this one of Edwin's, to re-establish the salmon in the
Thames. The tale of these well-intentioned efforts
may be read in the Conservancy's records and in
many other places. Smolts have been enlarged in
the middle Thames, spawn, I think, also has been
artificially laid down to become alevins of Windsor
weir. But the hope that the salmon's well-known
affection for the home of his childhood would, did he
survive to taste the clean salt water beyond the Nore,

bring him homing back through the foul tides of London Bridge, has not been justified, so far, by events. And a very good thing too say I and all other thoughtful Thames anglers.

And what, you say, ails me at the Thames salmon ? Consider, please. Thames does not belong to the nation, nor even to his loving and excellent Conservators. He and his fishing rights are the property of Squire This, Sir Thomas That and my Lord So-and-So. And none of these three good sportsmen and landlords are much use with a roach pole, and my lord, so I hear, has never angled with a leger and a lobworm in his noble life. Therefore they trouble not to exercise their overlordship, either on the Berks bank or on the Bucks, nor yet in middle river. And so far as they are concerned you and I may catch their roach and their pike, even their trouts and their chavenders, and good luck to us. And, meanwhile, Squire goes to the Helmsdale, Sir Thomas to Simon's Yat on Wye, and my Lord, in April, to cast a Jock Scott under the shadow of Lochnagar. For they are salmon fishers all three of them. And did they read, in the Olympus Club, that Mr. Jones had brought to bank at Windsor (fishing with Ned Andrews) five salmon $37\frac{1}{2}$ lb., 22 lb., 20 lb., 17 lb. and 15 lb., and that Dr. Smith (fishing with A. Wells) at Wallingford had, on Saturday last, landed three salmon, largest 42 lb., what do you think they'd do about it ?

You don't know ? Well I do. There would be such a looking up of title-deeds and old parchments as never was since Doomsday Book was made. And next time that you went out to get a few roach a big man in velveteens would happen along followed by

a curly-coat retriever and—well, if you gave him any
of your lip he'd chuck you into the water and clump
you over the head as you climbed out again. Which
would but serve you right for a poaching cockney.
And if your fishing club got together with my fishing
club and all the other fishing clubs and fought, even
unto the House of Lords, for Thames as he was yesterday, why, we should lose and the lawyers would
make fortunes out of us.

And so if it happens, as it might happen, that you,
you spinning a blue phantom at the tail of Goring
weir and a May flood clearing, hook something that
takes with a smash and, in the brightest silver, leaps
and fights you for half-a-mile and comes, at length,
to hand, his deep flank flushed with that faint breath
of silvery-rose that is only worn by a salmon headlong
out of the salt water—*say nothing about it*. Do not,
if you value your Father Thames, boast yourself to
The Field, *The Fishing Gazette* or *The Angler's News*.
Take the—er—what you've got there, home at once,
say that it comes to you ' in a present ' from Montrose
in Angus, and into the pot with it. And don't talk
any more heedless and ungrateful rubbish about wish-
ing that the Thames was a salmon river. For, if you
do, you may wake up some morning and find that
your wish is granted.

There have been attempts to make the huchen,
from the Blue Danube, a Thames fish. But somehow
the huchen has not responded. I do not know why
for he is a ' lannart ' fellow and the sea makes no call
to him. I cannot say at what age and size these fish
were put into the river, but I have heard of two, each
of about four pounds' weight. The one was picked

up dead and I forget where. Of the other Lord Boston's keeper told me. It was found, also dead, in the eel-bucks at Hedsor. The huchen grows to a great weight and is a fine fighter, so he might, if established here, be an addition to the river. On the other hand he too is a salmon and should be suspect as such.

But a little Thames creature whom I would welcome back is the crayfish. I do not say that there are none in the Thames but only that I have not seen one for years. But within living memory the crayfishes were as common as minnows. The cray was, and I hope he may be again, a little lobster of some four inches long. He is not the black-and-pink lobster of the lobster pot and the fishmonger's slab. He is a little olive-brown fellow with a mustard-coloured underneath—French mustard, I mean. He lived in the cracks of the masonry of weirs, between the boards of camp sheathing, and in hundreds of little holes in the bank which he made for himself and out of which he would loll like a hermit crab out of a snail shell at Looe. When boiled he did not become the vivid scarlet of the Epsom Downs lobster, rather did he change to a sort of salmon-pink *cum* red coral hue. He was easily caught in a basket trap, baited with a dead rat, for he had a passion for carrion. But easier still was it to put a gloved finger into the hole he sat in. The crayfish would lay hold of your finger and you then pulled him out, for, like the lobster in *The Water Babies*, it is a point of honour among crayfish never to let go. And as the crayfish is small and the Thames tidal only up to Richmond the fate that so nearly befell the Mayor of Plymouth, who went lobster-catching to the Mewstone at low tide, cannot

well be ours who merely go to catch crayfish at Caversham.

Alas for the Thames crayfish, thirty, forty years
ago, there came an epidemic to the river.   How it
came, and whence, I know not—men say from France
where such a crayfish scourge occasionally wipes out
a whole river bank of crays.   In Thames it began in
the lower reaches and ran, like the pestilence it was,
to the sources of the river.   The poor little crayfish
came out of their nooks and crannies, turned pink and
died.   Their countless corpses made the sorrowful
river edges and backwaters pink to see.   However,
the crayfish still exists in some of the Thames tributaries, the Pang for instance, and I hope that I may
live to see him established once more a familiar of the
river, a delicacy of the family board.

The female crayfish carries her roe on her person
in the same manner as does the female lobster.   But
there is this difference, that the lobster is born in an
intermediate, alevin state and the crayfish is born all
crayfish.   A crayfish mother carries a swarm of tiny replicas of herself clinging about her as thickly as bees.

A strange thing about the baby crays is that though
their bodies grow, and grow a-pace, their shells remain
in statu.   The result is that the little crayfish must
shed their armour about ten times in the first year of
their existence or ever Father Thames supplies them
with their final suit.   I believe that the barbel used
to eat quantities of the crayfish, crunching the same
in his pharynx where he keeps teeth of tremendous
crushing power.   The barbel must miss the crayfish
even more than most of us do.

The lamprey is another once inhabitant of the

river who has gone. I have never seen a lamprey in
the Thames and no angler of to-day is likely to die of
a surfeit of him, but I am told that of old-time he was
known and that Hambledon and the streams below
Hambledon were favourite haunts of his.   And I for
one applaud his taste.

Hambledon weir is famous as a trouting weir, yet
I mostly remember Hambledon as a beauty spot, as
a place where I saw a record catch of roach made by
a celebrated actor, as the place where I had an adven-
ture with a cat and, on another occasion, an adven-
ture with Irish terriers.

As for the beauties of Hambledon, its background
of hills and summer woods, its white and dragon-
green streams, why,

> I met a man mowing
>   A meadow of hay,
> So smoothly and flowing
>   His swathes fell away
>   At break of the day
>   Up Hambledon way ;
> A yellow-eyed collie
>   Was guarding his coat—
> Loose-limbed and lob-lolly,
>   But wise and remote.
>
> The morning came leaping,—
>   'Twas five of the clock,
> The world was still sleeping
>   At Hambledon Lock,—
>   As sound as a rock
>   Slept village and Lock ;
> ' Fine morning ! ' the man says,
>   And I says, ' Fine day ! '
> Then I to my fancies
>   And he to his hay !

> And lovely and quiet,
>   And lonely and chill,
> Lay river and eyot,
>   And meadow and mill ;
>   I think of them still—
>   Mead, river, and mill ;
> For wasn't it jolly
>   With only us three—
> The yellow-eyed collie,
>   The mower and me ?

I have told you of the matinée idol and the sack full of roach. And I will now tell my cat story as a warning to all anglers.

No man would leave a loaded gun lying about lest the children play with it. And no man ought to leave a spinning-rod with a mounted Thames flight suspended from it propped against a blossomed apple tree. Yet this last I did while I took a cup of tea in the garden. And there walked the great, red, tiger Tom of the lock-keeper. And a zephyr woke and, out of sheer mischief, caused the bleak on the Thames flight to swing, ever so gently to and fro, to——

An arc of orange fur, the playful catamount sprung. And the reel (just like in fishing stories) screamed and the rod bent. The cat, every bristle erect, took twenty yards of line in its first rush. I will not labour the situation. It was caught at length and wrapped in a tablecloth. I have said that no eel is really difficult till it is landed. The same applies to a ginger Tom cat. The only difference is that an eel has no paws and a cat has four, and all four are tipped with steel. But we extracted the hook, staunched the bleeding (our own), and appeased the patient with milk. And now when I see an angler engaged, blasphemously, with an eel, I know that he is fortunate in not having caught a Tom cat.

Early one Sunday morning I was fishing at Hambledon weir. I was young in my river days and I did not know the neighbourhood. I had a pug puppy with me who was bored because, like most dogs, it hated fishing. So I stopped spinning and took it for a short walk. I crossed the footbridge and followed the right-of-way through the mill. Of a sudden I and the puppy were surrounded by quite twenty couple of Irish terriers. I picked the puppy up and stood with my back to the wall. There was no one about and I was very frightened indeed. Most of the pack were doubtless peaceable enough, but one member was dangerous ; I could see that by his stiff carriage, his slightly lowered head. And by pack law, one is all. I stood quite still ; had I moved, the old red fiend would have pinned me. And doing so he'd have given the ' tear him and eat him ' cue to his co-mates and brothers in exile.

And one by one the Paddies dispersed on their occasions. All except the old dog, who, red and grizzled, sat on motionless. And still no kennelman came. I edged along the wall. The dog followed but kept his distance. I got on to the narrow bridge and, facing him, backed along it. And so we came to the middle river and there he stopped and sat down. I was off his beat. I and the pug went our ways. The old Irishman threw his grey snout up, ' woof,' said he. He turned and, stiff-legged, he stalked back whence he came.

I began this chapter by deploring the absence of legend and fable anent the Thames waterman as com-

pared with the Scots ghillie or the Irish. But this
pug puppy of mine reminds me of something. It is
an absurd thing. Also it has nothing very much to
do with the Thames except that Lady Skrimshire was
rather like the heron who was catching frogs on the
meadow above Cleeve just now and all Thames dabchicks remind me of Harriet.

But I admit that I should never have remembered
this story had it not been for the pug puppy. And I
should never have remembered the pug puppy had
it not first been for Father Thames and Hambledon
weir. And, anyhow, from a weir to a were-wolf is the
merest step, the most natural sequence in the world.
So then :

Harriet Hepplewhite was a spinster who made no
secret of being forty-five years of age. Harriet had
leanings towards the occult unusual in a lady's-maid.
That is, she enjoyed *Dracula*, and she liked Miss Fyle-
man's poetry. But mostly was she interested in a
little old Russian tale that she had lately read, in
which a beautiful Countess was accustomed to get
out of her own mouth of an evening and, leaving her
day self at home, go roaming in the gloaming as a
pretty white wolf. Harriet gathered that to do this
properly you must have a working knowledge of
magic or else you must have effected a sale of yourself to the Devil. Still, the notion was a romantic one,
and to be able to get out and about as and when you
chose was certainly intriguing.

Harriet's was a simple nature and an affectionate.
She was quite unsoured even after seven years' servi-
tude with Lady Skrimshire. Lady Skrimshire, the
widow of a knight, was a tall, thin-lipped, famishy-

looking lady who played a fine game of Bridge and went from watering-place to watering-place like an acquisitive old heron. But would you look among the water-fowl for the prototype of Harriet, you would, I think, decide without difficulty upon the dabchick, so roundabout was Harriet, so plump, so pleasing. But Harriet was not cocksure as is the dabchick, nor was she self-assertive as he is. On the contrary she was good-hearted and easily put upon.

For instance, if Lady Skrimshire said, as she frequently did say, ' Oh, Harriet, I wonder if you would mind putting off your evening until to-morrow, because I shall be out myself to-night and shall want you to be at home to answer the telephone ? ' then Harriet would reply, ' That will be *quite* all right, my lady.' And Lady Skrimshire would say, ' Thank you, Harriet, I was sure you would oblige me.' But of course the obligation didn't amount to much really, for poor Harriet had few friends and nowhere particular to go when she *did* go out.

Lady Skrimshire was well-to-do, but this time, when she went to Cheltington Spa, she stayed in rooms and not at the Majestic Hotel. Harriet was sorry for this, because there was a band in the lounge at the Majestic and she loved bands. But, if you know Cheltington, you'll remember that there is also a band that plays in the Council Gardens of an afternoon and, May to September, from 7.30 to 9.30 of an evening. Chairs cost tuppence and the music goes down your back like pins and ices. And so when Lady Skrimshire said that day, ' Oh, Harriet, etc.,' it was a *shame* it was, for was not to-night the last band night of the season and was not the programme a

gala programme ?   It was indeed.   For a minute poor
Harriet felt quite cross and said to herself, ' Silly old
devil, I've been sold to her for seven years.'   Then she
was sorry and she said as cheerfully as she could,
' That will be *quite* all right, my lady.'   So just about
7.30 she saw Lady Skrimshire into the taxicab and
then she sat down to have a nice read.

About the time for ' God Save the King ' (a tune
which always gave her a lump in her throat), Harriet
had unhooked Lady Skrimshire, who had come home
early with a violent indigestion, and was putting her
to bed with a hot-water bottle.   But Harriet did not
feel inclined for bed herself.   She wished that she
could go out for a nice long walk in the moonlight, an
impossibility, alas, for Harriet, unless of course she
were a were-wolf.   In this case then, what would look
like Harriet's everyday self would be lying in the
little room on the other side of the passage, while the
real Harriet, in the form of a lovely and elegant white
wolf with a long bushy tail, would wander, free of all
black and silver magic, under the dark and the stars.
Of course Harriet in the metamorphosis she so suddenly contemplated had no intention of *biting* anybody, for, as I have told you, she was of a gentle and
an affectionate nature.   But she did think, with a
sudden pretty independence, that if she *had*, as she'd
declared earlier in the day, sold herself she might as
well——

Harriet peeped into Lady Skrimshire's room.   Her
ladyship slept well.   ' Poor soul,' said Harriet kindly.

Now to become a were-wolf, even when you are,
like Harriet, qualified, is not quite so simple as is
generally imagined.   Mistakes are easily made, and

once made cannot be rectified until the spell has spent
itself. And let the cub-beginner, the amateur were-
wolf, beware (despite all hereinafter related) lest the
influence run down while he or she is still about and
abroad.

Sergeant Coppinger of the Cheltington Police was
due to retire upon a pension. He was a widower and
childless, a big jovial man of great good-humour and
of some private means. He had moreover an excellent appointment in prospect as lodge-keeper to the
Council Gardens.

It was, then, when Sergeant Coppinger was ' visit-
ing points ' between 10.30 and 11 p.m., that he
bumped right into Harriet Hepplewhite. Now had
Harriet been completely successful in her magic I feel
that the Sergeant would never have ventured to
address her. It is no part of a policeman's duty to
interfere with a promenading were-wolf, neither is
there, as far as I know, any bye-law broken if the
were-wolf is without a collar. The case of pug-dogs
is of course entirely different.

' 'Ullo, Fido ! ' said Sergeant Coppinger, flashing
his bull's-eye ; ' out after sunset are you, and without
a collar too ? You come along to the station, Fido.'
He clipped a finger and thumb in so truly friendly
a manner that he won Harriet's heart at once. She
wagged her curly tail and trotted up to him. The
Sergeant felt leisurely in all his pockets for the official
piece of string.

' No string, Fido,' he said ; ' well, I'll have to carry
you.'

And he tucked a blue and a comfortable arm round
Harriet's plump waist and walked off with her.

Harriet licked his hand shyly.   And so they came to the station.

' One minute, Fido,' said Sergeant Coppinger, and he put Harriet down in the space between the double-swinging entrance doors, where nobody could see her. He then went to get the bit of string with which every officer on duty should be provided.   When he came back to report Harriet into the Inspector's office he found her blushing very prettily, because the magic had run down, and Harriet in her everyday self was thinking that she *was* a lucky one in that the power had lasted till they got to the station.   But, though painfully fluttered, Harriet had presence of mind. She spoke up as quick as quick and as truthful as truthful.   She said rather breathlessly, ' I was just coming in because a little pug-dog ran out of the house and disappeared ; and, oh dear, I forgot to put my hat on, *there* now ! '

For of course Harriet was dressed just as she was when she made the magic.   Sergeant Coppinger knew at once what had happened.   He knew that when the young lady had pushed open the first swing-door to come in, Fido had, unseen by her, escaped once more.   But he didn't let on to Harriet, or to the In-spector, the hand he thought that he had played in this latest departure.   But he *did* walk home with Harriet, looking about for Fido all the way.   And Harriet let him look and then let herself in with the latchkey that was in her pocket ; and next evening she had her evening out, and Sergeant Coppinger, in mufti, called for her and took her to the pictures.

When Harriet became Mrs. Coppinger, which she did three months later, Lady Skrimshire gave her twenty-five pounds and said she hoped that Harriet wasn't being foolish.

Now that's the end, except that some day Harriet means to tell her husband about when she was a were-wolf. You see Harriet feels that when Coppinger talks of their first meeting, which he often does, the happiness of the recollection is slightly dimmed for him (since she knows that he is the kindest man in all the world) when he reflects that poor little lost Fido was never found.

Moreover Harriet feels sure that he *hates* to have a secret which he thinks he does not share with his wife.

XVI. THE FLOWERS OF THAMES

Of flowers—the frail-leaf'd, white anemone—
Dark bluebells drench'd with dews of summer eves—
And purple orchises with spotted leaves—

MATTHEW ARNOLD.

YOU, in your punt, who pay your pennies to pass through the lock on the seventh Sunday after Trinity, the Gods of Tin shouting, the pretty girls the prettier for the ardent sunshine and a golden freckle or so on a white arm, may possibly spare a moment to admire the flowers in the lock-keeper's garden— roses, geraniums, hollyhocks and the massed and brilliant blue of lobelia along the border.

And if you say to the ex-bo'sun—all lock-keepers are sailors, R.N., that the garden looks a treat, he will look pleased and say, 'It's Inspection week, you know, Sir.' And you will say, as if surprised by your own forgetfulness, 'Why, so it is.' But in reality you will not have the least idea what the fellow is talking about. And here am I to tell you.

Of course every lock-keeper (something like Mr. Kipling's sea-faring Uncle Salters) is a gardener at heart.   It's his garden that he loves, and I fear that Father Thames takes second place to a seed catalogue every time.   But our Philosopher comforts himself with the reflection that these occasional Edens upon his road redound to his honour and add to his ancient beauty.   And his Conservators encourage him in this belief.   They want every lock-keeper to be a son of Adam, they offer cups and prizes, they advance money for the erection of glass houses, and their gods are Flora and the young Vertumnus.   And just about now, they put on their becoming dark-blue uniforms, their white yachting caps, and, a-wink with brass buttons, they go aboard the official steamer and sail to judge all lock gardens from Dan to Beersheba, from the top of the river down to where they hand over their Authority to that of the Port of London, at Royal Richmond.

It is a fine sight to see a lock judged.   At the lock where most often I see it, the Conservators arrive about 5 p.m.   By four o'clock everything is in man-o'-war order, the lock-keeper, meticulously shaven, wears his best uniform, his shoes are pipeclayed, he is as agitated as a bride and you could probably get through the lock for nothing if you were the sort of fellow who would want to.   The flowers themselves, from the crimson riot of ramblers high above the gate to the lowliest and most modest pansy, seem to be looking upstream.   A poetical blue lupin is mis-quoting *Maud*, something like this :

> There has fallen a splendid tear
>   From the passion flower at the gate,
> He is coming is Desborough's peer
>   And many a noble mate,

And the red rose calls, ' they are near, they are near,'
  And the white rose weeps, ' they are late,'
The larkspur listens, 'I hear, I hear,'
  The lily whispers, 'I wait.'

And thereupon, silver clear, a whistle blows beyond the bend, and the muffle of green woods above Hardwick picks it up and echoes it back. A coquettish ripple of foam about her bows, a house flag flying free, the steamer approaches. The gates swing open ; the shining craft comes alongside ; their lordships land, sunburnt, handsome gentlemen of whom Father Thames is justly proud and to whom he is very justly grateful. For their labour on his behalf is a labour of love and so it is done, even to the judging of a geranium, with the heart and to perfection.

And presently away they go again down river and the lock gardener can unbend and give great glowing bouquets to me and to his friends and wait the word (he will get it within the week) which says that the Challenge Cup is his, and that for a year it shall adorn his sideboard and be the envy of those others, his colleagues in the service, upstream of him and down.

But to wait a word of that sort is the nerve-racking thing if a man really *cares*. I know of only one thing worse. And that is to be, as I am, a man who shoots occasionally and—well, what I want you to do for a moment is to come up into the woods (which you will remember that hounds were drawing as we came home from perch fishing last winter) and look, with me, into the state of mind of the owner or tenant of a shoot when the hounds are coming to his coverts. If he is a vulpicidal egoist with two guns and a hide like a rhinoceros he will welcome the Hunt, in February, with smiles and cherry brandy and a winning bet, taken with himself, of a £1000 sterling to a false French franc against a find.

But if you are no vulpicide but merely a vacillating and easy fellow who wants to be thought kindly of by all honest men you will be full of anxieties. You will remember that you enquired, in May, as to the welfare of the vixen and her family in Friar's Hill-sides. You will remember that Bagwell made evasive reply. And you will recall, you will recall uncomfortably, that there you let the matter rest. And you will recollect that you lunched (was it at Goodwood ?) with your Master. Blazier had indeed been most hospitable to a comparative stranger. You had spoken to Blazier on that occasion a little as if——. Well, it will be a bore if they don't find. And, of course, the fox that Henrietta said she saw when we were shooting might just as well have been a hare— or a squirrel. You will summon the gamekeeper. Oh yes, Bagwell (he has a face like a block of wood sometimes) knows of the meet. The gates shall be open, the wire down. A fox ? Why, yes, if hounds do but draw properly. Mr Spratt, however, is always afraid of laming his hounds in our thick stuff and bramble. Spratt is content, it appears, to trot about the rides horn-blowing and his hounds dragging at his horse's heels. A huntsman can't expect to move a fox in *them* woods just by cheering. Nor by his lads whip-banging all up and a-down. At Grassington, where Bagwell has lived, he always had foxes. But the Duke's hounds would go through a bramble bed like spaniels. Like spaniels they would go through. And His Grace once said to Tom Woodcock——

So *you* say to Bagwell, ' Thank you, Bagwell ; have a glass of beer before you go home.' And the day comes. You will wake feeling worried. For after all you have some personal pride. And what is more tonic to a manly self-esteem than to have hounds find a fox in one's own preserves ? I do not know why this should be so. Possibly because one thus becomes the direct benefactor of the multitude. It is said that all the world loves a lover. It would be equally true to say that the shooting man who shows a fox, a perhaps not altogether expected fox, to a hundred or so of horse folk and foot folk and to twenty couple of genuinely surprised hounds, may be similarly sure of universal popularity. And a scarcely less evanescent popularity either than is that of your Romeo who is a kaleidoscopic sort of fellow and woefully infirm of purpose.

You will walk to Pilkington Cross Roads at 11 a.m. There will be a crowd out because it is Christmas time. You will see Bagwell in his best clothes. He is talking to Spratt who, in his holiday scarlet, bends upon a neck of shining chestnut to hear. Blazier sees you and adds a cordial question to a seasonable wish. You feel that you hate the fellow as much as if you'd robbed him. And you'll slip away before they move off. You'll slip into Friar's Hillsides and feel positively ashamed of the cartridge cases winking in the rides. You'll go to the top of the hill and watch the opposite side of the valley. If they don't find on the south face they won't find at all. Hark, Spratt's drawing now—the far side. He blows a long, complaining note. Nothing doing ? Of course not—Damn ! They are coming down the hill. Bagwell was right, hounds don't seem to try a blessed yard. . . .

He is dark red ; dark, coppery red. He has a great full brush with a white tag to it. He is sleek and shiny and subtle. He has black velvet ears. In fact he is a real beauty of a fox and no mistake. He lopes up the ride all diamond dainty. And, as he melts through the hedge and away for Watson's as cool as cucumbers, you signify the same in the usual manner.

' Viewed him yourself too, did you ? Well done ! ' Blazier tells you, he hugging the brown horse up the hill. Now if, anon, when you would strike a match, your hand wobbles up and down ? Well, the sight of a fox always serves me in exactly the same silly way. Whereas I can see a cock pheasant, I can see five hundred cock pheasants, without a tremor.

But to-day it is summer, a time not of foxes and pheasants but of fishes and flowers, and to the latter we will, if you please, return. For Thames is famous for his flowers and for his wild flowers, and I have walked, at Goring, from Streatley church to *The Beetle and the Wedge* at Moulsford, the while an expert gathered, in the going there and back again, fifty distinct species of summer flowers. And on Friar's Hillsides, where we viewed the fox and where the badgers earth, there grow, in April, the primroses, the wood anemones and the violets. And in May such carpets of bluebells as never you saw. I cannot describe them but they are as heavenly blue, under the beeches, as the robes of the Madonna and it gives me a lump in my throat to be looking at them.

And when they pass you may find, on the same

hillside, and the old river sliding below you silvery blue, the purple orchis and her paler sister. Also you may find the bee orchis and the white butterfly orchis and the rare soldier orchis, for Friar's Hillsides is on the Berkshire chalk. And you may add the last three to the total of fifty Thames flowers that we picked between Streatley and Moulsford, and then we will walk by Hart's Lock woods to Whitchurch and if you do truly and earnestly want to poison Aunt Elizabeth now is your chance. For here grows the dwale and the yew and the fool's parsley. And the foxglove, the pink foxglove and the white. But the dwale (I prefer ' dwale ' to ' nightshade ' though both titles are expressive) is the aunt-killer I should most recommend. But on so jolly a day who would want to kill anything or anybody ?

Now I am no expert of wild flowers except in that I am expert at loving them, and if you ask me of Thames flowers I will show you, upon his banks, king-cup, forget-me-not and iris, and upon his surface the golden water-lily and no lily is she at all, so the learned say, but neither the carp who lives in her shelter nor I who fish for the carp care. There is also, who is typical of Thames, the leucojum, the little friend of April and the daffodil, whom you call, and I, both wrongly, of course, the Lodden Lily. There is meadowsweet too and the loosestrife, always the loosestrife. And there is the honeysuckle at the gate.

But mostly my Thames flowers are the buttercups and the daisies that make cloth of gold and silver on the watermeadows and up the hill where the white mays climb. There is the cowslip too of which (I

seem to remember) men make wine.   Something of
this sort :

> The river ran unheeding ;
>   The cuckoo made his mock ;
> The big trout wasn't feeding ;
>   I drowsed beside the lock ;
> It might have been the weather,
>   It might have been the stream,
> Perhaps the two together
>   That made me dream a dream.
>
> I dreamed a dream of Maytime,
>   Of hawthorns white as snow,
> The village green at playtime
>   A hundred years ago ;
> A dream of bow and fiddle
>   And dancing on the green,
> A maypole in the middle,
>   The finest ever seen.
>
> The maids were red as roses
>   That took each ribbon rope ;
> The lads who held their posies,
>   They shone with health and soap ;
> Each lass had got her lover,
>   Save one I did espy
> As plump as any plover,
>   As sweet as cherry pie.
>
> I slipped an arm around her ;
>   The fiddles called to me ;
> As light of foot I found her
>   As e'er a lass could be ;
> 'Sir Roger,' and the same was
>   Most wonderful to tread ;
> I asked her what her name was,
>   And, 'Hephzibah,' she said.

The fiddlers were in fettle ;
 Too soon the dance was done ;
I sat her on a settle,
 All dimpling in the sun ;
I found for her a fairing,
 This pretty maid of mine,
A kerchief for her wearing,
 And cake and cowslip wine.

I said, ' My dear, I love you
 Most tender and most true ;
You little, pretty dove, you,
 Oh, won't you love me too ? '
White lids the blue eyes beaming
 Swift shadowed as I spoke ;
'Twas then—so much for dreaming—
 'Twas then that I awoke.

The cuckoos still were calling ;
 In amber, jade and pearls
The splashing weir was falling,
 To spin in silver swirls
As gaily as a dancer ;
 I rubbed my eyes—but ah,
I never had her answer,
 My little Hephzibah !

XVII. THE BIRDS OF THAMES

As I came down from Bablock Hythe
Through meads yet virgin of the scythe
The air was sweet, the birds were blithe
Along the stream to Eynsham :

ST. JOHN LUCAS.

NOW see how Thames flowers suggest Thames butterflies. And I think that they ought to for the flowers, in ages forgotten, brought the butterflies and the birds to the Thames Valley. There is a bush of buddleia in our garden and there, in August, come all the Thames butterflies there are, except the blues and the heaths. The rarer sorts are the occasional (I have seen him twice in ten years) White Admiral, Comma (last summer three visited us) and Marbled White who is, as a rule, a fairly regular caller. The loveliest are the Peacocks and the Painted Ladies—if indeed you can call either lovelier than Red Admiral and Tortoiseshell who match so with the gold and blue of late summer and the last of the halcyon days.

The downs above the river are for the Blues and

the Heaths, and the downs, the Grey Men, are very, very old and wise. Upon the downs and Berkshire hills once came the earliest butterfly of all if I may call, for my purpose, a Sphinx moth a butterfly, and there too, no doubt, was the earliest of the Thames birds, the archæopteryx, the first of all the birds. He was almost the size of a kestrel hawk and he had a tail like a dragon, but he was a true bird and the only one of his era. And I am thus reminded that, æons later, came man to shoot birds. And, almost as I write, comes to me by post an early evidence of Thames man and the shooting of shots. I will not say evidence of the earliest shots of all, for in that case I'd need to have had access to the armoury of the brat Cupid, and that I cannot have, although indeed, myself when young, I have many times been the target for his aim. And glad I am to acknowledge the same to-day. But I have here an arrow head that seems, so says a professor, to have been made of meteorite, and to have belonged, beyond any doubt, once upon a time to a Palæolithic sportsman and artist. At least I imagine that the fashioner of my arrow head was an artist because he has fashioned it so beautifully.

And I shall imagine (after all it is *my* arrow head, for the moment, and it shall make such magic for me as I require), I shall further imagine that its maker was a red-skinned little artist who had just learned to walk on his hind legs. But he still walks ape-like and stoopingly ; stoopingly, but very agile, he can go, flit and crouch, through the dreadful oak swamps. I do not know what my artist's name is—I doubt if he has one—so I will call him Man. And I will watch him slip, like an ugly little shadow, through the tree trunks and climb upon a terrible hillside.

He is being very brave. He is looking for magic. For his Totem has told him that if he will dare to seek where the Fire Ball fell he will find the magic stone of the gods, the stone of which the ghosts who hunt the ghost buffaloes fashion their arrow heads. And now he has found what he sought, and he pounces upon it like a dog, and paws it and snuffs it and howls an incantation.

The stone he has found lies among the boulders, and it is other than mortal flint. It has a colour like —a little like—dry blood and dust, so Man thinks. It has, only Man does not recognize the fact, iron in its constitution. And it is of a size to make a quiverful of elegant, dead-shot arrow heads.

And now the scene changes. I see Man who sits to make his magic a lethiferous magic. He hammers it with mortal flint. He rubs it and flakes it on a polishing piece of elk-horn. And as he rubs and flakes he grunts to himself the earliest Song of Shooting, which begins something like this :

> Nock and Feather
> Pile and Shaft
> Grew together
> By Man's craft.

And presently (' Where's Sabre Tooth ? ' said Man), presently this very actual arrow head of ours fell with a tinkle between Man's naked and calloused knees all new and smoking hot.

And so Man made the arrow head, and, strong in its magic, got up (perhaps) and went and looked for

Sabre Tooth. But whether Sabre Tooth saw Man before Man saw Sabre Tooth I do not know. I only know that Man went to the barrows above Moulsford and Sabre Tooth to extinction long, long ago. And that his arrow head, by magic, remains. For it *is* a strange and magic thing to think that here am I who shoot and there was Man who shot, and that this small worked stone of the dawning, that fell between his naked knees, has fallen on and on and down the ages until, the other day, it dropped into my letter-box to link Man and me, two shooting gentlemen together, in this most comradely fashion.

But I cannot think that the magic has come direct from Man to myself. The archer of crossbow and quarrel has held it, may happen, and smiled condescendingly and passed it on to his brother-to-be of the early sporting arquebus, who was whimsical, and, sniffingly, let it fall into the æons again so that it tumbled on to the table of Mr. Joseph Manton himself. And our Joe handled it gently, I imagine, and half understood and then turned to his beloved flints again and wholly forgot it. And so the arrow got started on a fresh flight.

But Fancy still goes back to my funny little red, hairy, half-ape who was Man, and sat on Streatley Hill and worked arrow head on elk-horn and sang the first Song of Shooting. Did he really seek Sabre Tooth with this our so very tiny arrow head? Or was he just content to draw a picture of Tiger upon the cave wall and shoot his arrow at that and shout, ' *There's* for thee, Man Eater ! ' ? Again I cannot say, but he was singer and artist, as we've seen, and Apollo is ever unpractical.

And therefore I will wink at Man, just as I am sure that he would have winked brotherly at me, and his arrow head, his magic, shall come in my pocket next time that I go to shoot cock pheasants. May happen that I shall hold more straightly than usual.

But this summer day the gun is in eclipse and seclusion. And what a neatly turned and compact piece of goods a gun-case is compared with a rod-box! As an epitome of the whole art of shooting it has more application than even the weapon herself. In a gun-case there is no room for anything else than the gun, which implies that the 12-bore is an exacting mistress with but small use for the man who holds her and admires, at the same time and to absent-mindedness, the view over the braes of Angus or the autumn colours on a Berkshire hillside. A gun-case looks as businesslike as a bee or a bunch of stock-brokers in a good market. A double gun-case assures the respect of railway porters and chauffeurs, and gives that nameless cachet to its possessor of which the rod-box is incapable.

Romance, too; for a traveller with a double gun-case might be coming from, or going to, any stately home of England that Fancy prefers. And what a picture of prosperity and good sport can a double gun-case upon a London taxicab be—Tottenham Court Road, say, for background, and, for frame, a sultry August evening!

And yet, and yet I would go back to where I started and say that a double gun-case has no real room for anything other than two guns. Yet it holds the entire business of the happy day, or the happy fortnight, in which you must be busy before you can be happy. I mean that if you go out to shoot and do not be shooting, then, with one gun or with two, you cannot be *quite* care-free because you will be sympathising, not with yourself in the smallest degree, but with your host, let us say, or your guests or with the gamekeeper or, last but not least, with the idle dog at your heels. A gun-case, too, is purely practical and has no partition for Imagination. Whereas into a rod-box you may pack much besides rods, indeed, from tooth-paste to daisy-chains and hope, all sorts may find place.

But the rod-box does not inspire the respect that the gun-case inspires. There may be roach poles in rod-boxes, there may even be the legs of a theodolite. But a gun-case implies a game licence, and being met by liveried chauffeurs, by footmen even, on October Friday evenings and country platforms, and by the Rolls that purrs beyond the station gate whose guardian, touching his cap, will insult no visitor to the Hall by naming a ticket.

Last spring I, on my way home from Deeside, waited with a rod-box upon a Paddington platform. And it was a means of introducing me to a brother of the angle who takes his pleasure, and his fishes, off the towpath at Isleworth. Now this courteous wayside meeting could not have occurred out of a gun-case. In fact, I fancy that a gun-case, a double one anyhow, would have inspired my friend with nothing but a feeling of dislike for me. And that is a strange thing but, I fear, a true one.

Now do you not notice that everybody loves a fox-hunter, and will do all that is humanly possible to head a fox on his behalf? And that the serene and simple angler is popular on the settle or in the railway carriage ? But about the man with the gun-case I am not sure. Gun-cases gain for you place and politeness as I have said, but further I would not commit myself. They imply (that too I have said) an exclusiveness in sport which makes for Envy. Anybody with a pair of boots and a Burberry can go a-foot and see something of a fox-hunting run—more of it often than the man in pink sees. And, in some way or another, everyone whose heart desires the water brooks can go a-fishing. But did I go shooting in the same popular manner I'd end in the police courts.

For shooting, in however simple a form you may shoot, is, more than all the field sports, a matter of money or friends. Even rabbits and wood-pigeons, if not strictly preserved, are strictly encompassed. And we live in an age of Envy. And gun-cases, in their sleek importance, invite a throwing of half-bricks. Yet, in a river book, the gun-case will, in the nature of things, not be too intrusive.

But there should be room in a river book for the birds of the river other than the archæopteryx. And you will say what are the birds of Thames ? And I will tell you that all possible British birds, except some of the sea-birds and sea-ducks, except the golden eagle and the crested tit, except the capercailzie, the red grouse and the black, except the ptarmigan, are the Thames birds. And though I have excepted the coastal ducks, yet the pochard is common in hard weather, nay more, a year or so back we had a pochard pair who hatched out a brood of little pochards in Cleeve reach. You thought that they were ordinary wild duck, did you ? You thought wrongly. And in that terrible February of 1929 I saw a pair of male smew with a great company of pochard and other fowl. The river was dark with duck above Mapledurham lock. They sat and, rising with a roar of wings, swung past me at under forty yards. Easily were the white and spectacled smew to be discerned. No doubt their wives were with them but, less conspicuous, they went unnoticed among the multitude.

There are the coots, the dabchicks and the moorhens, there are the teal and the mallard, to be the continual birds of Thames. There are the swans, the black and the white. Quarrelsome and pugnacious creatures are all except the teal, except the mallard, and the swans are murderous. Only the other day I saw the cob swan on Goring reach kill its own cygnet of last year. It chased the poor ' ugly duckling ' till the latter took refuge in a boat-house on the further bank where I could not rescue it. Its savage sire followed it in and killed it while its mother looked on and preened herself. And the swans, black and white, who look to be such excellent parents to their callow broods when they bring them alongside the punt for what's left of the lunch and even allow them first go at the sodden seed-cake and the flotsam ham sandwich are, in reality, the very greatest of fools. They will swim along the lip of the lasher sculling powerfully and as graceful as lilies. But over the wash of the weir the little ones go and, ten times out of eleven, that's the end of them. For they cannot get back and so they either starve or are killed by the pair of swans who own the water below. For all the river birds, from the swans to the dabchicks, have their beats and boundaries, and furious are the encounters when, respectively, one of their own species over-swims the margin of good manners, commits a tres-pass, presumes, in the case of a swan, to sneak up to the tea party under the trees and it *just* off his water. Ruffling and raging the rightful owner will come from afar with prodigious commotion and the wave of a steam-boat. And the poacher, snatching a last ginger-bread nut, will, the coward of his conscience, slip off as fast as he can without looking too undignified.

The dabchicks are just as bad. When you see furious splashings under the trees on the Berks side these mean that the dabchick of above Temple island has found the perch spawn which is the property of the dabchick of below Temple island and that the former, feasting, has in turn been discovered by the latter.

Once I saw two baby swans lost by their careless parents. They were carried over the weir and into Marlow pool. They looked so infantile and made such pathetic little squeals as they vainly tried to go home again that I had to stop fishing and go to their rescue. It took the whole morning to catch them with the landing-net in the fast white water and bubble-shoots. But, thanks entirely to the consummate watermanship of Walter Coster, this was accomplished and the two squeaking bundles of swan's-down were returned intact to the family flotilla.

But if the white swan is careless the black swan is worse. Last summer the two black swans above Mapledurham lost all their brood but one. They lost them in the main river. Whether the otter who haunted there in frogging time took them I do not know. But the parents turned up in the mill-cutting with their one surviving piccaninny. I knew that they would lose it over the weir and I spent an hour in stoning them away. But they would not move for me and, next morning, the chick was not with them.

The only intelligence the black swans have ever exhibited is in that they recognize they are no longer in Australia and alter their natural breeding days to suit the topsy-turveydom of Thames.

Swans have, however, one pleasant virtue. They mate for life and they miss one another if parted. Indeed they, ducks too, suffer dreadfully from loneliness and it is a cruel thing to keep a single swan on a lake, or an artificial water, as is sometimes thoughtlessly done. I knew a case of a lonely swan who attached itself to the gardener who used to mow the lawn about its pond. It never left the man's side, and when he gave up his situation the swan died of a broken heart.

Mr. Englefield (I think it is Mr. Englefield) tells of a cob swan who, while his mate sat on her eggs and his, fell in love with a pretty girl who used to be on the river daily. In a follow-my-Leda mood he swam continually and as closely to the punt as possible. He fished up for his Miss Lucy long wavy bits of delicious green weed which he laid on the till of her punt. He took her sleeve, very gently, in his beak and tried to coax her to come into the water. He was a perfect scandal of a swan. Mr. Englefield does not give us the end of this romance, perhaps he did not know it, but I am glad to think that such almost human infidelity is rare among swans.

Thames is abundant with the lovely kingfishers. At least they are lovely at a little distance. They are lovely when they go, burning bright, in the greyness of a winter day. They are lovely when, blue and orange, they chase each other among the green willow boughs of May. But when a kingfisher comes and sits on the end of the punt do not look at his villainous red eye, his retreating forehead, his stiletto beak, or you will never again think him as lovely as you did before you knew him all intimately and in the same boat.

The heron, like the halcyon, is a Thames fisherman too and he is a typical river sight as he stands on the sill of a weir in the early summer morning when you come downstream with a trout rod to stand beside him. He looks at you ; then, *flap flap*, he gives you best and is off to Whitchurch Pool where anglers don't get up so early to interfere with each other's sport. So plentiful are the Thames herons that one wonders why Thames heronries are so few and far between—the only two that I know are at Richmond and near Nuneham respectively, though the last I have never seen. There is something prehistoric in the appearance of a nestful of snapping, hissing young herons, something that suggests pterodactyls and dinotheriums, and a dinosaur who heaves his fearful length from the primal mud of Thames to munch a green herbage dead a million years ago.

Last summer another fisher, much more of a rival than the riparian heron, shared Mapledurham Pool with me all one afternoon. He was a merganser and I do not know if he caught anything, but I expect that he did. He saw to it that I did not. The merganser is a not uncommon bird, but he is an uncommon nuisance in a pool when you are fishing it too. He dives a hundred yards away and then up he comes, his snaky neck in the white water at your feet ; side to side it sways and then, in a flash, it is gone again. A shoal of bleak spring in a scatter of silver, a chain of bubbles mark the urgent business of the destroyer, and every trout takes cover who is not a ten-pounder.

How different are the terns who visit us occasionally, six, twelve, sea-swallows at a time. How the bright air is full of bright and sudden wings ! *Splash* and, silverly, *splash* again, sea-swallows after ' river-swallows '—the darting green-backed bleak—*splash* again, and lo, the lovely visitors are gone, full-cropped and kindly welcome to return on any fine day that they feel inclined to do so.

I very nearly caught a tern once. It saw my blue phantom come back to me, spinning in the stream below ' The Anglers ' at Marlow. The tern made the most sparkling of stoops, saw her error, twisted like a snipe and shot aloft falcon-winged and white as snow. But I fancy that she was very nearly deceived.

The rarest water bird I have met on the river came about in this way. I was fishing at Cleeve and the lock-keeper, knowing that I was as fond of birds as he himself was, told me that there was a bird who beat him on Temple island. I waded along the weir and peeped about in the reeds. Then, within a couple of yards of me, I saw a big, brown, owl-coloured bird who stood stock-still and cocked a short, green beak in air. The bird looked at me with a mild, un-flurried eye. I looked at the bird with a reverence and an awe, for was it not the first bittern that I had ever seen ? I saw him on a Saturday ; on the Sunday afternoon he was still there. But when the bells were ringing for an up-river evensong the big brown bird rose, heavily flapping, into the chill September dusk and went on his mysterious way. And, as far as I know, he has never returned.

Wild geese I have seen on the marshes at South Stoke and, about every third winter, the golden plover come. Five went, *swish*, past me within a few yards and I ' feeding ' the partridges in the hungry days of last February.

There is a larch wood at, shall we say, Friar's Hill-sides, where, if you are lucky, you shall see crossbills, golden crests, titmice and long-tailed titmice all on one tree. It was within this wood that I saw the rarest Thames bird that I have seen in my Thames days.

It was a covert shoot, the beaters, yet afar, were coming, to a *tap*, *tap* of sticks. A jay scolded in a tree near me. I looked up and saw the irritated one, but it was no jay. It was a chocolate-coloured bird, of the jay size, chocolate and white ; and the joint knowledge of my lady-loader and myself told us that it was a nutcracker. It flitted off, jerkily, from tree to tree, harshly querulous.

Our woodpeckers, green and spotted, are not un-common garden birds, but the green are by far the more numerous.

We have water-rails in plenty and an occasional corncrake, and I have heard of quail upon the down-lands of Moulsford but have never seen them, or, if I have, I have mistaken them for a covey of ' cheepers.'

And of the hawks and the falcons I can tell nothing new. But still the hen sparrow-hawk knocks a par-tridge over and I do not grudge it to her. And still the kestrel, I am glad to think, battens on the fat, field voles, and still the merlin outflies, or is outflown by, the brown, down skylark. The peregrine I saw here last autumn. She was in two minds about stooping at a pack of partridges who came to the Guns. She did not but, instead, lifted into the West Wind and was gone. And the year before last a game-keeper, who wagged his tail, brought me an immature peregrine which he had shot that morning. I tried to be congratulatory, for after all one pays a keeper to shoot peregrines, but I failed.

And last summer there was a river-side fellow who shot a hobby hawk, the lovely little falcon who catches beetles and bumble-bees. I do not like to think of this slaying.

And of nightingales, nuthatches and nightjars we never fail. And, in April, the cuckoo calls from Basildon woods across the broad river to the green heights of Hart's Lock. And with singing birds all Thames gardens and orchards are musical and the goldfinch sits on the thistle tops of October and the 'bully,' the beauty, opens the pods of the autumn delphiniums outside my window, up and down, up and down.

And, from the blackcap, Gilbert White, and all Thames anglers, have heard ' a full, sweet, deep, loud, and wild pipe ; yet that strain is of short con-tinuance and his motions are desultory ; but when that bird sits calmly and engages in song in earnest, he pours forth very sweet, but inward melody, and expresses great variety of soft and gentle modula-tions, superior perhaps to those of any of our Warb-lers, the Nightingale excepted.'

And of that famous vocalist, the blackbird, Mr.

Eric Parker says : ' And when the blackbird of black-birds rouses himself from indolent happiness to sing the fullness of his heart out into the April morning, it is a song of such jubilant joy as must overpower even the passion of the nightingale. I have heard two such blackbirds, and never a nightingale that could equal either. One of them sang many years ago for two springs running in a wood above a lake in Sussex, and I listened from a boat morning after morning to such a song as I did not know a bird could sing, and a song that I have never heard since and can never hear again, for its power to touch the heart of those that listened. And the other I have only heard once and I hope to hear again, for as I write he may still be waiting for another February. When I heard him it was an afternoon in April, and I had left Kew Gardens to walk to the station. As I went down the road there suddenly broke out the loudest and most wonderful bird's singing that I have ever heard so close to me. I looked round for an open window, for I could not decide what the bird could be ; the song was like that of an Indian orange-headed thrush that I used to listen to in the Western Aviary in Regent's Park, but far richer and more powerful. I could see no cage, and became more and more puzzled, for the bird was certainly singing quite near, but I could not determine where ; the song so flooded the air that it seemed to be coming from anywhere and everywhere. It ceased as suddenly as it began, and from the top of a pol-larded lime above my head there dropped down a blackbird to a garden hedge. Was that the bird ? I could only wait to see ; I had never heard a blackbird with such a voice. My train became unimportant ;

I went to have tea in a shop near, where I could hear him if he started to sing again. And when he began again I found him and watched and listened; until the train became a necessity.'

But Mr. Parker's minstrel boy will not sing before St. Valentine's Day and sometimes not even then. And for me no song of spring sung in the rising year is to compare with a song of April sung in the dark of a December morning. And who but the Thrush, the speckled beauty, can sing it?

Myself (*in December*).—Oh, Mr. Thrush, what a song you sing!
    Never a passer-by but cocks his
    Eye to the orchard which you ring
        With a roundelay
        On a Winter day
    As if you'd springtime over the way
    And little Miss April come to stay
        With her green and her gold band-boxes.

Mr. Thrush.—But amn't I right to sing a song
    When the days are dark and a song amazes?
    Don't the gold ghost daffodils chime ding-dong
        In each bubbly note
        Of my bursting throat
    Till you catch the rustle—not *too* remote—
    Of little Miss April's petticoat
        And the chink of her chain of daisies?

Myself.—Good Mr. Thrush, but of course you're right,
    And a song sung now finds a thousand thankers
    For one who'll turn when your orchard's white;
        So lift your head
        To our skies of lead
    And fill 'em with gold to wake the dead,
    Or little Miss April a-bed, a-bed,
        Her daisy-chain down at her bankers.

XVIII. A KETTLE OF THAMES FISH

The careful angler chose his nook
At morning by the lilied brook,
And all the noon his rod he plied
By that romantic riverside.
Soon as the evening hours decline
Tranquilly he'll return to dine,
And, breathing forth a pious wish,
Will cram his belly full of fish.

R. L. STEVENSON.

'IT was the *riding* that did it,' said the Borgian, but always philosophical and sporting, Mr. Wainwright when the Lord Chief Justice condemned him to be hanged. By that he meant that Mr. Cockburn for the Crown had been one too many for the prisoner's counsel. And the best rider is not the lad who wins the race upon the best horse running but the horseman on the fifth best who runs the winner to a head for it. And after all Mr. Wainwright had not, I imagine, much of a case.

What I mean is that anybody can cook a salmon or a trout and make a feast of the one or the other. I could do so myself. I'd ask a handful of salt, a big black pot or kettle, a sharp knife and a brisk fire. These for the salmon. And for the trout a frying-pan instead of the kettle and a *daud* of butter. Or I could be doing without the pan and still cook you a dish of trouts among the hotted stones by the burn side. But I'd want last week's *Field* to wrap them in, buttered, of course, or larded with the surplus fat from the ham sandwiches. And if you've no salt and happen to have a 16-bore cartridge in your pocket (boys often happen to have one), a pinch of gunpowder will make a gallant and sportsmanly seasoning. I know, any-how, that the old black powder of the eighties did, but whether the high velocity article of 1932 is equally gallant I cannot tell.

It was a fine manly stuff the old black powder and it went nobly with the smell of wet ' neeps ' and the keen air of an East Coast October. And if there is anyone who, with black powder, began his stalking days will he ever forget how the high hills of Breadal-bane would roll the roar of it in thunder about the corries till Starav echoed back to Stob an Ruaidh ? To a *bang* that is less than the crack of a hunting crop do the stags of these degenerate Septembers die, but it was the great-mouthed black powder that brought the Muckle Hart home from the hill, that made trophy of Glen Fiddich's famous monster.

But it was minnow tansy and fried gudgeon that I had in mind when I began this chapter, and the food value and kitchen of Thames fishes in general. And fine entertainment they make in the hands of an artist or even without the aid of a *cordon bleu* so be that you are of simple tastes and as hungry as a man ought to be who has breathed the Berkshire air from 9 a.m. to 4 p.m. of a November day.

And let the epicure beware of prejudice. Lots of *viveurs* will exclaim at a course of freshwater fish other than *truite au bleu*, other than *saumon à la sauce Hollandaise* and the latter not a freshwater fish at all. I will tell you a little memory of my own to illustrate the folly of prejudging any case before it is tried.

There was a salmon angler whose Silver Doctor was taken by a pike as sometimes happens even in the best of salmon rivers. The pike was gaffed, landed and, in due course, went ' up to the house.'

' What,' asked the lady of the latter, ' shall I do with the pike ? ' ' Pitch it away,' replied her lord. ' Pitch it away,' echoed Lieutenant-General Sir Currie Rice of the Allahabad Command, ' pitch it away, at once, my dear lady, pike is poison, poison.'

But the lady was not one to ' pitch away ' any of heaven's mercies. Next evening the menu cards announced a cold mayonnaise of turbot. And a lovely-looking mayonnaise it was that the butler handed, golden with the grated yolks of eggs and crisp with green lettuce. And smooth and creamy and bland was the sauce that accompanied it. Here let me wonder who it was who invented mayonnaise ? A Frenchman of course, but exactly *who* that great

Frenchman was I do not know. But I have heard an ingenious gourmet and patriotic son of Erin declare that mayonnaise sauce was no Gallic inspiration at all, at all, but the brain-child of an Irishman, chef to the Earl of Mayo. And that the artist named his creation for his master and for his master's heir, my Lord Naas. It is a pretty notion is it not and one that deserves to have been founded on fact ?

But, whoever was creator of the dish, this is a glorious mayonnaise that the butler is handing. Sir Currie has had two goes at it and is looking hopefully over his shoulder even now to see if Crichton is to hand it a third time, while the master of the house, scraping his platter, exclaims at the excellence of the turbot and says that one gets devilish tired of salmon, morning, noon and night.

And of course it was the boned pike that they ate so gladly. But the lady was not telling till breakfast time next day.

And if there's a moral to this story it is that there is no one so mortal as an expert. And both Sir Currie and his host considered themselves no small beer in the kitchen arts. But here is an even more dreadful example of my contention.

Last year there came to stay with me on the eve of a shooting party two friends. The one has earned for himself, in the words of his calling, a reputation as the ' best judge of port wine in the trade.' The other, by studious endeavour, has acquired an amateur status equal, almost, to that of the professional.

I asked my two guests what wine they would drink at dinner. They asked in return to see the menu.

They saw it and nodded gravely. They asked the vintage of the port that was to follow. They spoke guardedly to each other and said, ' Burgundy.'

Now I myself take little or no wine at all, until a Port or a Madeira crowns the dessert. Through this meal I drank gin and soda-water while my friends, trolling the jolly bowl about, finished the decanter and spoke not unkindly of its contents. And thus dinner drew to an end in good cheer and good fellowship and good hopes for the sport of to-morrow.

Before pushing the port along I poured out half a glass and sipped to assure myself of temperature and bouquet or ever the critics criticized it, and me. I sipped and sipped again and the situation slowly dawned upon me. The port and the burgundy had been decanted into twin decanters. The port, a wine chosen to suit the expert company who was to taste it, had been, without detection, enjoyed throughout dinner as the beverage burgundy that now sat facing me.

You may say that politeness and good breeding may have kept my friends silent as to a mistake of my household ? I will reply that they have known me long and, by custom, where I am concerned, they dispense with both these shams.

And so I will say, once more, that in the eating of ' coarse ' fishes much lies in the cooking, that it is indeed ' the riding that does it.' And, by the way, burgundy is no fish wine. With fish drink always a white wine and a dry ; or else an old ale.

And for every fish the first step to table is, after the landing-net part, the preparing for the kettle. All fish should be eaten *quam celerrime*, ' oot o' the watter an' intill the pot,' as men said of the salmon in Mr. Scrope's day. But this all possible speed is more important in application to the coarser fishes than to those of the *sea* or of the *game*. And here are the rules of preparation which apply to all freshwater fish.

In choosing a fish to cook prefer, if choice there is, a hen to a cock fish, the flesh of the latter being less delicate than that of the female. A rule which is in flat contradiction to the rule of the salmon, where always would I pick a cock fish to eat in preference to a hen.

When cleaning care should be taken to keep the fish on its back. If this is not done there is a grave risk that the gall bladder breaking may embitter the *plat* to be. If the fish must, perforce, be kept overnight, clean it but do not leave it to soak in either fresh water or in water to which salt has been added. Even an hour in soak will destroy much of its natural flavour and nutritive quality. When cleaned it should be rubbed, at once, the inside and the out, with salt and vinegar, in the proportion of a teaspoonful of vinegar and a heaped teaspoonful of salt to each pound that the fish weighs. A medium-sized fish will generally taste better than a slocdolager, so do not send away, in compliment, any of your four-pound perch and three-pound roaches. And if you go out with the avowed intention of catching a dish of coarse fish wherewith to dumbfound some gourmet Didymus with the excellence of our river harvest, I would recommend that a bottle of vinegar go with you and, as each fish is taken and rapped on the head, a *coup* of the same be poured into its mouth and allowed to permeate within its person. This will effectively dispel any suspicion of *muddiness* which some coarse fishes, the tench, for instance, are occasionally subject to.

And the next thing to consider is which of our Thames fish are best worth the cooking and eating, which of them, failing the blackbird pie as pictured by Mr. Caldecott (for any other form of blackbird pie than his would be unthinkable), would you choose to ' set before a king ' ?

Well, if the king likes to sit down and feast royally I'd set before him a smoking bowl, a blue-and-white crock, of stewed eel, and to flank it a dish of boiled potatoes, big, mealy potatoes. For I think that I would put the eel first of all the coarse fish, and here, if your king is a ' nasty particular ' king, are some of the ' nicer ' modes of eel for him.

This, for instance, is how to ' collar ' eels :

Take two large (say 2 lb. each) eels. Your king, if he is anything of a trencherman, can eat a whole eel at a sitting and heaven knows that you can. Take, then, two eels. Skin them in the prescribed manner. Cut them down the back in spatchcocking mode and remove bone and trail. Rub them with salt and vinegar and much care. Dry them now with a clean cloth. Take chopped, finely chopped, parsley, thyme and sweet marjoram, take grated nutmeg, take ginger, salt and pepper and, mixing herbs and condiments together, strew the whole over the eels. Now roll the eels up as though you made a collar of brawn, sew each in a separate cloth and boil in water, salt and vinegar with a blade of mace and a bouquet of sweet herbs. Serve them with a ' bree ' of the boiling set apart in a sauce-boat, as though they were salmon that you served.

And here is a delightful and nourishing dish of eel *à al'llemande*. Skin and remove head, tail and trail, being ever careful to remove the clot of blood that the eel wears in his innards. Clean as directed. Now cut the fish into transverse sections of about three inches each. Steam it to softness and, when the flesh falls easily away from the spinal column, remove the former to a casserole containing a smooth, hot sauce of white Rhine wine, flour and fennel. Serve at once.

And for an eel galantine, prepare the eel as though you would ' collar ' it. Let the eel become cold and then cut it into thicknesses of an inch and a bittock. Pack it into a mould which has been painted with salad oil within and which contains some of the liquid jelly, or stock, from the boiling. Pour some more of this stock over the whole. And, when set, turn out on to a platter. Decorate and garnish with green cucumber and pink prawns and serve with a *sauce verte*.

There are many ways of serving eel. There is eel-pie, beneath a flaky pastry, served cold along with a salad of cucumber, served with sliced hard-boiled eggs between the jellied layers of eel.

There is fried eel—boned sections of three inches fried in fat to a beautiful brown hue and served with tartare sauce—fried eel is a delicate fare. Yet it requires *riding*, so the connoisseurs of it say, before it can be eaten to supreme perfection.

But, by two hungry people, the blue-and-white bowl of stewed eel, the big, hot potatoes, the coarse white kitchen tablecloth, the coarse white kitchen salt, will be remembered when many a more elaborate course has gone to the limboland of meals forgotten.

There is a dining club in London. It is an association formed solely in the honour of the eel. Can trout and salmon say as much ?

Next to the eel in point of excellence comes, surely, a winter pike. I have spoken of pike mayonnaise *à la* turbot. Pike *à la* whitebait may be prepared by boning a boiled or parboiled pike, cutting the snowy flakes of flesh into oblongs of an inch or so, and frying them in egg and bread crumbs. Serve, of course, very hot with lemon and thin slices of brown bread and butter.

And here's the how of a baked pike. Clean the fish, an eight-pounder, let's say. Scale it and dry it in each part with a clean towel. Take a pound of beef suet, take a pound of grated bread ; mix and season with pepper, salt and nutmeg. Work into the suet and the spiced bread shredded lemon peel, thyme, three shredded anchovies and the yolks of three eggs. Squeeze lemon juice over the whole and place it, like Jonah, in the belly of the fish. Sew the latter up and bake in an oven until the skin cracks. Serve with a sauce which is half the battle of a baked pike. To make it take a pint of beef gravy, a quart of stewed oysters, a pint of peeled shrimps and half a pint of stewed mushrooms. Melt a pound of fresh butter and mix the rest into it. This sauce may be served separate (as I prefer it to be) or poured over the pike, from whom the thread that sewed him should be removed ere he comes to table.

Perhaps the best method of all for a smallish pike is this one : Clean the fish carefully, but *do not scale.*

Rub it, outside and in, with a solution of salt and vinegar. Bend it, head to tail, like a chaplet and, to keep it so, fasten end to end with a small wooden skewer. Place the pike, its back uppermost, in the fish kettle with just enough of salt and water to cover it. Boil slowly for half an hour. Garnish with small portions of the liver and serve with a piping hot brown butter to which add a few drops of vinegar. And be careful to serve along with this dish, but separately, a supply of *finely grated horse-radish*.

The pike, I may say, or ever we leave him, is best suited of all the coarse fish to a soufflé since his flesh is light and firm.

The perch to many folk is the best of the Thames fishes when the gong goes. He is certainly a very good one and if he were not so bony I think that I would agree with his admirers who say that he is as good, almost, as the brook trout. As a trout, a burn or a brook trout, a trout of small size, I eat the perch. Clean, split and *scale*. Roll in salt and oatmeal and fry in fresh butter over a slow fire. And here is a sauce in sufficient quantity to suit six perch of, say, three-quarters of a pound each. Take six tablespoonfuls of melted butter, the yolks of four eggs, two tablespoonfuls of chopped parsley, three tablespoonfuls of lemon juice, one tablespoonful of grated lemon rind, three tablespoonfuls of cream. Mix well together and whisk over a fire *but do not allow to boil*. Pour over fish before serving or, if you will, serve in a sauce-boat.

And here is a Dutch dressing for three one-pounder perches. Scale and clean and remove the heads. Boil the fish with bay leaves, parsley, salt and vinegar.

Take one onion, one stick of celery, one bunch of parsley, two tablespoonfuls of butter, two tablespoonfuls of flour. The vegetables must be finely chopped and the whole fried lightly and then mixed with one pint of boiled meat stock. Thicken if necessary with flour and butter and pour over the perch before serving. And serve along with them thin bread and butter.

It was once the fashion to mix the trail of the perch with the vegetables before frying them, but I have never tried out this early epicurism.

A perch is the easier to scale if it is dipped first into boiling water.

The roach may be fried in the perch manner, but he is a tasteless wretch, I fear. Mustard sauce (as with grilled herrings) helps him out a little, but not much. The cat will eat him, if she is hungry.

To give you Thames carp recipes will, I imagine, be of little practical use ; for when you've taken the seventeen-pound carp, who has lived at Mapledurham since 1837, it will go to a taxidermist and not to the kitchen. But a barbel, if properly treated, is as good as a carp ; a fine slabsided fellow is a barbel and much underrated by most anglers, who are content to make fish curries of him, fish rissoles and fish pudding. Try the next six-pound barbel you catch to this carp recipe of mine and you'll tell me what a good fish he is after all.

Draw the trail without cutting the fish entirely open. Clean meticulously within and without. Make the following stuffing in suitable quantities and place it within the barbel. Chopped boiled sweetbreads, chopped crayfish (or lobster or crab), the *fonds* of six artichokes, *fines herbes*, white grated bread, the yolks of six eggs, salt and pepper. Fill the barbel with this stuffing and sew it up. Brown it lightly and ' lard ' its back as though it was a guinea-fowl. Cook it slowly in a long earthenware dish, basting it the while with white wine and a bay leaf. Serve the liquor of the basting separately in a sauce-boat. The chef should not aim at achieving here, what is called, *haut goût*, but his masterpiece should have a simple yet noble flavour, a smooth and velvety suggestion. With the barbel should appear the driest of the golden brands of Chablis.

The chub is a poor enough table fish. The smaller chubs, however, split, grilled and served with tartare sauce, are not too contemptible. The larger may, boiled and boned, be treated as a fish to curry, along with a feather of the Bombay Duck, or to make a fish pudding of. Moreover a big chub, *carefully* boned, makes a useful change of diet to mix in with the dog's dinner. Most dogs get cod's head once a week and a whole chub does equally nicely.

If you want to boast that you have eaten bream proceed thus : scale and clean the fish (and remember that the *tongue* of a bream and the *roe* of a bream are esteemed to be *de bonnes bouches*) and stew in melted butter, bread crumbs, salt and sugar. Add two cups of white wine and cook slowly. Serve on a hot dish and pour the ' bree ' over the bream, thickened with the yolks of three eggs. Garnish with cubes of roe and olives.

The tench, though he looks like a trout, tastes of mud (a little), of turtle (a trifle), and of eel (no great deal). The whole effect is a rich one. Boil him in salt and water ; enough water to cover a tench is enough water to boil him. The tench should be put into the pan *before* the water boils or his skin will crack and his appearance become unsightly. With him should be boiled thyme, onion, lemon peel, horse-radish and a quarter of a pint of vinegar. Serve a sauce of shrimps or oysters with your tench ; garnish him about with lemon and mushroom.

Of the smaller fishes the gudgeon of our grandsires is best. Indeed the gudgeon still is, as *The Gentleman Angler* said of him in 1726, ' a pleasant, sweet and delicate fish ' and he may be fried and served as though he were that other delicate Thames fish, the smelt, who used to be caught (and may be still for all I know) in plenty at Chiswick.

The dace I have eaten grilled *à la* fresh herring and as such he is excellent. A sauce of melted butter and anchovies suits him well. So also does the ordinary herring sauce of mustard.

Of the littlest fish, of minnows and of the fry of most others, *tansies* may be made. A Thames tansy is no more or no less than a dish of Greenwich white-bait, cooked and served either as usual or *au diable* ; the latter is, I think, the better mode. Brown bread and butter, lemon and red pepper, please. Mr. Marston has declared the minnow to be a somewhat *bitter* little fish but I have not found him so. Mr. Marston's minnows were, however, not Thames minnows.

Of the cookery of a Thames trout I have said noth-ing. I will now say only that what is good enough for a salmon is good enough for a Thames trout. Boil or broil and a sauce to suit and who shall say the differ-ence between *salar* and Thames *fario* ?

And the motto to cook either by is, *Simplicity*.

But have I said enough of my coarse fishes to dispel any ' pins and cotton-wool ' ideas that might, previously to this reading, have been yours ? I hope so.

If I have not, why, then, remember two things about eating. Firstly, that ' scornful cats eat horrid mice,' and secondly that, whether you sit down to a Dee salmon, a Dover sole, or a Thames roach, the rhyme and the reason to all three lies in the girl who, I hope, sits opposite to you when you draw your chair in. Indeed I hope that you'll be telling her,

> But meals, past, present and to come,
>   On these old Solomon still wants beating—
> His *herbs* and his *stalled* ox, in sum
>   His is the inwardness of eating
> That leaves me nothing to be said
>   Save prayer, sincere if light as a feather,
> ' Give us,' I'll pray, 'our daily bread
>   And may we eat it oft together.'

THE END